Gateway

B1

Workbook

David Spencer

Contents

MACMILLAN

1 Family matters

Grammar ‣ Present simple and present continuous ‣ Articles
Vocabulary ‣ Ages and stages of life ‣ The family
‣ Noun suffixes *-ment*, *-ion*, *-ence*
Speaking ‣ Asking for personal information
Writing ‣ An informal email

‣ Vocabulary

Ages and stages of life

1 Read the clues and complete the puzzle. Which word appears in the shaded column?

1 He's 72. He's a senior citizen.
2 and 3 She's 55. She's a middle - aged adult.
4 the period of life when you change from being a child to being a young adult
5 a very young child who can't talk or walk
6 the stage of life when you are 70, for example
7 the opposite of life
8 the beginning of life
9 teenager

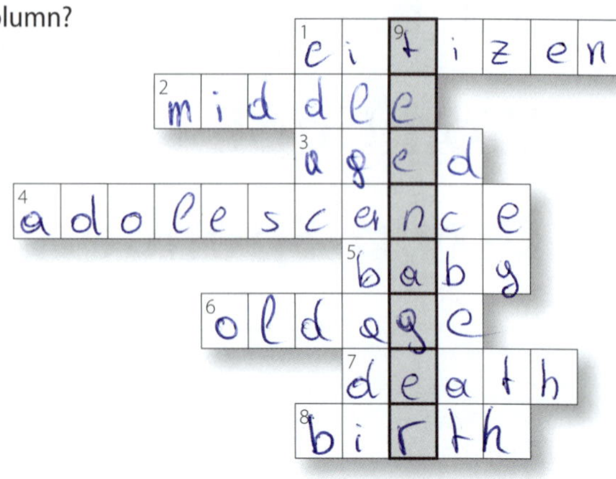

The family

2 Look at the family tree and complete the sentences.

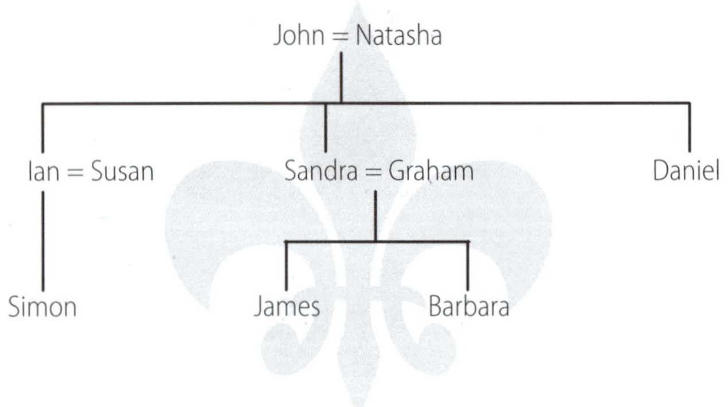

1 John and Natasha are Simon's *grandparents*.
2 Susan is Ian's sister.
3 James is Simon's .
4 Natasha is Graham's mother.
5 Graham is Ian's brother.
6 Daniel is Simon's uncle.
7 Barbara is Ian's cousin.
8 James is Daniel's cousin.
9 Barbara is John's grand-daughter.
10 Graham is Sandra's brother.

3 Match the halves of the sentences.

1 I've got a **stepfather** …
2 My aunt is 50 and **single** …
3 She's my **niece** …
4 Paul is an **only child** …
5 I come from a **one-parent family** …
6 Peter is my cousin's **partner**, not her husband …
7 Samuel is **divorced** …

a because his parents didn't want any more children.
b because they don't want to get married at the moment.
c because my parents got divorced and I live with my mum.
d because after my father's death my mum got married again.
e because she's my sister Elizabeth's daughter.
f because he separated from his wife legally last year.
g because she never wants to get married.

4 Write definitions or explanations of the words in bold from 3.

1 stepfather *your mother's new husband in a later marriage*
2 single
3 niece
4 only child
5 one-parent family
6 partner
7 divorced

1 Read this text from a website. What do you think the website does?

1 It gives news about social changes.
2 It's a place where you can buy new products.
3 It gives descriptions of and opinions about new products.
4 It explains the science behind new technology.

File Edit View History Tools Window Help

TECHNOWORLD

PRODUCT DESCRIPTION: A new high-tech coat for young children

A You know that here at Technoworld our job is to tell you all about new sorts of products that are about to appear in a shop near you. Well, this week we're looking at a coat called the EZ-Find coat. Riley Electronics are working on it and they hope that it will be in the shops by next December.

B Losing your child is a terrible experience. This coat can tell you where your young child is by computer or mobile phone. You can receive GPS data from it every 15 seconds. The coat also has an alarm which you can use to tell your child to come home. Some of you are probably thinking that this is spying. Maybe. But remember that this coat is for very young children and the idea is, above all, to protect them. Another nice thing about the coat is that when your child loses it, the GPS can help you to find it again.

C OK, so now you're waiting for next December to come so that you can run out and buy the coat. But first we need to tell you about one or two problems we had when we tested it. For a start, it's *very* warm. That means that, except for people who live in Alaska, your child probably won't be able to wear it very often. And then there's the other big problem. The coat is very expensive, especially if you pay for the monthly service to be able to track the GPS signal.

COMMENTS

By **Einheit** | 01.23PM | 24/10
This is great news for my family. I have a child with a disability. I think the idea of the coat is to give the children extra independence and help parents to relax. That sounds perfect for us!

By **Jabber** | 01.45PM | 24/10
What a 'great' idea! Put a GPS in the first thing that your son or daughter takes off – their coat!

By **Inkedfusion** | 03.45PM | 24/10
Great for little children but we all know that this doesn't work with teenagers. When they have GPS technology in their mobile phones, they take their phone and leave it in the library. You think they're studying but then they go away and do what they want!

By **Stammer** | 04.05PM | 24/10
This is the perfect coat for me. For me, not my children. I always take my coat off and leave it. Then I never remember where it is! With this GPS coat, it's the end of that problem!

2 Who (the Technoworld website, Einheit, Jabber, Inkedfusion or Stammer) thinks that the coat …

1 is good for people with a bad memory? ...., ...
2 is ideal for their child? ....
3 is a bad idea because children always take their coats off first? ....
4 isn't a good idea when it's warm? ....
5 is a stupid idea for adolescents? ....
6 costs a lot? ....

3 In your own words, explain what these different people think of the coat.

1 Jabber ....
2 Einheit ....
3 Inkedfusion ....
4 Stammer ....

4 Find words in the text which have similar meanings to these words or explanations.

1 types (*paragraph A*) ....
2 something that happens to you (*paragraph B*) ....
3 principally, most importantly (*paragraph B*) ....
4 follow or find someone or something (*paragraph C*) ....
5 the ability to take your own decisions (*comment by Einheit*) ....

5 What about *you*?

Write a comment for the Technoworld website and give your opinion about the coat.

....

Present simple and present continuous

1 Look at these sentences. Choose the correct alternative and explain why we use the present simple or present continuous in each sentence.

1 My friends are listening to the concert at the moment.
Present *simple*/***continuous*** because *it describes an action that's happening now*.

2 You never listen to me.
Present ***simple***/*continuous* because he/she never does it

3 My dad works at the weekend.
Present ***simple***/*continuous* because she's always doing this

4 Water turns to ice when it's below 0ºC.
Present ***simple***/*continuous* because it's always like that

5 My brother is spending the weekend with my grandparents.
Present *simple*/***continuous*** because it's only this weekend

6 Ah! Now I understand.
Present ***simple***/*continuous* because ....

7 A: Do you like this programme? B: Yeah, I love it.
Present ***simple***/*continuous* because ....

8 They go swimming twice a week.
Present ***simple***/*continuous* because they do that twice a week

2 Complete the sentences with the present simple or the present continuous form of the verbs given.

1 A: Why has he got his hand up?
B: He wants (want) the teacher to ask him.
He knows (know) the answer.

2 A: Why are you studying (study)?
B: I've got an exam tomorrow.

3 A: How do you prepare for exams?
B: I am reading (read) my notes and then I am writing (write) questions for myself.

4 A: Who is singing (sing) downstairs?
B: That's my sister. She's good, isn't she?

5 A: Bonjour, mademoiselle.
B: Sorry, I don't speak (not speak) French.

6 A: Mmmm. What's that smell? Is it pizza?
B: Yes. My dad makes (make) the dinner.

7 A: Why isn't your mum here at the moment?
B: She finishes (finish) work late on Thursdays.

8 A: Can I speak to the director?
B: No. He is speaking (speak) to someone else.

3 All the questions are in the present simple (PS) or the present continuous (PC), but one word is missing. Add a word to each question and write PS or PC next to it.

1 Where you live?
Where do you live? – PS

2 What your mother do?
What does your mother do? – PS

3 What your friends doing now?
are your friends doing – PC

4 Does your friend English well?
....

5 Are you your homework at the moment?
....

6 What sports you do?
....

7 What is your friend at the moment?
....

8 Who do you usually next to in English lessons?
....

4 Write your own true answers to your questions in 3.

1 ....
2 ....
3 ....
4 ....
5 ....
6 ....
7 ....
8 ....

Grammar extension

5 Are these sentences correct? If not, correct them.

1 Are you writting your essay at the moment?
....

2 She doesn't have her books with her today?
isn't having

3 Do you studying for your exam now?
Are

4 Why are you and Joe walking to school today?
....

5 Do your brother plays in the basketball team?
....

6 My cousin studies at this school.
....

7 My sister and I are having two bikes at the moment.
....

8 A: What do you do now? B: I listen to my MP3 player.
....

Noun suffixes *-ment*, *-ion*, *-ence*

1 Write the noun form of these words.

1 equip (v.) *equipment*
2 invent (v.) invention
3 protect (v.) protection
4 improve (v.) improvement
5 adolescent (adj.) adolescence
6 retire (v.) retirement
7 inform (v.) information
8 different (adj.) difference
9 move (v.) movement
10 discuss (v.) discussion
11 independent (adj.) independence
12 confident (adj.) confidence

2 Match words in 1 with these definitions. Make sure you write the correct form of the word: noun, verb or adjective.

1 facts about someone or something information
2 to make something better improve
3 things and materials that you need to do something equipment
4 to keep someone or something safe protect
5 something that makes one person or thing not the same as another
difference

3 Write a definition to explain the meaning of these words.

1 invention ....
2 movement ....
3 retire ....

Vocabulary extension: noun suffixes *-er*, *-or*, *-ist*

4 We can add the suffixes *-er*, *-or*, *-ist* to verbs or nouns to make nouns that describe people. We usually add *-er* and *-or* to verbs and *-ist* to nouns. Write the nouns for these words. Use your dictionary if necessary.

1 art *artist*
2 sing singer
3 drive driver
4 invent ....
5 science ....
6 economy ....
7 teach teacher
8 play player
9 photograph photographer
10 direct co
11 write writer
12 build ....

5 Complete the sentences with words in 4.

1 He always wins at tennis. He's a very good
player
2 Steven Spielberg is a very famous film
....
3 Albert Einstein was a great ....
4 Is your dad a taxi-..........?
5 I hate that .... All her songs are the same.
6 I'd like to be an .... one day. I love studying finance and markets.
7 It was his job to discover new things. He was an
....

6 Who are these people? Use the words in 4.

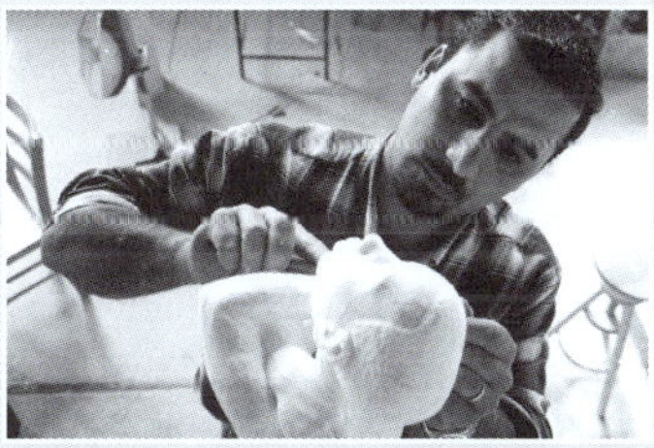
1 ....

2 ....

3 ....

4 ....

5 ....

Click onto... Family names

International cultural knowledge
The origin of British family names

1 Answer the questions.

1 Write down three British family names you know.

Jackson,

2 Can you guess the origin of any of these names?

I think Jackson is 'the son of Jack'.

2 Read this text about the origin of British family names. What are the four origins that the text talks about?

1 *They explain who the person's father or grandfather was.*

2

3

4

▸ WORD BOOSTER

Match the words and definitions.

1	generation	a	from Scotland
2	Scottish	b	an area of green land, often with animals
3	field	c	a group of people who are born/live around the same time
4	seashore	d	land next to the sea

The origin of British family names

Some people think that names aren't important. They're probably right, but they *can* be very interesting. Take British surnames, for example. A surname is a name that you and your family all have, and that you pass from one generation to another.

When we start to look at the meaning of different surnames, we soon discover that many of them answer one of these basic questions:

a) **Who is this person's father or grandfather?**
This gives us British surnames like Peters or Peterson. There are many surnames which begin with Mc or Mac, for example McCartney or Macdonald. This has a Scottish origin and also means 'son of', the same as O' in Ireland, like the surnames O'Connor or O'Brien.

b) **Where is this person from?**
Some people have a country for their surname, for example England. Field, House, Lake and Hill are all common family names in Britain too. In fact, some experts think that 50% of all surnames come from some type of geographic description.

c) **What is this person's job?**
The very common surname Smith (five million people in the world have got this surname!) comes from 'blacksmith', the traditional job of making objects such as horseshoes from metal. Baker (someone who makes bread), Shepherd (someone who looks after sheep) and Carpenter (someone who works with wood) are all common British surnames.

d) **What is special about this person?**
If your surname is Small, there's probably a small person in your family's history. If your surname is Armstrong, then somebody in your family's past probably had strong arms. And the surname Reid comes from the word red, so you probably had a family member with red hair or a red face.

When you start to investigate, you soon find that British surnames can be really interesting. And when you discover that there is a book called *A Student's Guide to the Seashore* by John and Susan Fish, you soon see that they can be funny too!

3 Read the text again and answer the questions.

1 What is a surname?

2 Where is the surname Macdonald from originally and what does it mean?

3 Where does the family name Smith come from?

4 What does a carpenter do?

5 What does it mean if your surname is Reid?

6 What is funny about the surname of the authors of *A Student's Guide to the Seashore*?

4 Write down two surnames from your country (but *not* your surname!). Then write down a possible origin. Is it one of the four origins from the text?

1 Surname
Possible origin

2 Surname
Possible origin

5 What about *you*?

Do you like your family name? Why/Why not? Do you know the origin of your family name?

Articles

1 Match these sentences with the rules.

1. My friend's dad is an engineer. .... e
2. I love animals.
3. That isn't the problem.
4. The sun is hot today.
5. Parents can be difficult.
6. They've got a car.
7. (They've got a car.) The car's blue.
8. She's the new president.

a We use ***no article*** when we talk about things in general.
b We use ***the*** to talk about a specific person or thing or a previously mentioned person or thing.
c We use ***a/an*** to talk about a singular, countable person or thing for the first time, or to say that the person or thing is one of a number of people or things.
d We use ***the*** to talk about someone or something that is unique.
e We use ***a/an*** to say what somebody's profession is.

2 Complete the sentences with *a, an* or *the*.

1. Yes, you're right! He *has* got ...a... mobile phone!
2. ...The... walkers in ...the... picture look very surprised.
3. What's ...the... title of that song?
4. He works for ...an... organisation that helps people with no home.
5. ...The... boy behind you is Paul's cousin.
6. What's on TV? Can you pass ...the... remote control?
7. She's single. She hasn't got ...a... husband.
8. I have ...an... idea! Why don't we go to see Uncle George tomorrow?
9. Alex is ...the... name of my nephew.
10. My stepfather is ...a... carpenter.
11. He is ...the... director of the film we saw yesterday.
12. My sister wants to be ...an... economist.
13. Have you got ...a... new computer? I haven't seen it before.
14. ...the... coat you are wearing looks very warm.

3 Complete the famous quotes with *a/an*, *the* or *0* (no article).

1. 'I have ...a... dream.' *Martin Luther King*
2. '...The... earth goes round ...the... sun.' *Copernicus*
3. 'I paint .... objects as I think them, not as I see them.' *Pablo Picasso*
4. 'To be or not to be, that is .... question.' *William Shakespeare*
5. '........ (I/i)magination is more important than .... knowledge.' *Albert Einstein*
6. 'Nothing is more responsible for .... good old days than .... bad memory.' *Franklin Pierce Adams*
7. '........ (O/o)nly problem with common sense is that it is not very common.' *Voltaire*
8. '........ (L/l)ife is .... dream.' *Calderón de la Barca*

Grammar extension

4 Look at these sentences. Cross out *the* when you think it is not necessary.

1. I love ~~*the*~~ Italian food.
2. *The* English people I know are really nice.
3. All you need is ~~*the*~~ love.
4. *The* food in this restaurant is terrible!
5. *The* money isn't *the* problem. *The* problem is not having *the* money!
6. *The* problem today is that *the* families don't spend enough time together.
7. *The* vegetarians don't eat ~~*the*~~ meat.
8. *The* man who lives next door is *the* headmaster's uncle.

Asking for personal information

1 You meet an English boy. Use these prompts to write questions to ask him.

1 Find out if he has brothers or sisters.
Have you got any brothers or sisters?

2 Find out their ages.

3 Find out if they go to the boy's school.

4 Find out if they all go out together at the weekend.

5 Find out what the boy does on Saturdays.

2 Match these answers to your questions in 1.

a Yes, they do. ......

b Yes, I've got two sisters and a brother. ......

c I usually go out with my friends on Saturday afternoon or evening. We go to the cinema, or bowling. ......

d Not usually. We sometimes go out together on Sundays. We just get in the car and drive out into the country to spend the day there. ......

e My sisters are 15 and 13 and my brother is 12. ......

3 Write your own true answers to the questions in 1.

1

2

3

4

5

Describing photos

4 Look at this photo and answer the questions. If you are not sure of something, use *I think* and/or *I imagine*.

1 Who can you see in the photo?

2 Where are they?

3 What are they doing?

4 How do you think the people are feeling? Why?

5 Use the questions in 4 to think of things to say about this photo. Make notes and then practise orally.

An informal email

1 Read this student's paragraph plan and email. Then put his email in the order of his paragraph plan.

Paragraph plan

Informal email giving personal information

Paragraph 1: Basic personal information
Paragraph 2: Information about my family
Paragraph 3: Hobbies
Paragraph 4: Favourite subject(s) at school
Paragraph 5: Asking for a reply

A In my free time, I like doing sport with my friends. We play all types of sport – football, basketball, tennis. We aren't very good, but we enjoy ourselves ☺. I also enjoy reading and watching TV.

B I live with my mum and my little brother. His name is Tom and he's only nine years old. My mum is an artist. She does illustrations for books and magazines. She's very good and she loves her job! My parents are divorced and I don't see my father very often.

C **Anyway**, it's time to do my homework. Write back soon and tell me about yourself.
Best wishes

D Hi!
I'm Steve. **I'm** 17 and I'm from Oxford in England.
Let me tell you about myself.

E At school my favourite subject is English. At the moment we're studying American literature and I'm really enjoying it. I also like studying art. My mum helps me with that, of course!

1 *D* ....
2 ....
3 ....
4 ....
5 ....
Steve

2 Look at the words or expressions in bold in the email. Explain why they are important in informal emails.

Hi *We usually start informal emails with this word.*

I'm ....

Anyway ....

Best wishes ....

3 Look at this personal information. Imagine that you are this person. Write an informal email using the paragraph plan and email in 1 as a model. Add more information and write complete sentences.

Paragraph plan

Paragraph 1: Marianela, 16, Buenos Aires, Argentina
Paragraph 2: Mother and father, two sisters. One sister 21, other 19. Both at university. Go out with them at weekend.
Paragraph 3: Main hobby – cinema (American films). Go often. Also like books.
Paragraph 4: Favourite subjects – Geography. Good teacher. Also History.
Paragraph 5: Ask for a reply

....

2 Criminal records

Grammar ‣ Past simple ‣ Past continuous
Vocabulary ‣ Crimes ‣ Criminals
‣ Phrasal verbs connected with investigating and finding
Speaking ‣ Reporting a past event
Writing ‣ An informal letter

‣ Vocabulary

Crimes

1a Find eight crimes in the word search.

g	n	m	r	a	a	v	p	s	b	c	l	l	t
a	t	v	e	k	p	r	d	d	n	e	p	r	s
o	e	i	t	c	s	o	e	m	t	w	i	h	a
r	b	t	n	r	p	b	e	r	e	i	r	o	o
i	c	w	o	a	d	b	u	r	g	l	a	r	y
w	i	t	m	n	d	e	t	h	c	a	c	o	i
j	h	m	u	t	f	r	r	r	r	m	y	e	s
e	u	g	g	r	t	y	h	a	s	b	r	g	t
s	z	e	g	n	c	a	r	t	h	e	f	t	d
n	r	l	i	h	w	n	l	m	e	r	d	q	r
h	v	a	n	d	a	l	i	s	m	c	t	v	d
t	t	t	g	o	d	h	o	t	e	e	l	e	s
e	n	i	n	w	i	s	m	u	r	d	e	r	i
c	f	y	s	h	o	p	l	i	f	t	i	n	g
e	e	a	h	a	a	t	n	n	f	w	v	s	t
f	s	h	p	o	v	m	r	d	k	e	e	g	r
t	t	e	i	u	q	f	f	l	o	w	v	f	t

1b Write the words from 1a in column A. Put them in alphabetical order.

	A: crimes	B: verbs
1	*burglary*	
2		
3		
4		
5		
6		
7		
8		

2 Complete column B with these verbs. You can repeat verbs if necessary.

burgle kill mug pirate rob steal vandalise

Criminals

3 Put the letters in order to find the names of different criminals.

1 ruggem *mugger*
2 fieth thief
3 tripea ....
4 lavand vandal
5 redrumer murderer
6 boerbr robber
7 fitposherl shoplifter
8 blagrur burglar

4 Complete the sentences with the correct form of the words in 1, 2 and 3.

1 The .... stole money and objects from our home.
2 The police arrested a group of .... who were breaking shop windows in Main Street last night.
3 A .... attacked an old woman last night and took her handbag and watch.
4 In my opinion .... is a terrible crime because it's wrong to take someone's life.
5 They make thousands of illegal copies. They .... software, CDs and DVDs.
6 The .... stole CDs and DVDs from the department store.
7 Those two robbers .... thousands of dollars every month in spectacular robberies.

1 Look at the photo and the title of the text. What do you think happened?

I think ....

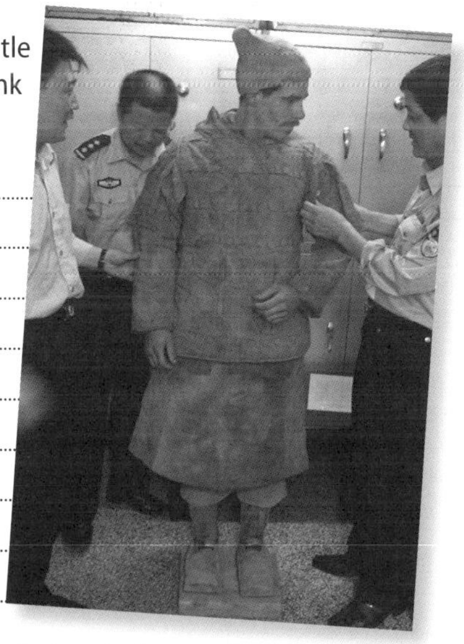

2 Read the text. Were your predictions in 1 correct?

A German student, the Chinese police and a 2000-year-old army

1 In 1974 two local farmers accidentally discovered the world-famous Terracotta Army near the ancient city of Xian in China. There were thousands of brown terracotta soldiers. They were there to guard the ancient emperor Xian Shi Huang, a job they began 2200 years ago. Archeologists immediately called the Terracotta Army the find of the century.

2 Thousands of people visit the Terracotta Army each day in the museum in Xian. On 18th September 2006 one of those visitors was a German art student called Pablo Wendel. Pablo, 26, looked like a normal tourist when he walked into the museum. But he was carrying a bag with something special in it. Inside was a brown costume that looked very old. It was an exact copy of the uniform that the terracotta soldiers were wearing.

3 Pablo quickly put on his soldier's uniform, covered his face in brown paint and jumped down into the area where the Terracotta Army was standing. Security officers saw him, but Pablo was well prepared and knew exactly what to do. He found a space in the lines of soldiers and stood completely still. The police arrived, but now that he wasn't moving, the officers didn't know which was the real person and which were the statues.

4 However, after two minutes, one of the policemen finally found him. Still Pablo didn't move a muscle. In the end, the police officers had to pick him up like a statue and carry him away. The officers asked Pablo a lot of questions to find out why he was there. He told them that he loved the Terracotta Army and wanted to be part of it for just one day.

5 The police decided not to arrest him, probably because Pablo didn't actually touch or break any of the terracotta soldiers. But they took away his uniform, told him not to do it again and sent him back to the eastern Chinese city of Hangzhou where he was studying.

3 Read the text again and choose a, b or c to complete the sentences.

1 Pablo Wendel wanted to
- a join the modern Chinese army.
- b be part of an ancient Chinese army.
- c be an expert in Chinese armies.

2 The Terracotta Army began their work
- a 100 years ago.
- b 30 years ago.
- c over 2,000 years ago.

3 It was difficult to find Pablo Wendel because
- a he was a good statue.
- b he was behind the soldiers.
- c the police weren't paying attention.

4 When the police found him, Pablo
- a started running.
- b didn't do anything.
- c attacked the police officers.

5 The police
- a said Pablo could stay in Xian.
- b carried Pablo away and questioned him.
- c thought the incident was funny and unimportant.

4 Answer the questions.

1 What did Pablo Wendel do on 18th September 2006? ....

2 Why did he do it? ....

3 Why did the police decide not to arrest him? ....

5 What is the meaning of these words from the text? Write a definition, explanation or synonym. Use your dictionary if necessary.

1 accidentally (*paragraph 1*) *without planning or wanting to do something*

2 century (*paragraph 1*) ....

3 costume (*paragraph 2*) ....

4 muscle (*paragraph 4*) ....

5 pick up (*paragraph 4*) ....

6 arrest (*paragraph 5*) ....

6 What about *you*?

Do you think that what Pablo did was right or wrong? Why?

....

Past simple

1 Match the puzzle pieces to make irregular forms of the past simple. How many irregular forms can you make? Write the present form of each verb in brackets.

bought (buy)

b | br | c | dr | h | l

p | s | sh | sp | t | th

-aught | -ang | -ank | -ew | -oke

-old | -ook | -ought | -ut

2 Complete the text with the past simple form of these verbs.

be   become   catch   go   not do   steal

Ronald, or Ronnie, Biggs **(a)** .... born in England in 1929. He **(b)** .... famous in 1963 for his part in the Great Train Robbery. In this robbery, a gang of criminals **(c)** .... 2.6 million pounds from a train. Biggs **(d)** .... much in the crime, he only had a small part in it, but the police **(e)** .... him and he **(f)** .... to prison.

change   escape   leave   see   work

Two years later he **(g)** .... He ran away to Paris and **(h)** .... his appearance thanks to plastic surgery. In 1970 he **(i)** .... France. Then, in Australia, he **(j)** .... in a television studio but a reporter **(k)** .... him and recognised him.

come   fly   live   make   sing

Because of this, Biggs **(l)** .... to Brazil, where he **(m)** .... with his new family for many years. He **(n)** .... a film with the Sex Pistols in 1980 and he **(o)** .... some songs with them. He **(p)** .... back to England in 2001 and had to go back to prison.

3 Use the question words and the verbs to write questions about Ronnie Biggs.

1 When/be born?
When was he born?
2 What crime/commit?
....
3 How much/steal?
....
4 police/catch him?
....
5 Where/go in 1970?
....
6 Why/fly to Brazil?
....
7 sing with/the Rolling Stones?
....
8 When/come back to England?
....

4 These statements are incorrect. Write one negative sentence and one correct sentence for each statement.

1 Ronnie Biggs was born in 1919.
Ronnie Biggs wasn't born in 1919. He was born in 1929.
2 Ronnie Biggs committed a murder.
....
....
3 Biggs stole 2.6 million dollars.
....
....
4 He ran away to Madrid.
....
....
5 A police officer saw him in Australia.
....
....
6 After Australia, Biggs flew to the USA.
....
....

Grammar extension

5 Use the answers to the questions in 3 to write a short text about Ronnie Biggs.

He was born in 1929.
....
....
....
....
....
....
....

Phrasal verbs connected with investigating and finding

1 Complete the phrasal verbs with these words.

come find look look turn work

1 .... out = discover
2 .... into = investigate
3 .... for = try to find
4 .... up = arrive or appear unexpectedly
5 .... across = find by accident
6 .... out = solve a problem by considering the facts

2 Choose the correct alternative.

1 Sir Isaac Newton saw an apple falling from a tree. He thought about it and *worked out/turned up* his theory of gravity.
2 When I lost a contact lens, I *looked for/looked into* it everywhere.
3 The maths problem was really difficult but after thinking hard, they *worked out/came across* the answer
4 Nobody usually went to her house but one Saturday one of her friends *turned up/came across*.
5 He wanted an original name for his new dog but he couldn't think of one. Then he *came across/looked into* the name Torak in a novel and he liked it.
6 When she *looked into/found out* that he was lying, it was a terrible shock.
7 They can't take a decision about this question yet. They need to *look for/look into* the facts in more detail.

Vocabulary extension: more phrasal verbs with *look*

3 Use your dictionary to match these phrasal verbs with *look* with their meanings.

1 look after	a plan what you are going to do in the future
2 look ahead	b feel happy or excited that something is going to happen
3 look back	c walk around a room, building or place and see what is there
4 look forward to	d look carefully at people or things around you to find a particular person or thing
5 look out for	e think about a time or event in the past
6 look round	f take care of someone or something

4 Complete the sentences with the correct prepositions.

after ahead back forward out round

1 Let's look .... this museum slowly. I think it will be interesting.
2 I'm looking .... to the football match tomorrow. I'm really excited about it.
3 We need to look .... and see what problems there could be in the next few years.
4 Mum and I are going out now. Look .... your little sister until we get back.
5 Stop spending your time looking .... The past is the past. It's time to carry on with your life.
6 When you go to the party, look .... for Helen and Kate because they said they were going too.

5 Answer the questions. Write complete sentences.

1 Do you ever look after anybody? If so, who?
....
....
2 Do you spend more time looking ahead or looking back?
....
....
3 What are you looking forward to doing this weekend?
....
....
4 Is there a house, building or museum that you would like to look round? Which one(s)?
....
....
5 When you go to a party, who is the first person you look out for?
....
....

Click onto... Private investigators

Cross-curricular – History
The first private detective

1 Look at the logo above the text. What do you think the agency did every day?

....

....

2 Read the text and choose the correct alternative.

1 The first detective, Allan Pinkerton, was born in *England/Scotland/America*.
2 From 1842 he lived in *England/Scotland/America*.
3 Pinkerton's National Detective Agency investigated *bank robberies/train robberies/murders* at the beginning.
4 Pinkerton's National Detective Agency *worked before the FBI/worked with the FBI/copied the FBI*.
5 Pinkerton's National Detective Agency was *very small/small/big*.

▶ WORD BOOSTER

Match the words and definitions.

1 gang	a kill an important person
2 logo	b gave money for something
3 paid	c group of criminals
4 assassinate	d walk behind somebody
5 follow	e symbol to represent a company or organisation

3 Complete the sentences with information from the text.

1 *Allan Pinkerton became a local hero* because he helped the police to find the leader of a gang of criminals.
2 ....
.... because there was money and gold on trains.
3 The Pinkertons' usual job was to ....
....
and they were very good at it.
4 Pinkerton's National Detective Agency became famous because the Pinkertons ....
....
5 ....
.... because Pinkerton's National Detective Agency had an eye for their logo.

4 What about *you*?

Who is your favourite famous detective from a book, TV series, film or cartoon? Why do you like him/her?

....

....

....

....

We all love films and books about private detectives. But who was the first private detective? In fact, his name was Allan Pinkerton and his story is as interesting as a detective novel.

Pinkerton was born in Scotland in 1819 but he went to live in America in 1842. He and his wife lived in Chicago. One day when he was walking by a river, he came across a small island. He saw that people were living there and he worked out that they were a gang of criminals. He went and told the police and they caught all the criminals except their leader. Pinkerton helped the police to look for the leader and he found him. Pinkerton became a local hero and the next year he became Chicago's first private detective.

In 1852 Allan Pinkerton and his brother Robert started their own detective agency. At the time, there were many train robbers because trains carried lots of money and gold. People usually paid the Pinkertons to find and catch train robbers. They were good at their job and soon criminals hated the name Pinkerton.

In 1861 the Pinkertons were investigating a train robbery when they discovered a plan to assassinate the American president, Abraham Lincoln. With this information, the Pinkertons saved Lincoln's life, and soon everybody knew about their agency, Pinkerton's National Detective Agency. In the American Civil War, Lincoln paid Pinkerton's National Detective Agency to organise a secret intelligence service. Before the creation of the FBI or the CIA in America, Pinkerton's National Detective Agency did exactly this type of work.

The Pinkertons soon had many men and women working for them. Allan Pinkerton taught them how to investigate crimes and how to follow people without them knowing about it. He was also the first person to keep a bank of information about different criminals, including their photos. On the side of Pinkerton's National Detective Agency's headquarters in Chicago they had a famous logo. It was a big black and white eye with the words 'We never sleep'. Private detectives are often called 'Private Eyes'. The Pinkerton eye was the origin of this name.

Past continuous

1 Complete the dialogue with the past continuous form of these verbs.

do do feel have not feel sit talk visit

HELEN: I rang you at 8pm last night but there was no answer. What **(a)** .... you ....?

LUKE: My mum and I **(b)** .... my grandmother in hospital.

HELEN: Why was she in hospital?

LUKE: Yesterday morning she **(c)** .... well so we called the doctor and he said that she needed to go to hospital.

HELEN: What **(d)** .... she .... last night when you visited her?

LUKE: She **(e)** .... on a chair, not lying in bed. All the patients **(f)** .... dinner and they **(g)** .... and laughing. She looked OK. When my mum phoned the hospital this morning, she **(h)** .... much better.

HELEN: That's good news.

2 Complete the text with the past simple or past continuous form of the verbs given.

One Saturday afternoon, a team of police officers **(a)** .... (play) football against a group of local people in Yorkshire, England. The police officers **(b)** .... (lose) 0–2 when suddenly an officer **(c)** .... (recognise) one of the men who **(d)** .... (play) in the other team. He **(e)** .... (know) that the man was a criminal. The police officers **(f)** .... (look) for him for several burglaries. The police officers **(g)** .... (stop) playing and **(h)** .... (arrest) the man. Then they **(i)** .... (start) the match again. In the end, the police officers **(j)** .... (win) the match 3–2! And the man **(k)** .... (go) to prison for a long time.

3 Write questions for these answers.

1 *What were you doing at 7pm last night?*
I was listening to my MP3 player at 7pm last night.

2 ....
My family was watching a film at 7pm.

3 ....
Later I took the dog out for a walk.

4 ....
No, I wasn't sleeping at 9pm.

5 ....
At 11pm I was reading.

6 ....
I went to sleep at about 12pm.

4 Write your own true answers to the questions in 3.

1 ....

2 ....

3 ....

4 ....

5 ....

6 ....

Grammar extension

5 Read the text. There are ten extra words in it. Find them and cross them out.

~~The~~ last night we were watching a film on TV when suddenly we did heard a sound like an explosion. At first we thought that it was came from the TV but then we realised the noise came from the kitchen.

My dad said us it could be a burglar and so he took a big stick and went to the kitchen to see if he was right. He was opening the door when that something jumped out really fast! It wasn't a burglar because it was only small.

Then there did was another sound. We went back to the living room. The lamp was on the floor. In the corner of the room there was a cat. My family and I we recognised it – it was my neighbour's cat. The cat was nervous and was knocking things onto the floor while it is was running through our house.

We did rang the neighbour and he came to take his cat back. In the end of we didn't see what happened in the film we were watching.

Reporting a past event – a crime

1 Complete the dialogue with these words.

after   at first   in the end   later   suddenly   then

AMY: Last night my friends and I went out to that new restaurant in Bank Street.
ADAM: Did you have a good time?
AMY: No, not really.
ADAM: Why not? What happened?
AMY: Well, we wanted to see if it was good or not. **(a)** .... we didn't like it because the waiter was really slow. But **(b)** .... we started eating and we loved it. When we were finishing our meal, a man **(c)** .... started shouting at the waiter. He was really angry and became violent. A few minutes **(d)** .... the manager of the restaurant called the police.
ADAM: Then what happened?
AMY: **(e)** .... that the man stopped shouting and sat down. **(f)** .... he paid and left.

2 Imagine that you were waiting outside the cinema last Saturday and that you saw this scene. Write the other half of the dialogue. Use some of the words from the box in 1.

YOUR FRIEND: Did you have a good time last Saturday?
YOU: **(a)** ....
YOUR FRIEND: Why not? What happened?
YOU: **(b)** ....
....
....
....
YOUR FRIEND: So what happened in the end?
YOU: **(c)** ....
....

Describing photos

3 Look at the photo and answer the questions. If you are not sure of something, use *I think* and/or *I imagine*.

1 Who can you see in the photo?
....
....

2 Where are they?
....
....

3 What are they doing?
....
....

4 What do you think of this crime? Why?
....
....

4 Use the questions in 3 to think of things to say about this photo. Make notes and then practise orally.

An informal letter

1 Read this letter from a girl called Georgina. What was Georgina's unusual experience?

....

....

....

....

(a) ....

(b) ....

(c) ....

(d) ....

It was great to hear from you.

Something really unusual happened to me yesterday. I was walking home after hockey practice when I saw a little boy on his own. He was crying because he was lost. He was only about four or five years old and he didn't know how to get home.

I didn't know what to do, but I couldn't just leave him there. I decided to take him to the police station. We were walking along the road when we got to some shops. Suddenly, a woman came running out of one of the shops. She looked very worried and was crying too. The boy shouted 'Mummy!' The woman was his mum! They both looked so happy, and I was happy for them.

(e) .... *and tell me about your week.*

(f) ....

Georgina

2 Put these words and expressions in the correct place in the letter in 1.

1 Thanks for your letter.

2 Dear Phil,

3 28th April 2011

4 Love,

5 70 Baxter Street,
Birmingham,
BO3 4RG.

6 Write back soon

3 Imagine that you found an animal some time ago. Write a letter to a friend telling them about what you found. Tell them:

- what kind of animal it was and what you were doing when you found it
- why you decided to take it home and how other family members reacted
- what problem you had with the animal and how you solved it
- how the animal changed your life.

....

....

....

....

4 When you finish, read your own letter and give yourself a mark from 0 (not very good) to 5 (excellent) for these criteria.

a It answers the questions. ....

b It has all the necessary information. ....

c It is easy to understand. ....

d It is well organised. ....

e I think the grammar is correct. ....

f I have used different words. ....

g I have used punctuation and capital letters. ....

5 Think about your marks in 4 and make changes to your letter to improve it.

Revision: Units 1–2

Grammar

1 Complete the sentences with the present simple form of the verbs given.

1 Elizabeth .... (watch) the news twice a day.
2 My friends .... (not read) magazines.
3 Sunny weather .... (make) me feel happy.
4 A: .... it .... (rain) a lot in your country?
B: Yes, it ....
5 My brother usually .... (study) in his bedroom.

/ 5 points

2 Complete the dialogue with the present continuous form of these verbs.

begin carry come not stay put

Katie: Why **(a)** .... you .... your books in your bag? The lesson **(b)** .... now.
Lucy: I **(c)** .... because I have an appointment at the doctor's.
Katie: Where's the teacher anyway?
Lucy: He **(d)** .... now. He's walking slowly because he **(e)** .... the CD player and some dictionaries.

/ 5 points

3 Complete the text with *a/an, the* or *0* (no article).

I've got **(a)** .... sister called Polly. My sister loves **(b)** .... Italian food. She's got **(c)** .... Italian friend who has **(d)** .... restaurant. **(e)** .... restaurant is near our house.

/ 5 points

4 Complete the text with the past simple or the past continuous form of the verbs given.

One day, when I **(a)** .... (walk) to school, I **(b)** .... (see) something unusual. A woman **(c)** .... (sing) and a lot of people **(d)** .... (watch) her. I didn't recognise her, so I **(e)** .... (continue) on my way to school but when I **(f)** .... (arrive), nobody **(g)** .... (be) there. Half an hour later all the other students **(h)** .... (come). They **(i)** .... (talk) about a surprise concert by our music teacher in the street and I was the only person who **(j)** .... (not see) it!

/ 10 points

Total / 25 points

Vocabulary

1 Write an explanation for each word or expression.

1 birth ....
2 adolescence ....
3 senior citizen ....
4 single ....
5 only child ....

/ 5 points

2 Who are these people in a family?

1 the brother of your father ....
2 the brother of your husband or wife ....
3 your father's new wife ....
4 your sister's daughter ....
5 the man a woman is married to ....

/ 5 points

3 Match the words with the suffixes to make nouns.

1 protect
2 different
3 improve
4 equip
5 invent

-ion
-ment
-ence

/ 5 points

4 Find words which match the definitions. They are all crimes or criminals.

1 somebody who steals from houses ....
2 the crime when you kill someone ....
3 somebody who attacks another person to steal from them ....
4 the crime of breaking and destroying public things for no reason ....
5 the crime of copying software, films, etc ....
6 the person who steals from a bank ....

/ 6 points

5 Complete the text with the correct present simple form of these verbs.

look look turn work

In this story, there is a mysterious theft. A detective **(a)** .... into the crime. He asks lots of questions and, by using logic, he **(b)** .... out that a man called Ron Carter is the criminal. He **(c)** .... for physical evidence that Carter did it. The detective can't find anything but when he suddenly **(d)** .... up at Carter's house, Carter admits he is the thief.

/ 4 points

Total / 25 points

Reading

1 Read the text and choose the best title for it.

1 School children and violent crime
2 Global solutions to the problem of absent students
3 Who is responsible for you travelling to school – you, your parents or the police?

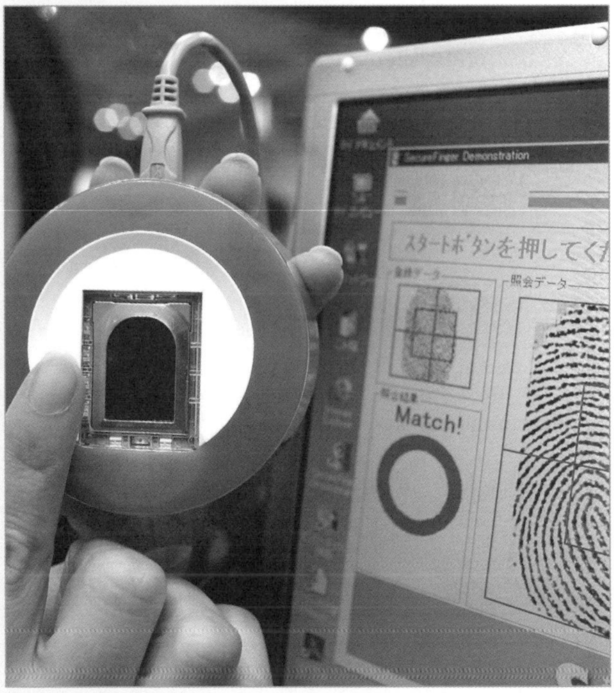

THE LAW IN Britain and many other countries says that children under 16 need to go to school. When they don't go to school, it's a crime. It's called 'truancy' and many different countries take truancy very seriously.

In a group of private schools in Tokyo, students put out their hands for examination every morning. A special computer looks at each student's fingers to check their fingerprints. Prison officers use the same technique with criminals in prison. It means that teachers know exactly who is in class and who isn't.

In some countries, truancy is the parents' problem and responsibility. At 5 am one morning in Miami, two policemen arrived at the house of Mindy Pearl Viera. They arrested her and took her to the police station because her teenage daughters didn't go to school more than 100 times that year.

In the Malaysian town of Seremban, when the police find a student who is in the street and not at school, they take them to the police station where there is now a special 'reading room'. The students read books while they are waiting for their parents to come and take them home. Students who don't finish the book take it home and then write a summary of it.

A school in Scotland uses an American system called Phonemaster. It automatically telephones parents when a student is 30 minutes late for school. The phone doesn't stop ringing until someone answers it.

2 Read the text. Are these statements true (T) or false (F)? Write down the line(s) where you found the answer.

1 Truancy is when children under 16 miss school for no reason. ....

2 Prison officers check fingerprints to know if criminals are present in the prison or not. ....

3 Mindy Pearl Viera had problems with the police because there were many times when she didn't go to school. ....

4 There are books at the Seremban police station. ....

5 All students in Seremban have to write a summary of their book. ....

6 With the Phonemaster system a person phones parents again and again until they pick up the phone. ....

/ 7 points

Writing

3 Last week you saw a crime. Write an informal letter to a friend telling them about it. Tell them:

- what the crime was
- what you were doing when you saw it
- who the criminal was
- if the police caught the criminal
- what happened in the end.

/ 8 points

Hi Luke,

Let me tell you what happened to me last week. I ...

Total / 15 points

3 Lost in translation

Grammar	▸ Countable and uncountable nouns ▸ Relative pronouns ▸ *Some, any, much, many, a lot of, a few, a little*
Vocabulary	▸ Countries, nationalities and languages ▸ Learning a language ▸ Negative prefixes *un-*, *in-*, *im-*, *ir-*, *il-*
Speaking	▸ Asking for information
Writing	▸ A language biography

▸ Vocabulary

Countries, nationalities and languages

1 Complete the table.

	Country	Nationality	Language(s)
	(a)	(b)	(c) ....
	(d)	(e)	(f) ....
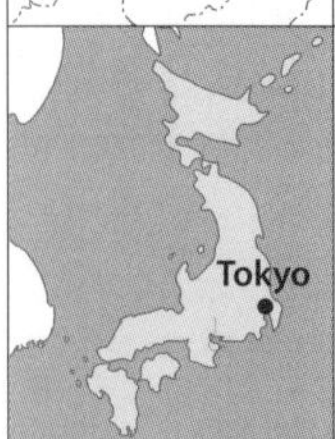	(g)	(h)	(i) ....
	(j)	(k)	(l) ....
	(m)	(n)	(o) ....
	(p)	(q)	(r) ....

2 Are these sentences true (T) or false (F)? If they are false, correct them.

1 In Russia they speak German. ....
2 In the Netherlands they speak Dutch. ....
3 People from Egypt are Egyptese. ....
4 People from Egypt speak Arabian. ....
5 Swiss people are from Switzerland. ....
6 In Switzerland they speak French. ....
7 In Brazil they speak Spanish. ....
8 Welsh people are from Wales. ....

Learning a language

3 Choose the correct alternative.

1 How often do you practice/practise your pronunciation?
2 Translate/Translation can be difficult sometimes.
3 It's natural to do/make mistakes.
4 Last week we made/took a listening exam.
5 I enjoy doing/making speaking exercises.
6 You need lots of practice/practise to speak and write well in English.
7 We're going to revise/revision for our exam.

4 Complete the questions with these words. There are eight words but only five gaps.

homework made mistake revise
skill translation write wrote

1 When was the last time you .... an essay in English? What was it about?
2 How do you .... grammar before an English exam?
3 Apart from ...., what else do you do in English outside school?
4 Which .... (reading, writing, listening or speaking) do you enjoy practising the most?
5 What is a typical .... you make in English (e.g. writing *english* instead of *English*)?

5 Write your own true answers to the questions in 4.

1 ....
2 ....
3 ....
4 ....
5 ....

1 Read this text and write a good title for it.

IN 2005 THE Chief Inspector of Schools, David Bell, said: 'Teenage boys in Britain don't really want to speak in English. So how are they going to learn to speak in other languages? Language learning in England's schools is becoming almost completely middle class and female. We know that girls are doing modern languages more than boys, and that schools in poor areas are not giving many opportunities to learn modern foreign languages.' But why aren't boys studying languages? Is it because they don't like making mistakes? Or is it because teenage boys just don't talk a lot, not even in their own language? 'It's not a good situation,' said Bell, 'because we want more people to learn a modern language.'

Mr Bell says secondary schools are already beginning to separate boys and girls for science lessons. He thinks it can also be a good idea for schools to do the same thing with modern language teaching. Mr Bell suggested that single-sex classes in modern languages could stop boys being embarrassed about speaking in another language. 'Some people think that it is a bad idea to separate boys and girls into different classes. But if the system produces good results for modern languages, let's do it.'

i INSIDE INFORMATION

- GCSEs are public examinations which English, Welsh and Northern Irish students usually do when they are 16. A-levels are the exams which 18-year-old students usually take. Grade A is the top mark.
- In Britain 'independent' schools are private schools. Parents pay to send their children to these types of schools.
- In Britain, the languages that secondary students normally study are French, German or Spanish – in that order.

Modern languages are not very popular in British secondary schools. Not many people are taking a GCSE in French this year. Recent investigation shows that there are problems with language learning in Britain. And those problems are making a difference to university language departments too. There are not many students who want to study languages, and so some university language departments now only have 10 or 12 students.

Other statistics also confirmed the idea that mostly rich students are now studying modern languages. The Independent Schools Council found out that last year 60% of all the top marks in A-level French came from students in independent schools.

2 Read the text again. Are these sentences true (T) or false (F)? Write the line(s) where you found the answer.

1 David Bell thinks teenage boys in Britain are good at modern languages because they like speaking. ....

2 David Bell is worried because in general children from poor families aren't studying modern languages. ....

3 David Bell thinks it's a good idea to have language classes with boys only because the boys won't be afraid to speak. ....

4 The number of students taking exams in modern languages is not high. ....

5 The number of students doing languages at university is going up. ....

6 You can only get a good mark in French if you go to an independent school. ....

3 Find these words in the text. Write a synonym, definition or explanation for each one. Use your dictionary if necessary.

1 completely (*line 5*) ....
2 opportunities (*line 8*) ....
3 separate (*line 15*) ....
4 single-sex (*line 18*) ....
5 embarrassed (*line 19*) ....
6 top marks (*line 34*) ....

4 What about *you*?

1 Is there any difference between the number of girls and boys studying languages in your country? What is the difference?

....

2 Do you think there is any difference in the way boys and girls learn languages?

....

3 What do you think about separating boys and girls into different classes in languages or in general?

....

Some, any, much, many, a lot of, a few, a little

1 Complete the table by ticking the correct boxes. Look at *some* as an example.

	some	any	much	many	a lot (of)	a few	a little
plural countable	✓						
uncountable	✓						
affirmative	✓						
negative & questions							
large quantity							
small quantity							

2 Are these words countable (C) or uncountable (U)?

1 close friend *C*
2 free time ....
3 problem ....
4 good idea ....
5 energy ....
6 niece ....
7 cousin ....
8 homework ....

3 Write questions with the words in 2 using either *much* or *many*. In your questions, make the countable nouns in 2 plural.

1 *Have you got many close friends?*
2 ....
3 ....
4 ....
5 ....
6 ....
7 ....
8 ....

4 Write your own true answers to your questions in 3 using *some, any, not much, not many, a lot of*.

1 *I've got some close friends but not many.*
2 ....
3 ....
4 ....
5 ....
6 ....
7 ....
8 ....

5 Look at the pictures and write sentences with *There is/are* and *a few* or *a little*.

1

There's a little water.

2

....

....

4

....

5

....

6

....

Grammar extension

6 Complete the sentences so they are true for you.

1 I've got some .... in my bedroom.
2 We haven't got any .... in our house.
3 I haven't got much ....
4 There aren't many .... in our family.
5 We've got a lot of .... at school.
6 I've got a few ....
7 We've got a little .... in our fridge.

Negative prefixes *un-*, *in-*, *im-*, *ir-*, *il-*

1 Complete the table by writing these words in the correct column.

correct formal happy ~~legal~~ official possible practical regular usual visible

un-	in-	im-	ir-	il-
....	....	....	....	*legal*
....	....	....	....	....
....	....	....	....	....
		Basic rule: *We use the prefix im- when a word starts with the letter*	Basic rule:	Basic rule: ....

2 Look at these words. Complete the basic rules in 1 to explain when we use the prefixes *im-*, *ir* and *il-*.

1 patient ➔ **im**patient
2 probable ➔ **im**probable
3 relevant ➔ **ir**relevant
4 responsible ➔ **ir**responsible
5 logical ➔ **il**logical
6 legible ➔ **il**legible

3 Match the words in 1 and 2 with these synonyms and definitions.

1 wrong ....
2 relaxed, friendly, not very serious ....
3 sad ....
4 not good at waiting ....
5 impossible to see ....
6 impossible to read ....

Vocabulary extension: negative prefixes *dis-* and *non-*

4 Look at these words. Which go with *dis-* and which go with *non-*? Which type of word is each one: a noun, verb or adjective? Use your dictionary if necessary.

1 *dis* like *noun, verb*
2 .... agree ....
3 .... alcoholic ....
4 .... appear ....
5 .... advantage ....
6 .... resident ....
7 .... stop ....
8 .... honest ....
9 .... obey ....
10 .... smoking ....
11 .... qualify ....

5 Complete the sentences with words in 4.

1 Cola is a .... drink.
2 Someone who doesn't usually tell the truth is ....
3 He doesn't normally live in this country, he only comes for short periods. He's a ....
4 When you .... someone, you don't do what they tell you to do.
5 If you do something against the rules in a competition, they can .... you.
6 You and I .... about nearly everything. Our ideas are almost always different.
7 One .... of mobile phones is the radiation that they can cause.
8 I hate cigarettes. Put me in the .... section.
9 The music on this radio station is .... It's one song, then another, then another.

Click onto... Latin

Cross-curricular – Languages
Latin ... in Finland!

INSIDE INFORMATION

- Finland is in Scandinavia. It's next to Sweden, Russia and Norway.
- The capital is Helsinki.
- Finland is a big country but only 5.3 million people live there.

1 Read the text and choose the best title for it.

1 School children in Finland want more Latin   2 The news in Latin   3 Latin isn't a dead language

File Edit View History Tools Window Help

In Finland they speak Finnish and a few people speak Swedish. But another language is popular there too, and that language is Latin.

Here's an example of Latin's popularity. A Finnish university professor called Tuomo Pekkanen has a radio programme where he reads the news every day ... in Latin. The title of the programme is *Nuntii Latini*. There are only one or two programmes like this in the world. 75,000 people listen to it, for example on the Internet. The programme receives letters from listeners in about 50 countries.

When he is making his news programme there are sometimes words which are difficult for Pekkanen to translate because, as you probably know, the Romans didn't have television, computers, emails or lasers, for example. But Pekkanen says that he can talk about any story on the news by inventing a few new Latin words if necessary.

And Professor Pekkanen doesn't just translate the news into Latin. He also translates the words for songs. And he isn't the only one. Dr Jukka Ammondt, another university professor, loves Latin and he loves the king of rock and roll, Elvis Presley. So what does he do? He sings Elvis in Latin. 'The legend of Elvis Presley lives forever, and it is of course very important to sing Elvis Presley's songs in the Latin language because Latin is the eternal language,' he says. So songs like *I can't help falling in love* become *Non adamare non possum*.

Elvis Presley

There is an important tradition of studying Latin in Finland. There was a Latin congress there recently and people had no problem talking in Latin. Nowadays English is the language which people all over the world use to communicate. But before English it was Latin. Tuomo Pekkanen says that around 15 million people in Europe speak or understand Latin. That's not bad for a 'dead' language.

WORD BOOSTER

Match the words and definitions.

1 legend	a big meeting of experts
2 eternal	b with no end
3 congress	c at the present time
4 nowadays	d very famous person

2 Read the text again and complete the sentences.

1 Tuomo Pekkanen is a professor who reads ....

2 Jukka Ammondt is a professor who sings ....

3 Finland is a place where there is ....

4 Latin is a language which around ....

3 Are these sentences true (T) or false (F)? Correct the false sentences.

1 There are many programmes like *Nuntii Latini* in the world.
....

2 It can be difficult to translate the news because there are not always Latin words for modern things. ....

3 Jukka Ammondt thinks there is a logical connection between Latin and Elvis Presley. ....

4 Today Latin has the same function as English. ....

4 What about *you*?

1 Do you, or did you, study Latin? Do/Did you like it?
....
....

2 Do you think it's a good idea to study Latin? Why/Why not?
....
....

Relative pronouns

1 Complete the rules with these relative pronouns.

that when where which who whose

1 We use *that* and .... for people.
2 We use .... and .... for things.
3 We use .... for possessions.
4 We use .... for times.
5 We use .... for places.

2 Choose the correct alternative. If you think both alternatives are possible, choose both.

1 Football is a sport *that/–* many people around the world watch.
2 He's an artist who *paint/paints* abstract paintings.
3 She's the girl *who/whose* cousin is at our school.
4 This is the town *that/where* he lives.
5 This is the room *that/where* I work.
6 That's the type of mistake *that/which* causes problems.
7 I remember the time *when/which* I first met you.
8 Those are the people who *come/comes* at the weekend.
9 He's the writer *who/whose* books are very popular at the moment.
10 This is the bus *which/–* goes to the city centre.

3 Complete the sentences with the correct relative pronoun.

1 Russia is a country .... it is very cold in winter.
2 The weekend is a time .... people can usually relax.
3 English is a language .... people speak all over the world.
4 Tennis is a sport .... has many fans in lots of different countries.
5 New York is a city .... they make a lot of films.
6 August is a month .... lots of people go on holiday.
7 Johnny Depp is the actor .... starred in *Pirates of the Caribbean*.
8 That's the man .... wife is famous.

4a Complete the definitions with the correct relative pronoun.

1 It's the nationality of a person .... comes from Wales.
2 It's the country .... Dutch people live.
3 It's the man .... father is your grandfather.
4 It's the crime .... thieves commit.
5 It's the person .... copies CDs and software illegally.
6 It's the period .... you are a child.
7 It's a country .... people speak Portuguese.
8 It's the thing .... you often do after school.

4b Now find the words which are being described in 4a in the word search. Be careful! There are 14 words in the word search but only eight definitions.

f	t	h	o	m	e	w	o	r	k
e	h	r	t	j	j	a	p	a	n
t	e	x	a	m	l	d	k	c	p
a	n	m	p	i	s	o	g	h	i
b	e	d	k	s	w	l	j	i	r
m	t	s	l	a	l	e	e	l	a
t	h	e	f	t	s	s	k	d	t
s	e	o	e	b	s	c	b	h	e
u	r	f	a	t	h	e	r	o	a
m	l	r	t	g	v	n	a	o	q
m	a	u	n	o	e	c	z	d	v
e	n	t	e	r	r	e	i	b	s
r	d	w	e	l	s	h	l	e	n
w	s	p	g	v	a	n	d	a	l
s	t	e	p	f	a	t	h	e	r
b	t	d	i	n	c	p	e	h	r

Grammar extension

5 Find six more words in the word search. The first letter of each word is in a grey box. Write definitions for them using relative pronouns. Use the definitions in 4a as a model.

1 Word: *a* ....
2 Word: *e* ....
3 Word: *J* ....
4 Word: *s* ....
5 Word: *s* ....
6 Word: *v* ....

Asking for information about a language course

1 Complete the questions used to ask for information about a language course with these words.

information last much organise pardon price registration repeat

1 Do you .... accommodation?
2 Does the .... include other activities?
3 Could you .... that?
4 Can you send me a .... form?
5 ....? Did you say on the 10th July?
6 Could you give me some .... about your summer courses?
7 How .... is the course?
8 How long does the course ....?

2 Complete the dialogue with the questions in 1.

RECEPTIONIST: Good morning. This is the Bradford School of English. How can I help you?
STUDENT: Good morning. I'm calling from Italy. (**a**) ....
RECEPTIONIST: Yes, of course. We have a course for teenagers which begins on the 13th July.
STUDENT: (**b**) ....
RECEPTIONIST: No, on the 13th.
STUDENT: Ah, I understand. (**c**) ....
RECEPTIONIST: 20 days.
STUDENT: (**d**) ....
RECEPTIONIST: Yes, we do. Students usually live with local families.
STUDENT: (**e**) ....
RECEPTIONIST: £950.
STUDENT: (**f**) ....
RECEPTIONIST: Yes, I said the price is £950.
STUDENT: (**g**) ....
RECEPTIONIST: Yes, it does. It includes excursions and social activities like parties and sports.
STUDENT: I'm very interested in the course. (**h**) ....
RECEPTIONIST: Yes, of course. Can you give me your name and address?
STUDENT: Yes, it's …

3 Which two questions in the dialogue in 2 do we use to check understanding?

1 ....
2 ....

Describing photos

4 Look at the photo and answer the questions. If you are not sure of something, use *I think* and/or *I imagine*.

1 Who can you see in the photo?
....
2 Where are they?
....
3 What are they doing?
....
4 What do you think they are talking about? Why?
....

5 Use the questions in 4 to think of things to say about this photo. Make notes and then practise orally.

A language biography

1 Read this language biography by a British student and put the paragraphs in a logical order.

Paragraph 1 .... Paragraph 3 ....
Paragraph 2 .... Paragraph 4 ....

A I still study French now at secondary school. We read books in French and then we talk and write about them. We also study difficult points of grammar and write down new words that we come across.

B I started learning French when I was at primary school. I was seven years old. I remember singing songs in French and playing games. We learnt a lot of French words, like colours, animals and clothes.

C My name is Luke Gallagher and I'm 17 years old. I'm British and my first language is English. Apart from English, I can speak French and German.

D Apart from doing French at school I also have some contact with French outside the classroom because I have a French e-pal. I send him messages every week and next summer I think I'm going to visit him. He lives in Brittany. I listen to some French singers too, and occasionally I watch French films at the cinema or on DVD.

2 Write a title to describe the aim of each paragraph.

Paragraph 1 *Personal details*
Paragraph 2 ....
Paragraph 3 ....
Paragraph 4 ....

3 You are going to write a language biography about yourself and your experiences of learning another language. Before you write, make notes here.

Paragraph 1: Topic ....
Notes ....

Paragraph 2: Topic ....
Notes ....

Paragraph 3: Topic ....
Notes ....

Paragraph 4: Topic ....
Notes ....

4 Use the notes to write your language biography.

4 Fit and well

Grammar	▸ Present perfect with *ever, never, for, since, just, yet, already* ▸ Present perfect and past simple
Vocabulary	▸ Parts of the body ▸ Health problems and illnesses ▸ Compound nouns connected with health and medicine
Speaking	▸ Describing a scene
Writing	▸ Notes and messages

▸ Vocabulary

Parts of the body

1 Complete the parts of the body.

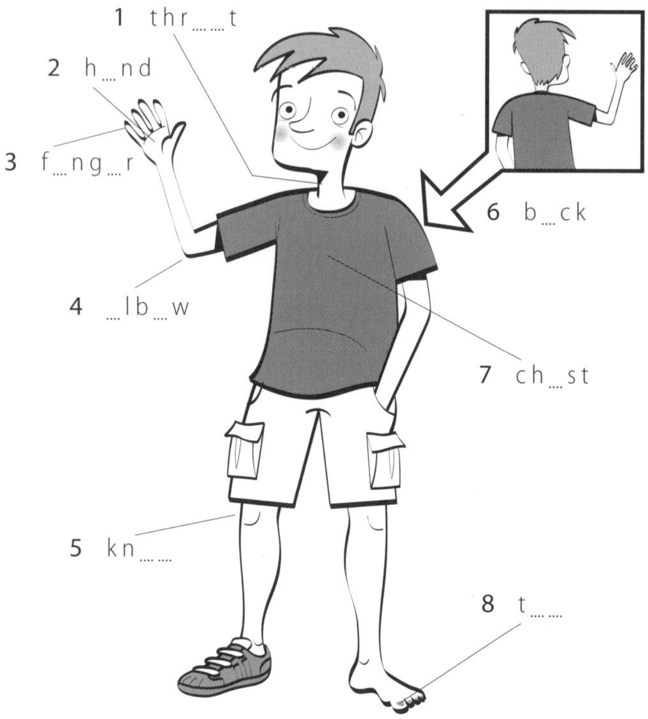

Health problems and illnesses

2 Look at the pictures and complete the sentences.

1 He's got a .... hand.

2 She's got a .... leg.

3 He's got ....

4 She's got .... in her leg.

5 His finger ....

3 Complete the crossword.

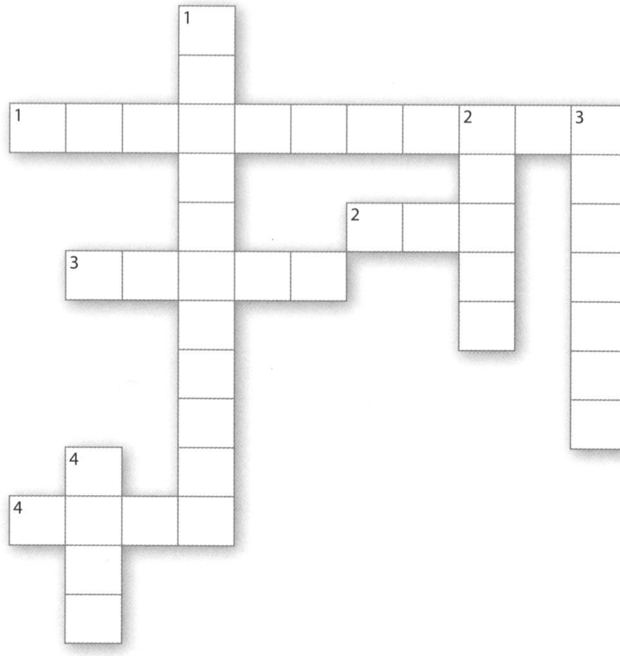

Across

1 When you eat too much of something, you often have this.
2 This is an illness which can make you very hot or cold and tired. It's common in the winter.
3 This is a very small living thing that can enter your body and make you ill.
4 When your throat hurts, you have a .... throat.

Down

1 You have this when your body is unusually hot, when you have a fever.
2 If you push air through your throat, it makes a sound, especially when you have a cold.
3 When your ear hurts, you have this.
4 This is a very common problem in the winter. It isn't as serious as 2 across.

4 Look at these questions and write the answers.

1 When do you need an aspirin?
You need an aspirin when you've got a headache.

2 When do you need to go to the dentist?
....
....

3 When do you need a tissue or handkerchief?
....
....

4 When do you need to stop eating for a short time?
....
....

1 Read this newspaper article and choose the best title for it.

1 The woman who stopped speaking
2 'That isn't me, is it?'
3 Why accents are not important

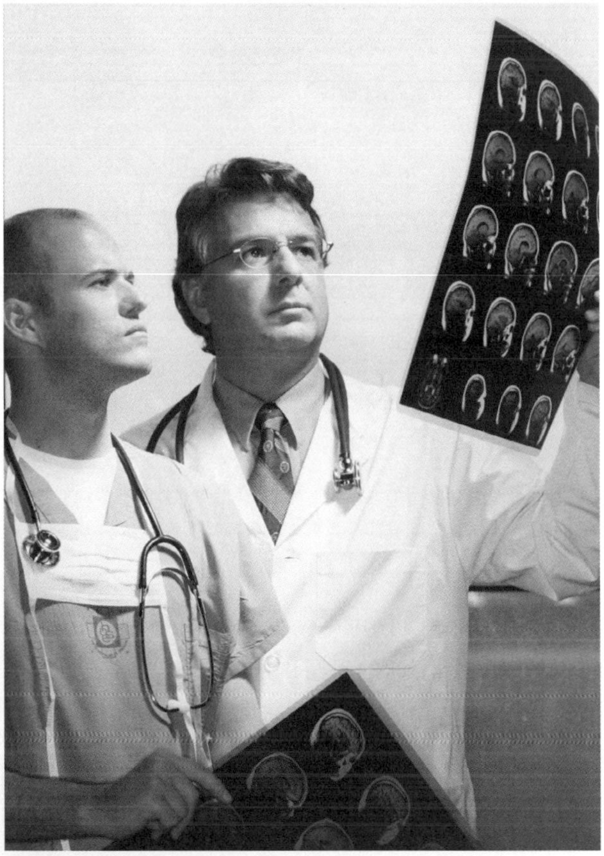

LINDA Walker is a 60-year-old woman from Newcastle. She has recently had a stroke. A stroke is a medical problem where blood suddenly cannot get to the brain. Often a stroke can stop people from speaking or from moving. In the case of Linda Walker it has caused something very unusual. Before, Linda spoke with a typical Newcastle accent. That's normal because she has always lived in Newcastle. But now her accent is a mixture of Jamaican, Italian and Slovakian.

It appears that Linda has Foreign Accent Syndrome. Patients speak differently after a problem like a stroke. They first discovered this medical problem in 1941 but it is not very common. Linda hates what has happened to her because she says she now feels like a different person. 'My sister-in-law says that I speak with an Italian accent. Then my brother says my accent is Slovakian. I spoke to him on the phone and he said, "Stop playing with me. Talk normally." Now someone has just told me that I sound Jamaican. I've never been to Jamaica. I don't know how to explain it,' she said. 'Everyone hears me differently. At first, I had no idea that I had this problem. Then my doctor played a recording of me talking. I couldn't believe it!'

Linda said: 'I've lost my identity because I never talked like this before. I'm a very different person and it's strange and I don't like it.' Is it possible for Linda Walker to go back to her original accent? It isn't going to be easy but she is having lessons to see if one day she can speak like the old Linda.

2 Read the text again and complete the sentences.

1 A stroke is when ....
2 .... patients can suffer from Foreign Accent Syndrome but it is not very common.
3 Different people say that Linda speaks with ....
4 It's very unusual that Linda speaks with a Jamaican accent because ....
5 Linda .... that she was speaking differently at first.
6 Linda couldn't believe it when ....
7 Linda isn't happy because she ....
8 Linda is having lessons because she wants ....

3 Find words in the text which have similar meanings to these explanations.

1 the way that people from an area pronounce words (*paragraph 1*) ....
2 two or more things mixed together (*paragraph 1*) ....
3 when you copy somebody's voice (e.g. on a CD) (*paragraph 2*) ....
4 first, the one that existed at the beginning (*paragraph 3*) ....

4 What about *you*?

1 Do you have an accent? If you do have one, what type is it?
....
....
....
2 Do you think accents are important? Why/Why not?
....
....
....

Present perfect with *ever*, *never*, *for* and *since*

1 Complete the sentences with the present perfect form of the verbs given.

1 I .... (see) a lot of films.
2 Sarah .... (do) her homework. Here it is.
3 Alfie and Holly .... (live) in Paris for two years.
4 We .... (buy) a dog.
5 Look! My dad .... (paint) this room green. It looks great!
6 Sam .... (have) this watch since he was 12.
7 She .... (read) that book.

2 Match the rules to the sentences in 1. Write a, b or c.

a an experience or experiences which happened at an unspecified moment in the past
b a past action which has a result in the present
c a situation that started in the past and continues to the present

Sentence 1 *a*
Sentence 2 ....
Sentence 3 ....
Sentence 4 ....
Sentence 5 ....
Sentence 6 ....
Sentence 7 ....

3 Complete this dialogue with the present perfect.

SOPHIE: (**a**) .... you met any Russian people?
BETHANY: Yes, I (**b**) ....
SOPHIE: Have you (**c**) .... Russian to them?
BETHANY: No, I (**d**) .... I can't speak Russian very well.
SOPHIE: (**e**) .... Joe told you that he can speak Russian?
BETHANY: No, he (**f**) ....

4 Write questions using the present perfect and *ever*. Then write your own true answers to the questions. If the answer is affirmative, write a short answer. If the answer is negative, write a complete sentence with *never*.

1 Question: you/climb a mountain?
Have you ever climbed a mountain?
Answer: *Yes, I have./No, I've never climbed a mountain.*

2 Question: your parents/visit the USA?
....
....
Answer: ....

3 Question: you/speak to a famous person?
....
....
Answer: ....

4 Question: your friend/win a competition?
....
....
Answer: ....

5 Question: you/ride a horse?
....
....
Answer: ....

6 Question: your English teacher/write a book?
....
....
Answer: ....

7 Question: you/sing in a concert?
....
....
Answer: ....

5 Choose the correct alternative.

1 I *live/have lived* in this house for two years.
2 We have been here *for/since* half past three.
3 William hasn't seen his friend *for/since* he left his school.
4 How *much time/long* have you waited to see him?
5 Liam has been the singer in the band since *three years/2009*.
6 My sister *has/has had* that bike since she was little.
7 I've loved that group *for/since* the start of their career.
8 She's waited for this moment for *nine months/January*.
9 Have you *ever/never* been to London?
10 He has *ever/never* met his Australian cousin.

Grammar extension

6 Rewrite the sentences by adding *ever*, *never*, *for* or *since*. Make sure you add the word in the correct place.

1 Have you been here a long time?
....
2 She's wanted to be a doctor she was seven.
....
3 Have you met my parents?
....
4 I've been to China but I'd like to go.
....
5 Have you worn a suit and tie?
....
6 She's been able to walk the operation.
....
7 We've known each other ages.
....
8 Humans have been able to live underwater permanently.
....

Compound nouns connected with health and medicine

1 Look at the pictures and use these words to say what each one shows.

aid attack centre first food health heart killers pain poisoning room waiting

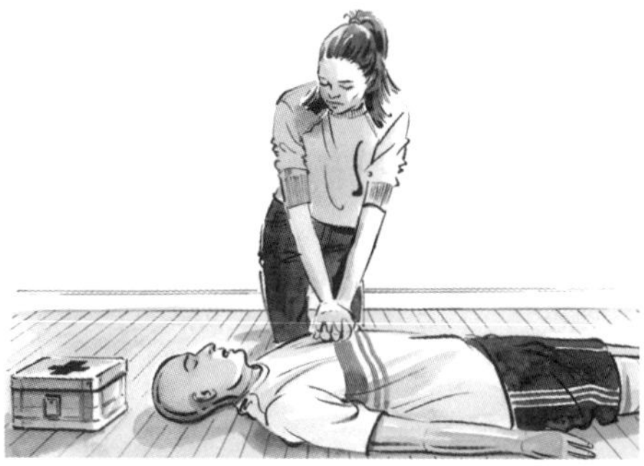

1 ....

2 ....

3 ....

4 ....

5 ....

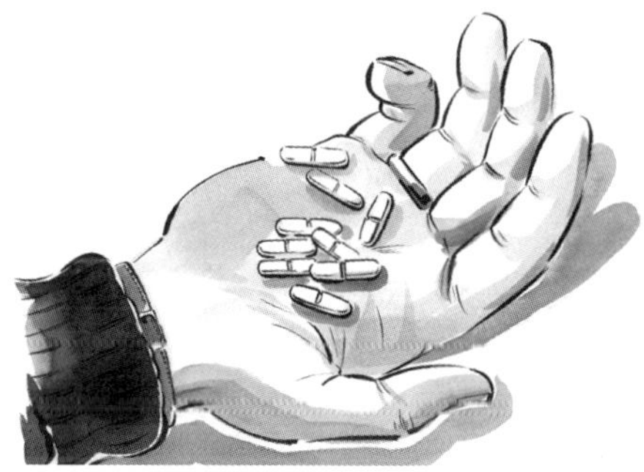

6 ....

2 Write simple definitions for the compound nouns in 1. Use *which, that, where, when* or *whose.*

1 *It's the help which you give to someone in an accident.*

2 ....

3 ....

4 ....

5 ....

6 ....

Vocabulary extension: compound nouns based on parts of the body

3 Match these words to make compound nouns. You can use words more than once. Use your dictionary if necessary.

1 arm	a bag
2 foot	b band
3 hair	c brush
4 hand	d chair
5 head	e dresser
6 tooth	f print

4 Complete the sentences with the compound nouns in 3.

1 He switched on the TV and sat down in his favourite ....
2 The detective followed the burglar's .... from the kitchen floor up to the bedroom.
3 He cuts people's hair. He's a ....
4 He's got long hair so when he does sport he often wears a ....
5 Dentists recommend using an electric ....
6 My mum puts everything in her .... – keys, money, mobile phone ...

5 Add parts of the body in 3 to complete these compound nouns. Use your dictionary if necessary.

1 ....ball or ....ball
2 ....teacher
3 ....writing
4 ....ache or ....ache
5 ....step

Click onto...

Famous doctors

Cross-curricular – Science
Gray's Anatomy

1 Read the text. What is *Grey's Anatomy* and what is *Gray's Anatomy*?

1 *Grey's Anatomy* ....

....

2 *Gray's Anatomy* ....

....

▸ WORD BOOSTER

Match the words and definitions.

1	full	a	different
2	colleague	b	process of producing a book
3	publication	c	someone who works with you
4	infectious	d	continuing now, after a long time
5	various	e	passing from one person to another
6	still	f	complete

Grey's Anatomy or *Gray's Anatomy*?

FOR SOME REASON, hospital dramas are incredibly popular with TV viewers all over the world. One series which has been especially popular in recent times is the American series *Grey's Anatomy*. Meredith Grey is a young doctor who works in a busy hospital. She's a central character in the series and this partly explains the title *Grey's Anatomy*. But there's another reason for the title. It's similar to the title *Gray's Anatomy*. But who was this Gray, and what exactly was *Gray's Anatomy*?

The full name of *Gray's Anatomy* is in fact *Henry Gray's Anatomy of the Human Body*. It's a human anatomy textbook which first appeared in 1858 and which people have considered a classic work since then.

Dr Henry Gray was British. He was born in 1827. In 1855 he had the idea of producing an anatomy textbook for medical students. He talked about his idea to a young colleague, Henry Vandyke Carter, who was an excellent artist. Gray wrote the text and Carter did the illustrations. They worked together on the book for 18 months, using dead bodies at the hospital for their work. Just three years after its publication, Gray died. He became ill while he was looking after a nephew who had an infectious illness. He was just 34 years old.

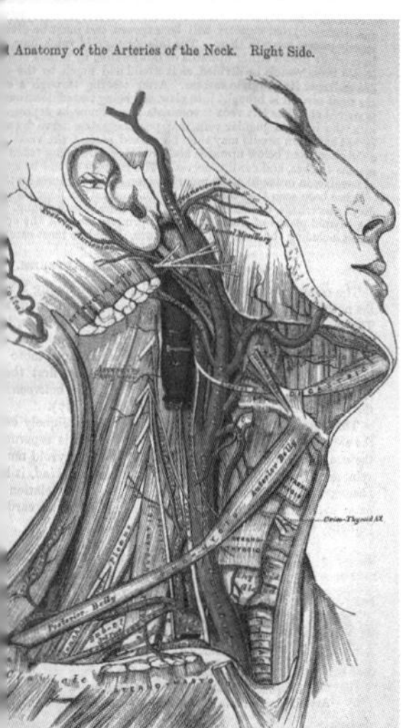

Gray's Anatomy quickly became very popular. This was for various reasons. The texts were very good, but people especially liked the illustrations. There were a lot of them in the book and they were of a very high quality. At this time, the medical profession was becoming more serious and students needed to know more to pass their exams and become doctors. *Gray's Anatomy* helped them to do this with all the information it contained.

Each new version of *Gray's Anatomy* has added to the original with recent discoveries. The book also exists now as a CD-ROM. Medical students all over the world still study *Gray's Anatomy*. Gray died many years ago but his work has continued to this day.

2 Read the text again and complete the fact file about Henry Gray.

Name: *Henry Gray*
Nationality: **(a)** ....
Born: **(b)** ....
Died: **(c)** ....
Cause of death: **(d)** ....
Famous work: **(e)** ....
Type of book: **(f)** ....
Illustrator: **(g)** ....
Year of publication: **(h)** ....

3 Answer the questions.

1 What is the origin of *Gray's Anatomy*?

....

2 What are the reasons for the popularity of *Gray's Anatomy*?

....

4 What about *you*?

1 Do you think it is difficult to become a doctor? Why/Why not?

....

2 Would you like to be a doctor? Why/Why not?

....

Present perfect with *just*, *yet* and *already*

1 Complete the table by ticking the correct boxes.

	Just	Yet	Already
1 We use it for very recent events.	✓	☐	☐
2 We use it for things that haven't happened, but we think will happen soon.	☐	☐	☐
3 We use it for something that has happened, possibly before we expected.	☐	☐	☐
4 We use it in affirmative sentences.	☐	☐	☐
5 We use it in negative sentences.	☐	☐	☐
6 We use it in questions.	☐	☐	☐
7 It usually goes at the end of the sentence.	☐	☐	☐
8 It usually goes immediately before the past participle.	☐	☐	☐

2 Write complete sentences saying what the people have *just* done.

1 She/have a shower.
She has just had a shower.

2 He/win a prize.
....

3 They/see a horror film.
....

4 We/do our homework.
....

5 I/finish this exercise.
....

3 Complete the sentences with the present perfect form of the verbs given. Put the words in bold in the correct place in the sentences.

1 I (not finish) this exercise. **YET**
I haven't finished this exercise yet.

2 My sister (have) an accident. **JUST**
....

3 Holly and Jack (eat) lunch. **ALREADY**
....

4 My mum (get) back from work. **JUST**
....

5 you (see) that film? **YET**
....

6 you (meet) the new teacher? **JUST**
....

7 the bus (go)? **ALREADY**
....

8 We (not study) for the exam. **YET**
....

Present perfect and past simple

4 Complete the sentences with the present perfect or the past simple form of the verbs given.

1 Oliver .... (be) at this school for five years but he doesn't like it here.

2 I .... (have) this jacket for two years and I always wear it when I go out.

3 My friend .... (go) on holiday to New York last year.

4 That team .... (win) the league in 2005.

5 She really enjoys reading. She .... (read) hundreds of books.

6 My friend .... (appear) on TV last summer.

7 .... you ever .... (eat) Indian food? Would you like to go to an Indian restaurant?

8 My parents .... (live) in our house for more than 15 years.

9 I .... (buy) a present for you yesterday.

10 We .... (fly) to New Zealand four years ago and we stayed there for a month.

Grammar extension

5 Each sentence contains a mistake. Find the mistake and rewrite the sentence correctly. Then explain the mistake.

1 My friend have lived in this city all of his life.
....
Explanation ....
....

2 Have you visited Rome ever?
....
Explanation ....
....

3 His parents have won the lottery in 2006.
....
Explanation ....
....

4 We have done the shopping yet.
....
Explanation ....
....

5 I've just seen my cousin ten hours ago.
....
Explanation ....
....

6 These are my favourite earrings because I had them since I was eight. ....
....
Explanation ....
....

Describing a scene

1 Look at the photo and read a description of it. Find three differences between the description and the photo and underline them.

There are six people in the picture and, er, they're in a waiting room. It's probably a waiting room in a health centre. I imagine it's the morning or the afternoon because that's when people usually go to the doctor's. Er, the people are patients, they're waiting to see the doctor. The doctor is also in the room. The patients are all looking at him. They look ill or, you know, have health problems. For example, I think one man has got a bad cold, or maybe the flu. I'm not sure but I think the businesswoman has got a sore shoulder or something because she's touching it.

The room isn't very exciting. There are, well, three pictures on the wall. I can also see some magazines. I think they're probably giving information to the patients. I've been in a waiting room like this when I've been ill. I don't like waiting rooms because they always seem sad and grey. The thing is, the picture makes me think about times when I've been ill so I don't really like it much.

2 Read the description again and put the questions in the order that the speaker answers them.

a What are the people doing? ☐
b When is the scene taking place (morning, night, summer, winter, etc)? ☐
c What do you think about the picture? ☐
d Who is in the picture and where are they? [1]
e What type of people are they? ☐
f What things or objects are in the picture? ☐
g Have you ever been in a situation like the one in the picture? ☐

3 In the description in 1, underline any words or expressions that the speaker uses as fillers to give them time to think.

4 Make notes of things to say about this photo. Use the questions in 2 to get ideas. Do not write complete sentences.

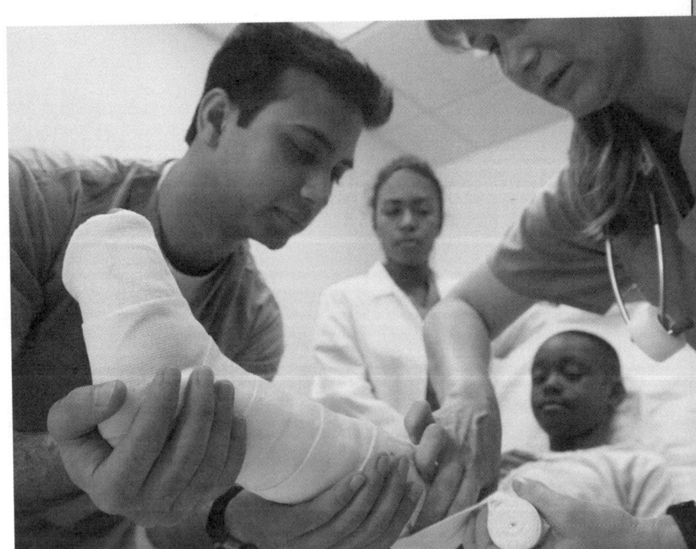

5 Practise describing the photo in 4. Here are some ideas of how you can practise.

1 Find a partner and take it in turns to describe the photo. If necessary, help your partner by asking questions.
2 Record yourself giving the description (e.g. with a mobile phone or MP3 player). Listen to yourself when you finish.
3 Practise on your own. Then do the activity again in class.

Notes and messages

1 Read these instructions. Then look at the note below. Does the writer follow the instructions? Do they write the note in the correct style?

It's your friend's birthday today. You have gone to his house to see him but he isn't there. Leave him a note. Include this information:

- wish him a happy birthday
- ask him to contact you when he gets home
- tell him that you have something for him
- arrange to meet him.

Marc,
Congratulations! Today's the big day, isn't it? 16 already. You're getting old. **Listen,** give me a call **asap**. I've bought you a small present (I haven't got enough money to buy you a big present – sorry!). I'd like to give you the present today. When can I see you? Let me know.
Jenny
PS Josh says Happy Birthday too!

2 Look at the words in bold in the note. Explain why they are important in notes and messages.

Marc. *We usually begin notes with just the name of the person we are writing to.*

Congratulations ....

Listen ....

asap. PS ....

3 What do these abbreviations mean?

1 St ....
2 tel. ....
3 etc ....
4 PS ....
5 asap ....
6 NB ....

4 Rewrite this note to make the style appropriate.

Dear Joe,
Would you please call me very quickly because somebody has burgled our house! They have taken the TV, the laptop, some money and other things. Please pay special attention – do not tell Philip at the moment because I do not want him to worry. By the way, I am not at home. I am at the police station at Farm Street.
Sam

Joe,

5 Read these instructions and write a note.

You usually go to an English language academy with your friend, Sarah. Today you can't go. Leave Sarah a note. Include this information:

- tell her why you can't go (an illness? an accident?)
- ask her to explain to the teacher
- tell her to call you quickly after the lesson to tell you what homework to do
- say thank you and arrange to meet somewhere soon.

Sarah,

Revision: Units 3–4

Grammar

1 Decide if the words in bold are correct in these sentences. If not, correct them.

1 I haven't got **many** money. ....
2 There isn't **some** bread on the table. ....
3 There's **much** orange juice in the fridge. ....
4 There were **a little** people at the party. ....
5 I've got **any** pencils that you can use. ....
6 Are there **a lot of** people in the shop? ....
7 Only **a few** people can win a Nobel Prize. ....

/7 points

2 Complete the sentences with the correct relative pronoun: *who, that, which, whose, when* or *where.*

1 He's the teacher .... helped me to pass the exam.
2 That's the school .... I went when I was five.
3 Do you remember the time .... I fell into the river?
4 She's the girl .... father is an actor.
5 Have you read the essay .... I wrote?
6 This is the email .... came yesterday.

/6 points

3 Write sentences in the present perfect. Put the words in bold in the correct place.

1 you/visit an art gallery? **EVER**
....
2 William/ride a horse. **NEVER**
....
3 Joe and Ellie/come back from their holiday. **JUST**
....
4 I/speak to George. **ALREADY**
....
5 you/write your email? **YET**
....
6 We/not buy bread. **YET**
....

/6 points

4 Complete the sentences with the present perfect or the past simple form of the verbs given.

1 I .... (have) this computer for ten years now.
2 She .... (visit) Argentina in 2006.
3 My uncle .... (live) in Germany since 2008.
4 I .... (be) in the basketball team two years ago.
5 I .... (buy) all of his CDs. I love his music.
6 He .... (forget) to do his homework yesterday.

/6 points

Total */25 points*

Vocabulary

1 Write the country or nationality.

Country	Nationality
(a)	Polish
Brazil	(b) ....
(c)	Swiss
(d)	Welsh
the Netherlands	(e) ....

/5 points

2 Decide if the words in bold are correct in these sentences. If not, correct them.

1 Oh no! I've **done** a mistake. ....
2 Have you **done** that exercise? ....
3 We need to **revision** before the test. ....
4 Do you want to **practise** this tomorrow? ....

/4 points

3 Make the words negative by adding prefixes.

1 ....possible 3 ....legal
2 ....regular 4 ....correct

/4 points

4 What are these parts of the body?

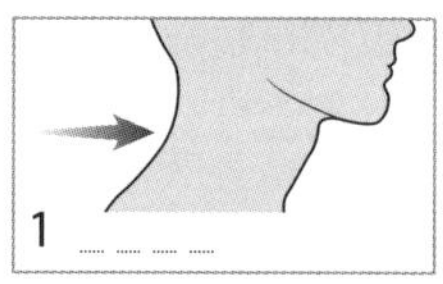

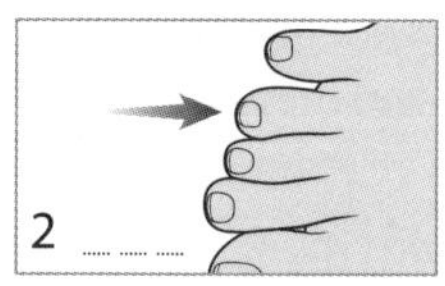

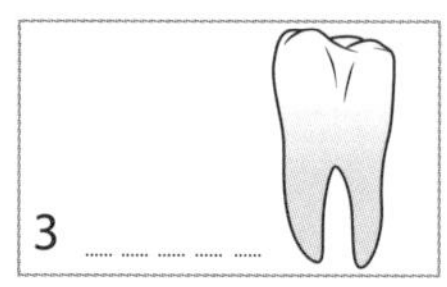

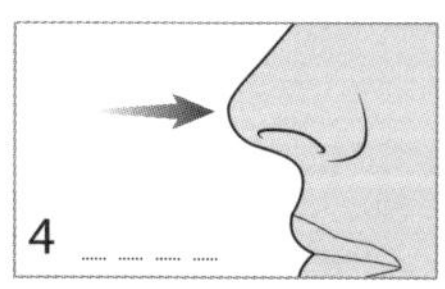

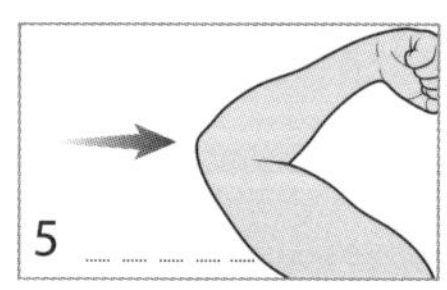

/5 points

5 Put the letters of the words in bold in order to find words connected with health.

1 I can't shout because I've got a **rose** throat.
....
2 Please take a seat in the **ingtawi moor** and the nurse will call you. ....
3 He had a skiing accident and he's got a **krenbo** arm.
....
4 When there's an accident, it's good to know **trifs dia**.
....
5 People who smoke often have a bad **gochu**. ....
6 Lots of people at school have caught a **survi**. ....
7 I can't get up because I've got **chackeab**. ....

/7 points

Total */25 points*

Reading

1 Read the text about an Ancient Greek called Hippocrates and choose a, b or c to complete the sentences.

There were many Ancient Greeks whose work helped to create the modern world we know today. One of these was an extraordinary man called Hippocrates, who changed the world of medicine with his ideas.

Hippocrates was an extremely intelligent man who is famous for being the 'father of medicine'. People called him the 'father of medicine' because he was the first person to make medicine a serious profession. Before Hippocrates, people thought that supernatural, mystical or divine factors were responsible for illnesses. Hippocrates didn't believe in these superstitious ideas. He watched his patients very carefully and saw that illnesses come from the things that we eat, the things around us and our habits.

Hippocrates was one of the first people to ask his patients questions and he wrote down the information to analyse it later. With this observation and information he worked out how to look after the patient. We now know that he sometimes made serious mistakes in his analysis, but in general his way of working was revolutionary for the time.

For example, Hippocrates believed that doctors needed to be serious, professional and, very importantly, to be clean. He told his student doctors to wash their hands all the time, and his patients were always clean too.

One of the many extraordinary things that Hippocrates did in his life was to discover and use an ingredient called salicin. He used salicin to cure headaches. Later people forgot about this medicine. But 2,200 years later a German scientist rediscovered salicin and it became an ingredient in today's typical cure for headaches – aspirin!

One final point about Hippocrates – he was clearly a good doctor because he himself lived until he was very old. Some people say he was 83 when he died, some say he was 90 and others say that he was 100 years old!

1 Before Hippocrates people didn't
  a want to be doctors.
  b look for natural explanations for illnesses.
  c like doctors because they were superstitious.

2 For Hippocrates, ______ was important to help his patients.
  a analysis
  b good food
  c time

3 Hippocrates
  a wasn't always right in his analysis.
  b didn't often wash his hands.
  c had a lot of enemies because of his ideas.

4 Hippocrates taught some people how to
  a wash correctly.
  b become doctors.
  c make mistakes.

5 We know that
  a Hippocrates created aspirin 2,200 years ago.
  b a German scientist discovered Hippocrates' instructions for how to make aspirin.
  c Hippocrates knew an ingredient to stop headaches.

/5 points

Writing

2 Write a paragraph about your English-learning experiences this year. Use these questions for ideas about what to write.

- What have you studied so far?
- What activities do you like the most?
- What are your strong points in English?
- How could you improve on any weak points?

....

....

....

....

....

....

....

....

....

....

/10 points

Total */15 points*

5 TV world

Grammar ‣ Comparatives and superlatives ‣ *Less ... than* and *(not) as ...*
‣ *Too* and *(not) enough*
Vocabulary ‣ TV programmes ‣ Adjectives describing TV programmes
‣ Adjectives ending in *-ing* and *-ed*
Speaking ‣ Negotiating
Writing ‣ A descriptions and opinions

‣ Vocabulary

TV programmes

1 Find eight types of TV programme in the word search. Then write them under the correct pictures. There are three types of programme that do not have a picture.

t	d	a	w	q	z	t	r	e	a	g	i	l	f	c
h	f	d	o	c	u	m	e	n	t	a	r	y	h	h
e	e	v	p	a	x	s	d	c	f	m	o	r	t	a
n	r	e	o	r	m	a	b	o	b	e	p	e	d	t
e	s	r	t	t	o	i	t	y	n	s	w	q	c	s
w	l	t	r	o	d	r	a	m	a	h	x	l	n	h
s	n	d	a	o	g	u	l	p	e	o	s	u	g	o
f	i	l	m	n	h	s	h	o	w	w	d	t	h	w

3 ....

4 ....

1 ....

2 ....

5 ....

2 Read the sentences. To complete them, add vowels to these words and then write them in the correct gap.

ch...nn...ls ...ff r...m...t... s...r...s t...rn pr...gr...mm...

1 ABC, CBS and Fox are American TV ....
2 The Simpsons and CSI are popular American TV ....
3 When you don't want to watch the TV, switch it ....
4 When people are bored, they often .... the TV on.
5 I don't want to watch this programme but I don't want to get up. Pass me the .... control.
6 Chat shows are my favourite type of ....

Adjectives describing TV programmes

3 Put the letters in order to make adjectives describing TV programmes.

cryas fromvinetia ginmov nuyfn ringbo rolpupa wulfa

1 .... 5 ....
2 .... 6 ....
3 .... 7 ....
4 ....

4 Write an example of a TV programme or film to describe each of the adjectives in 3.

1 *funny* – *The Simpsons*
2 .... – ....
3 .... – ....
4 .... – ....
5 .... – ....
6 .... – ....
7 .... – ....

1 Write two or three sentences with your opinion about adverts on TV. You can use these adjectives: funny, interesting, useful, boring.

I think adverts are ....

....

....

....

2 Read the text. Is it generally positive or negative about adverts? ....

Adverts turn TV viewers off

Recently fans of top soaps, dramas and reality shows in the USA have started to get angry about the number and frequency of the adverts in the middle of the programmes. Sometimes it seems that the adverts are more important than the programmes themselves. For example, American dramas aren't as long as they were in the past. Nowadays in the US, an 'hour-long' drama lasts about 40 minutes (in the 1980s they lasted 48 minutes). The rest is adverts. Or, in other words, for every two minutes of programme there's one minute of adverts.

The ABC channel had slightly more adverts than other channels. But recently they've changed … and what they do now is even worse than before! Before, all their dramas had four sections. But now ABC tells producers to separate each programme into six sections. Usually the first section is approximately ten minutes long. Then they have the first break. When people have watched a programme for ten minutes, it's much less probable that they will stop watching or change channels. But then, in the next 45 minutes, there are four more commercial breaks. Each break is about three and a half minutes long.

All of this makes it much more difficult for writers of dramas to write good stories. Quiet scenes make no impact because there are more and more adverts and the adverts are longer and longer. 'It's OK for game shows or more exciting adventure series,' says American TV producer David E. Kelley. 'But for programmes that don't depend on violence or melodramatic scenes, it's more difficult to make a story with six sections than to make one with four. The only thing you can do is be more aggressive, either with the music or the visual impact, just to attract people's attention after the adverts.'

3 Are these sentences true (T) or false (F)?

1 Today American dramas consist of around 40 minutes of programme and 20 minutes of adverts. ....
2 On the ABC channel dramas now have six parts. ....
3 After ten minutes, viewers often change channels. ....
4 It's difficult for game shows to have frequent breaks. ....
5 TV drama writers like having lots of different sections in a programme. ....
6 Some shows use exciting music to get people's attention after the adverts. ....

4 Match the questions with the answers.

1 Why do drama programmes have more sections now than before? ....
2 Why do they wait ten minutes before the first break? ....
3 Why is it more difficult for dramas than for game shows? ....
4 Why do dramas need fast music? ....

a Because it isn't easy writing a slow, non-violent story with a lot of different, short sections.
b Because after the adverts they need to make people pay attention.
c Because that way there are more adverts.
d Because they know that when people have watched the start of the programme they continue watching.

5 Find words in the text which have similar meanings to these words or explanations.

1 people who like something a lot (*paragraph 1*) ....
2 the best, most popular (*paragraph 1*) ....
3 short rest (*paragraph 2*) ....
4 very dramatic, too dramatic or emotional (*paragraph 3*)
....
5 strong or big effect (*paragraph 3*) ....

6 What about *you*?

Is advertising in your country the same as in the USA? Do you think there are more adverts now than before?

....

....

....

Comparatives and superlatives

1 Complete the table by putting these adjectives in the correct place and then writing the comparative and superlative forms.

boring brilliant cool easy far fit good scary ~~small~~ thin

Adjective	Rule	Comparative	Superlative
(a) *small*	one-syllable adjectives, add *-er* or *-est*	*smaller*	*the smallest* ....
(b)	one-syllable adjectives which end in one vowel + one consonant, double the last consonant and add *-er* or *-est*	....	....
(c)	two-syllable adjectives ending in *-y*, omit *-y* and add *-ier* or *-iest*	....	....
(d)	adjectives with two syllables or more, use *more* + the adjective or *the most* + the adjective	....	....
(e)	irregular adjectives with no set rules	....	....

2 Complete these sentences with the comparative or superlative form of the adjectives given.

1 This year is .... (hot) than last year.
2 She's the .... (beautiful) girl in the world.
3 London is .... (far) from Moscow than Berlin.
4 That was the .... (bad) day of my life!
5 Salad is .... (good) for you than chocolate.
6 She's the .... (intelligent) person I know.
7 I think it's .... (difficult) to write in Chinese than in English.

3 Look at this information about Jake, Ethan and Ryan and then complete the sentences using the comparative or superlative form of the adjectives given.

Jake **Ethan** **Ryan**

Name	Tall	Talkative	Good at sport
Jake	***	*	*
Ethan	*	***	**
Ryan	**	**	***

1 Ethan *is shorter than* .... (short) Jake.
2 Jake .... (tall) Ryan.
3 Jake .... (tall).
4 Ethan .... (talkative) Ryan.
5 Ryan .... (good at sport) Jake.
6 Ryan .... (good at sport).

4 Rewrite the sentences using comparatives and superlatives. Make sure the meaning stays the same.

1 No boy is taller than Jamie in this class.
Jamie is *the tallest boy in this class* ....
2 A bike is lighter than a motorbike.
A motorbike is ....
3 Becky is older than everybody in this class except Matthew.
Matthew is ....
4 No one in the 20th century was more intelligent than Einstein.
Einstein was ....
....
5 My bedroom is bigger than my brother's bedroom.
My brother's bedroom is ....
6 I think a Peugeot 507 is good but a Ferrari is very good.
I think a Ferrari is ....

Grammar extension

5 There is a word missing in each sentence. Write an appropriate word in the correct place.

1 Formula 1 racing is more dangerous playing football.
2 Everest is than any other mountain in the world.
3 The Nile is the river in the world.
4 Giraffes are taller elephants.
5 Motorbikes are dangerous than cars.
6 Jasmine is the best swimmer the class.
7 This is most exciting film I've ever seen.
8 Simon is younger Michael.

Adjectives ending in *-ing* and *-ed*

1 How are the people feeling? Match these words to the pictures.

bored confused ~~disappointed~~ embarrassed frightened interested relaxed surprised tired

1 *disappointed* ....

2 ....

3 ....

4 ....

5 ....

6 ....

7 ....

8 ....

9 ....

2 Complete the sentences about the people in the pictures in 1. Use the *-ed* and the *-ing* form of the adjective.

1 The student *is disappointed* because her exam mark *is disappointing*.
2 He .... because the programme ....
3 She .... because the ghost train ....
4 He .... because he thinks maths ....
5 They .... because the music ....
6 She .... because the situation ....
7 He .... because the class ....
8 She .... because the news in the letter ....
9 He .... because the race ....

Vocabulary extension

3 Match these *-ing* adjectives with their synonyms or explanations. Use your dictionary if necessary.

1 depressing	a very tiring
2 disgusting	b horrible, very bad
3 exhausting	c very sad
	d very good or surprising
4 worrying	e making you unhappy because you think of problems or bad things
5 terrifying	
6 amazing	f very frightening

4 Write the *-ed* form of the adjectives in 3. Check your answers in your dictionary if necessary.

1 .... 4 ....
2 .... 5 ....
3 .... 6 ....

5 Complete the sentences with *-ing* or *-ed* adjectives in 3 and 4.

1 Yuck! I think eating insects is ....
2 I haven't slept for two nights. I'm ....
3 This programme is very .... It's all about the terrible problems in the world.
4 She hasn't studied. Now she's thinking about her exams and she's very .... about them.
5 Wow! Look up there! It's the .... Spiderman!
6 I'm really afraid of high places so the idea of going up that mountain is .... for me.

Click onto... The Slovak Robin Hood

Cross-curricular – Literature
Juraj Jánošík

1 Read the text and match the titles to the correct paragraphs.

1 In the forest a legend is born
2 The legend continues
3 The young soldier
4 A Slovak hero
5 A tragic end

(a) ....

People sometimes call Juraj Jánošík the Slovak Robin Hood. He has been the topic of many Slovak and Polish legends, films, TV programmes, paintings, books and poems. 'He took from the rich and gave to the poor' are the famous words which people associate with him.

(b) ....

It all began in 1688 when Jánošík was born in Terchová, now in Slovakia. At the age of 18, he decided to join the troops of a man called Rákóczi Ferenc. These troops lost the battle and the Habsburg Emperor's army took Jánošík prisoner. Later he joined the troops of the Emperor.

(c) ....

While he was serving in the Emperor's army, Jánošík met a prisoner called Tomáš Uhorčík. Uhorčík was the leader of a gang of outlaws. One day Uhorčík escaped from prison and Jánošík joined his group. Later Jánošík became the captain of the group. They lived in the forest and took money from aristocrats, merchants and travellers and gave it to the poor. They did not kill any of their victims and sometimes they even helped them if they were ill.

(d) ....

In 1713 soldiers captured Jánošík. The legend says that in a pub a wicked old woman threw peas on the floor to make him fall and help the soldiers to catch him. They put him in prison and then killed him. He had an early and violent death, but his legend has survived and he is a very important person in Slovak folk history today.

(e) ....

Jánošík's legend was already getting bigger in the early 18th century, mainly because people considered him a symbol of resistance. People needed a hero, especially one who took from the rich and gave to the poor. In the end, the stories made him invincible, protected from bullets. The tales of Jánošík and his friend, Uhorčík, have everything that makes a great legend: love, adventure and the fight for justice.

▶ WORD BOOSTER

Match the words and definitions.

1	troops	a	an old story that was possibly true at first but then becomes fictional
2	merchant	b	groups of soldiers
3	capture	c	take somebody prisoner
4	legend	d	person that buys and sells things

2 Answer the questions.

Juraj Jánošík

1 Where was he from?

....

....

2 How did he become the captain of a group of outlaws?

....

....

3 How and when did he die?

....

....

4 Why did he become a legend?

....

....

3 Look at this scene from the legend of Juraj Jánošík. With information from the text, write about who the people are and what is happening.

....

....

....

4 What about *you*?

Describe a folk hero or legend from your country.

....

....

....

....

Less … than, (not) as … as

1 Read the sentences and put the correct symbol (> for *more than* or < for *less than*) after each one.

1 Wood is less heavy than metal. <
2 TV is more popular than the cinema. ......
3 Europe isn't as hot as Africa. ......
4 Learning Japanese is harder than learning English. ......
5 Eating chocolate is not as healthy as eating fruit. ......

2 Compare the two things using the adjective and *less … than* and *(not) as … as*.

1 Italy ➔ big ➔ Russia.
......
2 Hamsters ➔ dangerous ➔ snakes.
......
......
3 The River Thames ➔ long ➔ the Amazon.
......
4 A kilo of gold ➔ heavy ➔ a kilo of rice.
......
5 Chocolate ➔ expensive ➔ caviar.
......
......

Too and *(not) enough*

3 Complete the sentences with the correct words.

1 He's 50. He's ...... old to be a professional football player.
2 When you're 15, you aren't old ...... to drive.
3 I can't buy that computer. It's £600 and I've only got £450. It's too ....
4 She plays the guitar really well. She's ...... enough to become a professional musician.
5 Those shoes are size 10 and your feet are size 8. The shoes are too ...... for you.

4 Rewrite the sentences using *too* or *not … enough*.

1 He's too young to vote.
He ......
2 I'm not rich enough to buy that.
I ....
3 Megan isn't tall enough to close the top window.
Megan ......
....
4 Her car is too slow to win the race.
Her car ....
5 That documentary is too boring to watch twice.
That documentary ......
....

5 Rewrite the answers using *too* or *not … enough* in the correct place in the sentence.

1 Why don't you go to school now?
Because it's early. ➔
Because it's too early.
2 Why can't you carry that big bag?
Because it's heavy. ➔
......
3 Why isn't she a professional pianist?
Because she isn't good. ➔
......
4 Why can't you ride a motorbike?
Because I'm 15 – I'm not old. ➔
......
5 Why can't you finish reading that book?
Because it's got 800 pages – it's long. ➔
......
6 Why don't people swim in the Arctic Ocean?
Because the water isn't warm. ➔
......
7 Why can't you go to New Zealand?
Because the flight is expensive. ➔
......
8 Why isn't he in the school football team?
Because he isn't fit. ➔
......

Grammar extension

6 Put the words in order to make sentences. Then write true (T) or false (F) after each one.

1 I not vote old am enough to.
......
2 Bicycles expensive are motorbikes than less.
......
3 The in leopard fastest world the is the animal.
......
4 as tigers Dolphins dangerous are as.
......
5 I to too to school old am go.
......
6 important in Latin language the the now world is most.
......
......
7 high K2 not as as Everest is.
......
8 hot polar the Sahara It bears for is too in live to.
......

Negotiating

1 Choose the correct alternative.

1 How about *to watch/watch/watching* a film at the cinema?
2 Shall we *to go/go/going* out this afternoon?
3 Why don't we *to see/see/seeing* that?
4 Let's *to go/go/going* for a walk in the park.

2 Put sentences 1–4 in 1 in the correct place in the dialogue.

BOY: **(a)** ....
GIRL: OK. Where could we go?
BOY: **(b)** ....
GIRL: Hmm. I'm not sure. I'm a bit tired of walking.
BOY: Yeah, we walked a lot this morning, didn't we?
(c) ....
GIRL: That's a good idea. What's on?
BOY: There's a new comedy about Robin Hood.
(d) ....
GIRL: No, I prefer a drama.
BOY: OK. How about that new film with Charlize Theron?
GIRL: Great! I love Charlize Theron!

3a Read the dialogue again. Find different ways of responding to suggestions and write them in the table.

Yes	No	Maybe
OK.		

3b Complete the table with any other phrases you know.

4 Write a dialogue using the chart below.

Nick:
Suggest doing something tonight.
1 ....

Cathy:
Say yes. But what?
2 ....

Nick:
Suggest going to the cinema.
3 ....

Cathy:
Say no. Nothing good on at the moment.
4 ....

Nick:
Suggest eating out.
5 ....

Cathy:
Say yes. What type of restaurant?
6 ....

Nick:
Suggest Italian.
7 ....

Cathy:
Say no. Prefer Chinese.
8 ....

Nick:
Say yes to Chinese.
9 ....

Describing photos

5 Look at the photo and answer the questions. If you are not sure of something, use *I think* and/or *I imagine*.

1 Who can you see in the photo?
....
2 Where are they?
....
3 What are they doing?
....
4 How do you think the people are feeling? Why?
....

6 Use the questions in 5 to think of things to say about this photo. Make notes and then practise orally.

A description of a TV programme

1 Read this email from a boy called Adam. Match the correct title with the paragraphs in his email.

Paragraph 1 ....
Paragraph 2 ....
Paragraph 3 ....

1 General news
2 His opinion about watching too much television
3 A description of his favourite programme
4 A description of a recent programme he hated
5 Reason for writing
6 His suggestion for making TV better
7 His general opinion of TV at the moment
8 The good and bad things about adverts

Get Mail | Write | Contacts | Reply | Forward | Delete | Print

Hi Liz,

1 How are things? I'm writing about that new series which was on TV last night. Did you see it? I saw the adverts for it all week and it looked really cool so I decided to watch it. But I was really disappointed!

2 Personally, I don't like soaps but the adverts said that this one was different. It wasn't! As far as I'm concerned, it was as boring as every other soap I've seen. The actors were awful and the story just wasn't interesting. And another thing – they stopped for adverts every five or six minutes.

3 In my opinion, television in general is getting worse and worse. I think the new series aren't as good or original as the old ones. The only thing I watch are old films. But a 90-minute film takes two hours because of all the adverts! Is it just me or is that really annoying?

Let me know what you think.

Adam

2 Read the email again and underline any expressions of opinion you can find.

3 Find Adam's opinion of the programme he saw last night and his opinion of TV in general. What reasons does he give to explain his opinion?

1 He *liked/didn't like* the programme he saw last night because
....
....
....
....

2 He *likes/doesn't like* TV in general now because
....
....
....
....
....

4 Are these statements saying good things or bad things about adverts?

1 Adverts can be funny. *Good*
2 Adverts can be stereotypical. ....
3 Adverts can be informative. ....
4 Adverts interrupt programmes you want to watch. ....
5 Adverts can show lots of creativity. ....
6 Adverts give you time to get something to eat or drink. ....
7 Adverts can be very expensive. ....
8 Adverts can be boring. ....
9 Adverts are repeated too often. ....
10 Adverts can make you think. ....

5 Write an email to a friend using this paragraph plan. Use expressions of opinion and give reasons for your opinions.

Paragraph 1: Reason for writing – you saw an advert last night that was really good/bad
Paragraph 2: The good things about adverts
Paragraph 3: The bad things about adverts

Get Mail | Write | Contacts | Reply | Forward | Delete | Print

....

6 Living planet

Grammar	▸ *Be going to, will, may, might* ▸ Zero conditional and first conditio
Vocabulary	▸ Geographical features ▸ The environment ▸ Different uses of *get*
Speaking	▸ Making arrangements
Writing	▸ A formal letter

▸ Vocabulary

Geographical features

1 Complete the crossword.

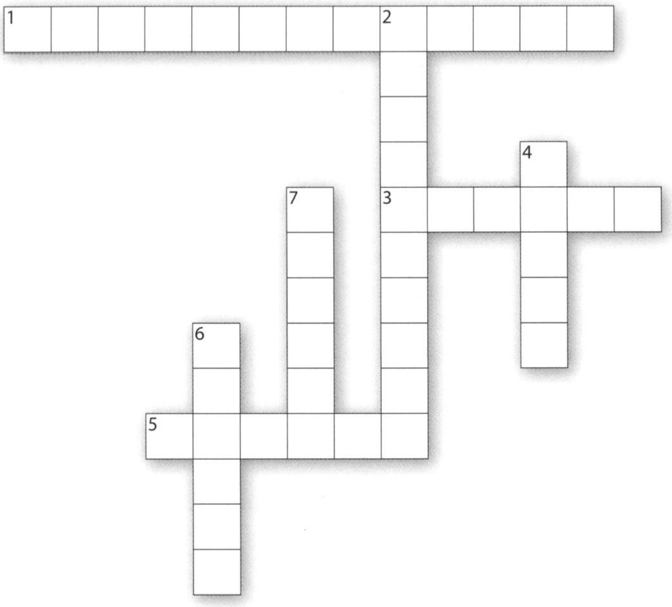

Across

1 a long line of very big hills
3 an area with a lot of trees
5 an area with a lot of sand, but not many plants and almost no water

Down

2 similar to 3 across, but here it rains a lot
4 an area next to the sea with sand, where some people go to spend their holidays
6 a big, cold area that covers the land and sea around the North and South Pole
7 a tropical area with a lot of plants, trees, animals and insects

2 Use the words in 1 to write about what there is or isn't in your country.

....

....

....

....

....

....

....

....

....

....

....

The environment

3 Complete these words and then match them to the correct pictures.

dr.... ....ght   fl.... ....d   gl....b....l w....rm....ng
gr.... ....nh.... ....s.... ....ff....ct   ....z....n....l....y....r
r....cycl....   s....v.... w....t....r   w....st.... w....t....r

1 ....

2 ....

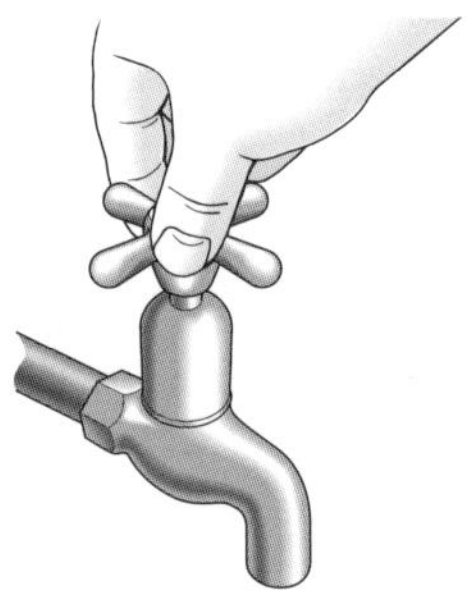

3 ....

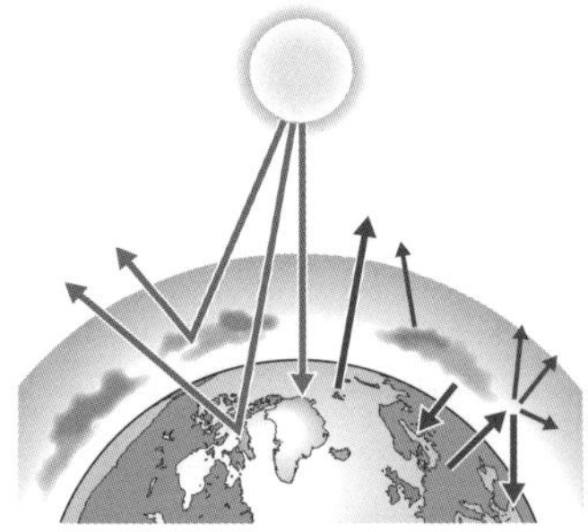

4 ....

5 ....

6 ....

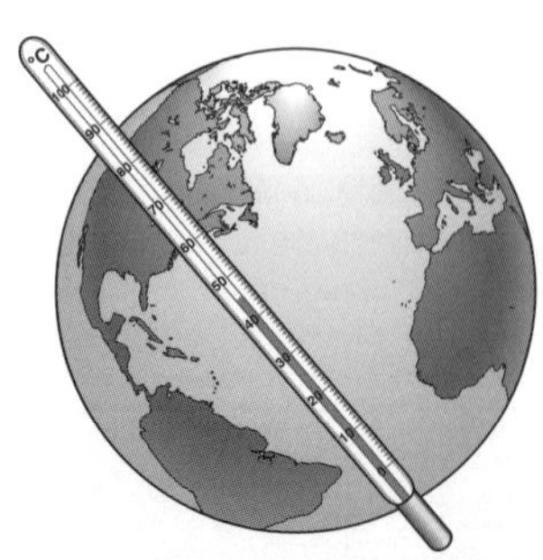

7 ....

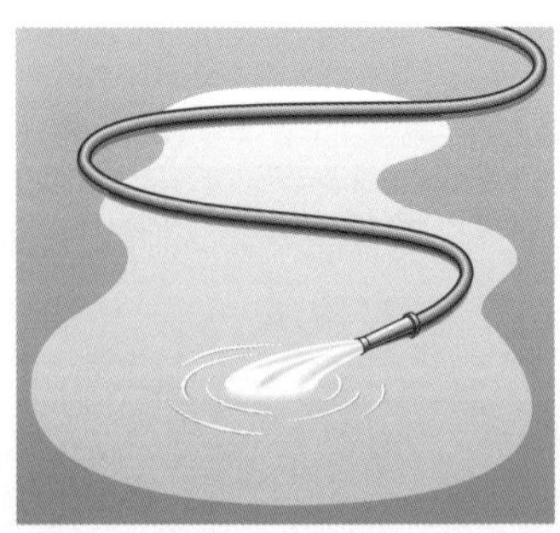

8 ....

1 Read this page from a website about rainforests and write a good title for each section.

File Edit View History Tools Window Help

FOUR THINGS KIDS CAN DO TO SAVE THE RAINFOREST

1 ....

Most paper comes from trees, so if you use less paper, you'll help to save the rainforests. Don't forget to use recycled paper whenever possible, or better still, use tree-free paper. As you can see from the name, tree-free paper doesn't come from trees, it's made from other types of plants. If you want to buy this type of paper, make sure you look closely at the packet. If paper really is recycled or tree-free, it will say so somewhere on the packet.

Another simple way of saving paper that many of us forget to do is by writing on both sides of the sheet. Meanwhile, there are other types of paper that we can save too. Paper tissues or paper towels are no good at all for the environment. Try not to use them. If you *do* use them, only use one at a time.

2 ....

As we all know, petrol and plastic are two things that come from petroleum, or oil. A lot of oil comes from the rainforests through a process called extraction. This has a very adverse effect on the rainforests, so using fewer oil products can help save them. Just think twice before asking your parents to use petrol to drive you somewhere in the car. Ride your bike, walk or take the bus whenever possible.

Save plastic by choosing glass bottles and by reusing the plastic containers and bottles that you already have. If you have a plastic water bottle, don't throw it away and buy a new one. Wash it and use it again and again.

3 ....

One big reason rainforests are disappearing is meat, or beef to be more specific. Big companies destroy millions of acres of rainforest and then cover it with grass for cows. The meat from the cows goes to make fast-food burgers, for example. What you may not know is that to make just one burger, they destroy an area similar to a small kitchen. Think about it – that's just for one burger!

4 ....

Rainforests are the most amazing places you can imagine, and they're important to every living thing on earth. Perhaps you think they're too far away to make any difference to you and your life. But, whether we live in the city, country, mountains or desert, rainforests affect all of us. Learn more about the rainforests and why they are so vital. Keep checking out our website to get more information, or go to a library for books on the rainforest. Tell your friends and family what you have learned and get them to join you in helping save the rainforests.

2 Look at these pictures. Match them to the correct section (1–4) in 1 and write an explanation of why they appear in the text.

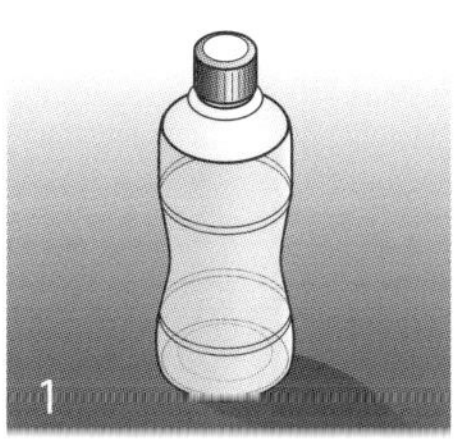

Section *2*

It's better to use glass bottles because plastic bottles are made from petroleum. Extracting petroleum can be bad for the rainforest. So we should use plastic bottles again and again, we shouldn't just throw them away.

Section ....

....

Section ....

....

Section ....

....

Section ....

....

Section ....

....

3 Find words in the text which have similar meanings to these words or explanations.

1 at any or every time (*Section 1*) ....
2 with no trees (*Section 1*) ....
3 a series of actions (*Section 2*) ....
4 put it in the bin (*Section 2*) ....
5 meat from a cow (*Section 3*) ....
6 very important, essential (*Section 4*) ....

4 What about *you*?

Would you like to visit a rainforest one day? Why/Why not?

....

Be going to and *will*

1 Complete the sentences and rules with the correct form of *be going to* or *will*.

1

Rule: We use .... to make predictions based on some sort of evidence.

2

Rule: We use .... for decisions that we take at the moment of speaking.

3

Rule: We use .... to talk about an objective truth.

4

Rule: We use .... to talk about future plans or intentions.

5

Rule: We use .... to make a general prediction, often after verbs like *think* or *hope*.

2 Choose the correct alternative.

1 A: The phone is ringing. B: I *'m going to/'ll* get it.
2 A: Do you want to come to a party on Saturday?
B: I can't. My family and I *are going to/will* go to London for the weekend.
3 How old *are you going to/will you* be on your next birthday?
4 Look. He's putting his coat on. He *'s going to/will* go out.
5 A: It's cold in here. B: OK. I *'m going to/'ll* close the window.

Will, may, might

3 Match these symbols with the sentences.

a  = Yes, certain.
b  = Yes, more or less certain.
c  = Maybe yes, maybe no.
d  = No, more or less certain.
e  = No, certain.

1 Perhaps it'll rain. ....c....
2 It definitely won't rain. ....
3 It may rain. ....
4 It's possible that it'll rain. ....
5 It might rain. ....
6 It'll probably rain. ....
7 It probably won't rain. ....
8 It'll definitely rain. ....

4 Put the words in order to make sentences. Then give an approximate percentage of certainty for each one.

1 team the win our Perhaps competition will.
.... = ...%
2 tonight won't It probably cold be
.... = ...%
3 will finish my homework soon I definitely.
.... = ...%
4 out tomorrow She won't definitely go.
.... = ...%
5 do the They week may exam next.
.... = ...%
6 this My probably call brother will afternoon.
.... = ...%

Grammar extension

5 Make predictions about your life when you are 35. Use the word given.

1 .... *may*
2 .... *probably*
3 .... *perhaps*
4 .... *possible*
5 .... *definitely*
6 .... *won't*
7 .... *might*

Different uses of *get*

1 Look at these possible meanings for *get*. Rewrite the sentences by omitting *get* or *get to* and using the correct form of these words.

arrive (at) become bring obtain/buy receive

1 When do you get angry?
When do you become angry?
2 How many emails do you get a week?
3 What time do you usually get to school?
4 Do you get presents for your parents when it's their birthday?
5 Are you going to get something to eat or drink on the way home after school?
6 Does your bedroom get hot in the summer?
7 What time do you usually get home after school?
8 Do you get tired of watching TV?
9 What did you get for your last birthday?
10 Did you get any letters in the post last week?
11 Please get me the pen that's on the table.

2 Write your own true answers to the questions in 1. Use *get* in your answer and write complete sentences.

1 ....
2 ....
3 ....
4 ....
5 ....
6 ....
7 ....
8 ....
9 ....
10 ....

Vocabulary extension: some phrasal verbs with *get*

3 Match the phrasal verbs with their meanings. Use your dictionary if necessary.

1 I get up at seven o'clock every day.
2 I get back from school at five o'clock.
3 I got out of the meeting just before lunch.
4 I'm getting behind with my project. I've only done half of it and I need to give it in tomorrow.
5 Why don't we get together at the weekend?

a return
b spend time together
c leave
d get out of bed after sleeping
e do something slower or later than necessary

4 Write your own true answers to these questions.

1 What time do you usually get up in the week?
2 What time do you usually get up at the weekend?
3 What time do you usually get back if you go out with friends on Friday or Saturday night?
4 What time do you get out of your house on a school morning?
5 How often do you get together with your grandparents and your uncles and aunts?
6 How often do you get behind with schoolwork or homework?

Click onto... An Australian novel

Cross-curricular – Literature
***After Summer* by Nick Earls**

INSIDE INFORMATION

- Nick Earls is a popular Australian writer. He has written books for teenagers and for adults.
- *After Summer* was Earls' first novel and it won a number of prizes. It is about a boy who is on his summer holidays. The extract below is from the start of the novel. The narrator is the teenage boy.
- In Australia the original title was *After January* because the summer holidays in Australia begin in December and end in January.

1 Read the extract. How does the writer feel?

1 very happy
2 excited
3 nervous
4 bored

WORD BOOSTER

Match the words and definitions.

1 waves
2 execution
3 turn
4 reflecting
5 showers

a killing somebody for doing a crime
b lines of water that go up and down in the sea
c shining back
d move 180º for example
e place where you wash with water

2 Read the extract again. Are these statements true (T) or false (F)?

1 This summer holiday is different from other summer holidays because the boy has just finished school. ....
2 The boy is waiting for some news which will make a difference to his future life. ....
3 The boy isn't having a good time because he's thinking so much about the 20th January. ....
4 The boy will get his results letter before he sees the newspaper. ....
5 The boy prefers swimming in the morning. ....
6 The boy finds it relaxing to enter the cold water. ....
7 The boy always looks for the place where the waves are the best. ....
8 Today the boy waits for one very big wave before he gets out. ....

3 Choose a good title for the extract and explain why.

Title ....

Explanation ....

....

4 What about *you*?

1 Do you like beach holidays? Why/Why not?

....

....

2 Have you ever been nervous waiting for exam results? When? What happened?

....

....

....

This begins in January, and January is OK. Sometimes it's as if the bright days of summer will last forever.

But the end of January is the end of the known world. It's been easy till now, relatively. I've had a new school year each January, but not this year.

This January I'm waiting for my offer, waiting for the message that will tell me what happens next. Waiting.

And the waiting is everywhere, in the waves and winds, in the familiar lights and sounds of the coastal summer, in the sun rising over the sea and going down through an orange sky into the Glasshouse Mountains.

The twentieth of January. Seventeen days from today. On the twentieth of January it comes out in the paper and I'll be there with the others from school around midnight at Newspaper House. I'll go down from the coast and I'll meet the others and we'll buy a paper and then we'll all know. And if the newspaper says I did it, I still won't believe it until I get the letter.

I need to stop thinking of this like an execution. I need to stop thinking and enjoy myself.

Whatever the weather is like I go to the beach early because I'm in the habit of it. It's the best time. I swim and the first cold wave always comes as a shock.

I swim in the sea right in front of the house. Even if there are better waves to the north or south, I usually swim here. These waves are mine.

This morning the waves aren't great but they're OK, coming in unspectacular threes and fours with long spaces between.

There are people out now, jogging, walking dogs, a girl in the surf. I see her when I turn and she's on a wave, lifting herself to a standing position on her board. And the sun is behind her, reflecting off the water so I don't see her well.

One more wave and I'll go in. I always want to wait for one last great wave but I know it won't come today. So I take the next one and go off to the showers. This is all part of my routine.

Zero conditional

1 Match the halves of the sentences.

1 If you leave a can of cola in a freezer, ...
2 If you run as fast as you can, ...
3 If you write too quickly, ...
4 If you read the newspaper every day, ...
5 If you look regularly at your vocabulary list, ...
6 If you work on a computer all day, ...
7 If you want to be a professional musician, ...

a you know what's happening in the world.
b it's a good idea to start playing when you're young.
c your eyes sometimes hurt.
d you often make mistakes.
e you remember words more easily.
f it explodes.
g you get tired very quickly.

2 Look at the sentences in 1 and choose the correct alternative.

1 We use the zero conditional to talk about *a specific, unique situation/something that is generally true*.
2 We use the present simple in *one half/both halves* of the sentence.

First conditional

3 Choose the correct alternative.

1 If I *like/will like* their next CD, I *buy/will buy* it.
2 She *doesn't/won't* come tonight if you *don't/won't* invite her.
3 If our car *doesn't/won't* work tomorrow, my dad *takes/will take* it to the garage.
4 If you *need/will need* help next week, I *come/will come*.
5 The police *arrest/will arrest* him tomorrow if they *find/will find* evidence.
6 If you *play/will play* that song again, I *go/will go* mad.
7 If she *doesn't/won't* play in the next match, her team *loses/will lose*.

4 Look at the sentences in 3 and choose the correct alternative.

1 We use the first conditional to talk about *possible/impossible* situations and their consequences.
2 We use the *present simple/will* in the half of the sentence with *if*.

5 Write complete sentences with the first conditional using the words given.

1 If/he/have a problem/he/speak to the teacher.
....
2 I/go to the doctor/if/my hand hurt tomorrow.
....
3 He/not be happy/if/he/miss the bus.
....
4 If/my sister/go to music lessons/my mum/buy her a guitar.
....
5 If/you/see the film tomorrow/you/know how the story ends.
....
6 The teacher/give me a bad mark/if/I/not give her my homework.
....
7 You/not see me/if/you/come late.
....
8 If/you/not switch off your mobile phone/people/get angry.
....
9 The picnic/be a disaster/if/the weather/be bad.
....
10 If/we/not go to the shops/we/not have enough food.
....

Grammar extension

6 Complete the sentences in a logical way with the first conditional.

1 If it rains, ...
2 ...., you won't pass your exams.
3 ...., I'll give you a present.
4 If my parents give me enough money, ...
5 If I don't speak English, ...
6 If the plane isn't late, ...
7 ...., perhaps she'll win the competition.
8 If the shop is open, ...
9 ...., I'll cry.
10 If that noise doesn't stop, ...

Weekend plans

1 Read this dialogue and complete the information below it.

KATIE: Hi, Lauren.
LAUREN: Hi, Katie.
KATIE: Listen. Are you **(a)** .... to anything tomorrow?
LAUREN: Not really. What **(b)** .... you?
KATIE: Do you **(c)** .... coming shopping with me?
LAUREN: Sure. What time **(d)** .... we meet?
KATIE: **(e)** .... about half past ten?
LAUREN: Fine. Why **(f)** .... we meet at the bus stop next to my house?
KATIE: OK, but where shall we meet if it rains?
LAUREN: Come straight to my house.
KATIE: Good idea. I'll ring Amy too and see if she wants to come.
LAUREN: **(g)** .... See you tomorrow.
KATIE: See you.

Katie, Lauren and possibly **(1)** .... *are going to go* **(2)** .... *tomorrow. They're going to meet at* **(3)** .... *at* **(4)** .... *But if it rains, they'll meet at* **(5)** ....

2 Read the dialogue again and complete it with these words.

about don't fancy Great How shall up

3 Complete the list with phrases from the dialogue. Then think of one more phrase for each box.

Asking about somebody's plans

a ....
b Do you ....?
c ....

Arranging to meet

d What time ....?
e ....
f ....
g ....

Responding to plans and arrangements

h Fine.
i ....
j ....
k ....

Describing photos

4 Look at the photo and answer the questions. If you are not sure of something, use *I think* and/or *I imagine*.

1 Who can you see in the photo?
....
....

2 Where are they?
....
....

3 What are they doing?
....
....

4 How do you think the people are feeling? Why?
....
....

5 Use the questions in 4 to think of things to say about this photo. Make notes and then practise orally.

A letter to a newspaper

1 Complete the table by putting the linkers in the correct place.

Finally   Firstly   Furthermore   However
Nevertheless   Next   What's more

Sequence	Addition	Contrast
....	....	....
....	....	....
....	....	....

2 Read this newspaper editorial. What reasons does the editor give for not wanting a new airport?

....

....

....

The Editor writes ...

Let's make it clear right from the start. The government wants to build a new airport here in the city but this newspaper is totally against the idea. Doesn't the government realise that another airport means more planes, and more planes mean more pollution? That means air pollution and noise pollution. And what about the people who live in the area where they want to build this new airport? How will they live with all this pollution from the sky? And how will they live with all the road traffic that this airport will bring to the area? A new airport? We say NO.

3 Complete these sentences in a logical way, not necessarily giving your own opinion.

1 I agree with what the editor says. Firstly, ... Next, ...

2 I think airports are important. However, ...

3 Airports create a lot of air pollution. Furthermore, ...

4 Plan a letter to the newspaper about the idea for a new airport. Make notes in the boxes. Do not write complete sentences.

Paragraph 1: *Express your opinion and explain your main reason for it.* ....

Paragraph 2: *Give an additional reason for your opinion.* ....

Paragraph 3: *Finish with one final reason for your opinion.* ....

5 Write your letter here. Use the linkers in 1.

Dear Editor,

I am writing in response to an article about airports which appeared in your newspaper last Wednesday.

Firstly, ...

Next, ...

Finally, ...

I will be interested in hearing other readers' opinions on this question.

Yours faithfully,

....

Revision: Units 5–6

Grammar

1 Choose the correct alternative.

1 Greece is *hotter/more hotter* than Britain in the summer.
2 I think Sam is thinner *than/that* Jake.
3 She's the best player *of/in* the team.
4 That's the *sillyest/silliest* thing I've ever seen.
5 Greg is the *more/most* intelligent person I know.
6 Do you think rainy weather is *more bad/worse* than sunny weather?

/6 points

2 Rewrite the sentences using the words in bold. Make sure the meaning stays the same.

1 Love is more important than money.
Money .... **LESS**
2 I think that biology is easier than maths.
I think that maths .... **AS**
3 We aren't old enough to see that film.
We're .... **TOO**
4 It's too cold to swim in the sea today.
It's .... **ENOUGH**
5 Her sister is very intelligent and she's very intelligent.
She's .... **AS**
6 He is too slow to win the race.
He .... **FAST**

/6 points

3 Choose the correct alternative.

1 I don't really know but Joe *may/will* win the competition.
2 It *won't probably/probably won't* rain tomorrow.
3 They say it *is snowing/is going to snow* next Christmas.
4 The effects *will definitely/definitely will* be terrible.
5 Nobody is certain, but humans *will/might* travel to Mars around 2050.
6 **A:** Someone's at the door! **B:** OK, I *'ll/'m going to* go.

/6 points

4 Complete the sentences with the first or zero conditional form of the verbs given.

1 If she .... (go) to London, she'll be able to see the London Eye.
2 She won't say anything if you .... (tell) her a secret.
3 If you put snow in your hand, your hand .... (get) cold.
4 If we have the chance, we .... (travel) all around Europe next summer.
5 If you look directly at the sun, it .... (be) bad for your eyes.
6 Sheila .... (do) well in tomorrow's exam if she .... (think) carefully.

/7 points

Total **/25 points**

Vocabulary

1 Complete the types of programme with the missing vowels.

1 g ... m ... sh ... w
2 c ... rt ... ... n
3 d ... c ... m ... nt ... ry
4 ... dv ... rt
5 ch ... t sh ... w
6 dr ... m ...

/6 points

2 Match these adjectives with the explanations. There are more adjectives than explanations.

confused confusing cool funny interested
interesting relaxing scary surprised surprising

1 It's when something makes you laugh. ....
2 It's how you feel when something happens but you didn't know it was going to happen. ....
3 It's when something makes you want to know more. ....
4 It's when something makes you feel frightened. ....
5 It's how you feel when you don't understand something or a situation. ....
6 It's when something is really good. ....

/6 points

3 Put the letters in order to find different geographical features.

1 leungj ....
2 tesdre ....
3 trsofe ....
4 mintoanu grean ....

/4 points

4 Match these words with the explanations. There are more words than explanations.

drought flood global warming greenhouse effect
ozone layer recycle save waste

1 when it rains a lot and rivers get too big ....
2 when you save old things to use the materials again ....
3 when you use things in an unnecessary way ....
4 the thing which protects the earth from the sun ....
5 when it doesn't rain and there is no water ....
6 when you stop using something or use very little ....

/6 points

5 Find a synonym for *get* in these sentences.

1 I'll *get* your bag. ....
2 Can you *get* me the newspaper when you go to the shops? ....
3 She usually *gets* home early. ....

/3 points

Total **/25 points**

Reading

1 Read about a cameraman called Matt Howard and choose a, b or c to complete the sentences.

Matt Howard is a cameraman who works on nature documentaries. He has filmed all over the world, in jungles, rainforests and deserts. Here he tells us about his job.

'To film nature documentaries, it's important to be good with a camera, obviously. But, in my opinion, it's more important to be interested in plants and animals. If you aren't, the work can be really boring. To make a two-minute film of a bird, insect or animal, you can sometimes spend a day or a week looking for them. And animals aren't like actors. They don't just appear when you want them to. Sometimes they never appear!'

Matt knows that his job is very important. When he travels to ice caps or deserts, he sees that the environment is changing. His job is to film a world that may disappear one day. 'If the environment continues to change because of global warming, the only place where you'll be able to see some animals and insects is in nature documentaries. I hope our work helps people to understand that we all need to do something to save the planet.'

Generally, changes in technology make Matt's life easier. 'High-definition (HD) cameras help to get better pictures. But if you make a small mistake with an HD camera, it looks much worse than with an old camera. It's true that the new cameras aren't as heavy as the old ones.' But sometimes Matt carries 35 kilos, climbs up a mountain, and tries to film at the same time!

Matt knows what he wants when he makes films. 'I want to film things that people have never seen before. Or I want to film things they've seen, but in a new way. I want it to be a unique experience for the people watching.'

And the scariest experience he's ever had? 'We were making a TV programme about polar bears in the Arctic ice cap. We weren't filming at the time, we were sleeping. Suddenly I heard the sound of a polar bear right next to my ear. I was too frightened to open my eyes. It stayed there for five minutes and then left. Believe me, they were the longest five minutes of my life!'

1 Matt says that
- a he doesn't like his job much because it isn't very exciting.
- b it can take a long time to make a short film.
- c the most important thing in his job is the camera.

2 Matt also says that animals
- a don't always do what you want.
- b don't like actors.
- c don't like appearing in films.

3 Matt thinks his work is important because
- a he is protecting some animals, insects and plants.
- b it may be the only way that people can see some animals and insects in the future.
- c he makes programmes about saving the planet.

4 Matt thinks that new HD cameras
- a always take better pictures than old cameras.
- b are lighter than old cameras.
- c usually take worse pictures than old cameras.

5 Matt
- a wants people to see something new and different when they watch his work.
- b once had a bad experience when he was watching a polar bear.
- c had a scary experience because he's very frightened of filming polar bears.

/5 points

Writing

2 Write a letter to a newspaper giving your opinion about something you saw on TV last week. Use these questions for ideas about what to write.

- What type of programme was it?
- Was it good or bad? Why?
- How did it make you feel – happy, angry, interested, frightened?
- What do you want? More programmes like this? To stop programmes like this?
- What are other people's opinions?

Dear Editor,
I am writing in response to a TV programme which I saw last week. The programme ...

/10 points

Total */15 points*

7 Odd jobs

Grammar ‣ Modal verbs of obligation, prohibition and advice *(must, have to, mustn't, don't have to, should, shouldn't)* ‣ Second conditional
Vocabulary ‣ Jobs, Personal qualities ‣ Compound adjectives
Speaking ‣ Making polite requests
Writing ‣ A letter of application and CV

‣ Vocabulary

Jobs

1 Complete the jobs with the missing vowels.

1 c...mp...t...r pr...gr...mm...r

2 r...c...pt......n...st

3 b......ld...r

4 p...l...c... ...ff...c...r

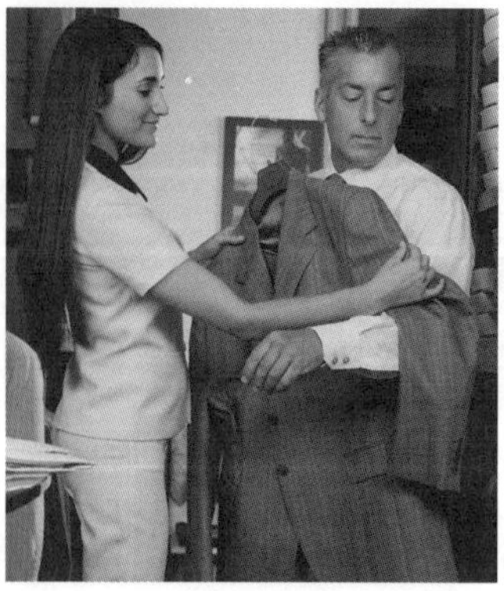

5 sh...p ...ss...st...nt

6 m...ch...n...c

7 f...sh......n d...s...gn...r

8 j......rn...l...st

2 Write true (T) or false (F) about the person in the photo.

1 He works with children. T/F
2 He works indoors. T/F
3 He does paperwork. T/F
4 He does manual work. T/F
5 He deals with the public. T/F
6 He travels a lot. T/F
7 He works in a team. T/F
8 He works in an office. T/F
9 He works with numbers. T/F
10 He works with a computer. T/F

Personal qualities

3 Find adjectives in the word search and write them next to the correct synonym or explanation.

c	d	c	n	c	d	v	c	s	b
r	e	l	i	a	b	l	e	t	p
e	r	e	m	r	i	c	o	r	y
a	f	v	b	i	n	a	i	o	u
t	i	e	u	n	g	l	k	n	e
i	t	r	o	g	h	m	j	g	r
v	s	o	c	i	a	b	l	e	a
e	a	m	b	i	t	i	o	u	s

1 with lots of imagination and new ideas: ....
2 healthy: ....
3 with lots of physical energy: ....
4 intelligent: ....
5 kind, helpful and sympathetic to other people: ....
6 a friendly person who likes being with other people: ....
7 somebody you can depend on: ....
8 somebody who doesn't easily get excited, worried or angry: ....
9 somebody who wants to be the best: ....

4 Write two personal qualities in 3 that you think are necessary in these jobs.

1 A sports teacher: ...., ...
2 A poet: ...., ...
3 A scientist: ...., ...
4 A shop assistant: ...., ...

1 Read the two texts and complete the titles to show what job each person did at first and in the end.

Text 1: Barry Cox – from .... to ....

Text 2: Aleksander Kudajczyk – from .... to ....

Text 1

BARRY COX IS a famous singer. He's from Liverpool but he isn't famous in England. In China it's a completely different matter. There he's a superstar. So how did that happen?

Barry is 30 years old. When he left school he wasn't happy and decided to do something different with his life. The first step was to learn a new language. He started with Spanish but he didn't enjoy the experience. Then one day in Liverpool's China Town he suddenly had an idea. Not many English people learn Chinese so he decided to try. He went into a local Chinese restaurant and ordered a meal … and some language lessons. He was lucky. The nephew of the restaurant owner wanted English lessons, so they helped each other and became friends. At that time Barry didn't know that there were different Chinese dialects. Barry learnt Cantonese, which is actually more difficult than Mandarin. He spoke it all day with his new Chinese friends and at a Chinese supermarket where he started working. Then one day he went to a concert by a famous singer from Hong Kong and it changed his life. He started singing in Cantonese. He took it more seriously, had singing lessons and entered singing competitions. One day he decided to move to Hong Kong. It was difficult to become a professional singer there but he moved to Macao, a sort of Chinese Las Vegas. That's where he became famous and where he lives now. He has to sing six days a week at a big casino but he loves it. And now they may make a film about his life!

Text 2

WHAT A CHANGE! At the moment Aleksander Kudajczyk has to clean the floors of Glasgow University but next week he is going to begin a new job, as a concert pianist. The surprising story of this 28-year-old Polish man is like a Hollywood film.

Mr Kudajczyk arrived in Scotland in January. He wanted to work as a teacher but all he found was a job as a cleaner at Glasgow University. He had to work there four hours a day, starting at 6am. One day in the university he discovered a grand piano and he asked permission to play on it. They gave him permission but nobody thought any more about it. What Mr Kudajczyk didn't know was that there was a webcam in the piano room. One day a university secretary was checking the webcam pictures and she saw Aleksander playing. The music was so perfect that she thought it was a CD. Then she saw it was the cleaner doing his daily piano practice. She immediately sent emails to other people at the university, telling them to watch. Soon after, Mr Kudajczyk was playing Chopin's music to hundreds of teachers and students. Since then he has played the piano at many special concerts and events but he has also continued to work as a cleaner. But next week that will change when he becomes a full-time professional musician and teacher.

2 Read the texts again. Are these sentences about Barry Cox (BC), Aleksander Kudajczyk (AK), both men (B) or neither (N) of them?

1 He lives and works in the country where he was born. ....
2 He has already started working full-time in the world of music. ....
3 He has found a new job because somebody discovered him by accident. ....
4 A woman played an important part in his change of career. ....
5 He practised a lot. ....
6 He's going to act in a film. ....

3 Write sentences with similarities or differences between Barry Cox and Aleksander Kudajczyk. Think about where they live, their old and new jobs and how they found their new jobs.

1 ....
2 ....
3 ....
4 ....

4 Look up in your dictionary three words from each text that you don't understand and write the meaning next to them.

Text 1

1 Word: .... Meaning: ....
2 Word: .... Meaning: ....
3 Word: .... Meaning: ....

Text 2

1 Word: .... Meaning: ....
2 Word: .... Meaning: ....
3 Word: .... Meaning: ....

5 What about *you*?

Which story did you like the most: 1 or 2? Explain why.

....

Modal verbs of obligation, prohibition and advice

1 Read the sentences and choose the alternative which describes the meaning of the sentence.

1 You don't have to be an expert to use a computer. *Obligation/ no obligation*
2 Doctors have to work at unusual times. *Obligation/prohibition*
3 You mustn't come home late. *No obligation/prohibition*
4 You should write down new vocabulary. *Recommendation/ obligation*
5 Your essay doesn't have to be perfect. *No obligation/ prohibition*
6 You must try your best. *Obligation/prohibition*
7 You shouldn't go to bed late the night before an exam. *Prohibition/advice*
8 You mustn't start crying when things go wrong. *No obligation/prohibition*

2 Write complete sentences using the words given and the correct form of *have to* or *don't have to*.

1 Normally teachers/wear a uniform.
....
2 Normally a police officer/wear a uniform.
....
3 I/go to school on Sunday.
....
4 A secretary/know how to use a computer.
....
5 Builders/wear hard hats.
....

3 Complete the sentences with *must* or *mustn't*.

1 You .... write carefully in exams.
2 People .... smoke in hospitals.
3 Students .... use mobile phones in class.
4 Professional musicians .... practise playing their instrument.

4 Complete the sentences with *should* or *shouldn't*.

1 People .... use violence to solve their problems.
2 You .... take medicine when you aren't ill.
3 You .... help your friends when they have problems.
4 When you aren't very good at something, you .... practise to get better.
5 People .... switch off their mobile phones in the cinema.

5 Choose the correct alternative. If you think two alternatives are correct, mark both of them.

1 Children *has to/have to/don't have to* go to school on Monday.
2 You *must/mustn't/don't have to* copy in exams.
3 Doctors *must/mustn't/have to* work hard.
4 You *has to/have to/must* wear good clothes if you work in a bank.
5 Visitors *mustn't/must/don't have to* talk in a loud voice or shout because it is prohibited.
6 You *must/don't have to/mustn't* use a mobile phone in a plane.

Grammar extension

6 Each sentence contains a mistake. Find the mistake and write the sentence correctly.

1 Children under 16 must to go to school.
....
2 This exercise is optional – you mustn't do it.
....
3 You should to do extra work if it's difficult.
....
4 Students haven't to wear a uniform in our school and so you can wear what you want.
....
....
5 You musn't drink and drive – it's illegal.
....
6 You don't have to open the car door when the car is moving.
....
7 You should eat chocolate just before you go to bed because it isn't good for your teeth.
....
....
8 Smoking is prohibited here. You don't have to do it.
....
9 It's essential to do this exercise. You mustn't do it.
....
10 You mustn't be 18 to ride a bike.
....

Compound adjectives

1 Complete the crossword.

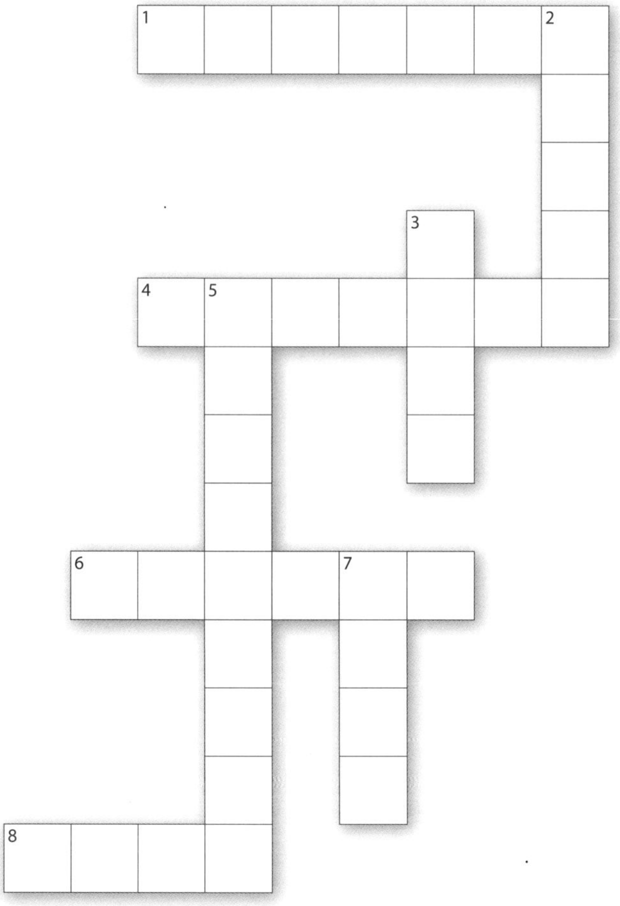

Across

1 He's the first person to arrive at work and the last person to go. He does more than anybody else. He's very hard-..........................

4 They're a beautiful couple. She's very beautiful and he's good-..........................

6 You've got the pen in your left hand. Are you left-..........................?

8 She's the director of a large multinational company. I'm sure she's well-..........................

Down

2 You should be more relaxed and easy-..........................

3 That teacher only teaches two lessons a day. He's part-..........................

5 She's well-.......................... She always knows where she should be and what she has to do.

7 People from Northern Europe sometimes have blonde hair and are blue-..........................

2 Look at the adjectives in 1. Write three which you think describe you and three which don't describe you.

1 I'm ...., ... and ....

2 I'm not ...., ... or ....

3 Think of a friend or family member and describe them using the adjectives in 1.

....

....

....

....

Vocabulary extension: more compound adjectives

4 Match these words to make compound adjectives. Then match them with the definitions. Use your dictionary if necessary.

1 self- dressed
2 open- known
3 well- reliant
4 bad- minded
5 well- off
6 well- tempered

a open to new ideas and different opinions
b rich, with a lot of money
c famous, many people know you
d you get angry often or quickly
e able to do things for yourself and not depend on other people
f wearing good clothes

5 Complete the sentences with the compound adjectives in 4.

1 Yes, she's very .... but that's because she spends all her money on clothes.
2 I like him because he's very .... He listens to you and thinks before he says yes or no.
3 She's very independent and .... She doesn't think her parents have to do everything for her.
4 My older brother is so .... He always shouts at me, and for no reason!
5 She's a .... writer. Lots of people have bought her books and seen her face.
6 I think his family is quite .... because they've got a really big house.

Click onto... Working in the UK

International cultural knowledge
Two traditional jobs

1 Read the texts about Ernie Wilkins and Penny Wilcox and write one sentence to explain what their jobs are.

1 Ernie Wilkins is a milkman. Milkmen bring ....
....

2 Penny Wilcox is a lollipop person. Lollipop people help ....
....

▸ WORD BOOSTER

Match the words and definitions.

1	float	a	not long ago
2	item	b	a large vehicle
3	official	c	an individual thing
4	recently	d	formal

2 Read the texts again and complete the table.

1 What Ernie likes about his job	**2** What Ernie doesn't like about his job
a *the peace and quiet of the early morning* b .... c	d ....
3 What Penny likes about her job	**4** What Penny doesn't like about her job
e .... f	g ....

3 Answer the questions.

1 What personal qualities do Ernie and Penny have?
Ernie: ....
Penny: ....

2 What is a School Crossing Guide?
....

3 Can Penny's job be dangerous or not? Why?
....

4 What about *you*?

Which of the two jobs would you prefer to do and why?

....
....
....

Text 1

Ernie Wilkins, Milkman

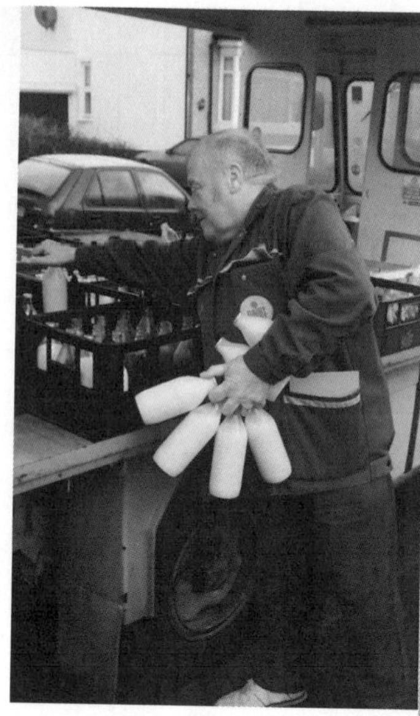

Ernie Wilkins has been a milkman for 20 years. He loves his job, but not everybody can understand why. For a start, he has to get up early every day. He gets up at one o'clock in the morning and starts work at two. That's when he puts all the milk onto his electric milk float. And nowadays milkmen don't just bring you milk. They often sell juice, cream, yoghurt, bread and potatoes. It usually takes him three quarters of an hour to prepare his float. Then he starts driving round the streets in his town, leaving bottles of milk and other items at his customers' doors. When they wake up, everything is there, waiting.

Ernie loves the peace and quiet of the early morning. He loves being outdoors, except when it's very cold in the winter. That's the one thing he doesn't enjoy. But watching the sun come up is always a special moment for him. Ernie is very caring. He loves the fact that everybody knows him and old people often ask him for help. When Ernie finishes work at 9am, he's tired but happy.

Text 2

Penny Wilcox, Lollipop person

Penny Wilcox is 55. She doesn't want to work long hours and so the job she started last year is perfect for her. She just works for half an hour in the morning and half an hour in the afternoon. The official name for her job is a School Crossing Guide. She works outside a school at the times when students arrive in the morning and leave in the afternoon. When there is a group of students waiting, she walks into the middle of the road and stops the traffic. She wears a bright yellow jacket and carries a sign which says 'STOP'. The sign looks like a lollipop, which is why everybody calls Penny and her colleagues 'lollipop people'. When drivers see her and her sign, they must stop and let the children cross. Penny is a very sociable person and she loves talking to the children each morning. The only thing she doesn't like is that some drivers get angry and shout when they have to stop. Penny thinks that in the past drivers were friendlier. She's unhappy that recently there have been some serious accidents and lollipop people have been hurt. But Penny knows a lot of the children and won't stop working if they need her.

Second conditional

1 Match the halves of the sentences.

1 If I were a president or prime minister, ...
2 If I had a boat, ...
3 In Australia it would be unusual ....
4 If they gave me a job in the summer, ...
5 We'd go to the USA in the summer ....
6 My parents would be really happy with me ....

a if we had enough money.
b I'd spend a lot of money on health, education and the environment.
c I'd take it because I need the money.
d if I became a famous singer.
e I'd spend my holidays at sea.
f if it snowed in the summer.

2 Look at the sentences in 1. Are these sentences about the second conditional true (T) or false (F)?

1 The second conditional talks about improbable and imaginary situations. ....
2 The second conditional talks about past situations. ....
3 We use *would* in the half of the sentence with *If*. ....
4 We can use *was* or *were* with *If I/he/she*. ....
5 The half of the sentence with *If* always comes first. ....

3 Choose the correct alternative.

1 If you *aren't/weren't* my brother, I'd be really angry with you.
2 If it was hot all year, I *won't/wouldn't* go out.
3 If I *were/am* you, I'd buy a new mobile phone.
4 If they *didn't/don't* have a pet, they'd be able to go away in the summer.
5 We *would/will* enjoy the concert more if we knew the songs.
6 They *would/will* continue running if they didn't get tired.
7 I'd do what he said if he *was/is* my boss.
8 Television would be better if there *aren't/weren't* all those adverts.
9 If I *could/can* sing, I'd start a band.
10 If you went out more, you *won't/wouldn't* be lonely.

4 Complete the sentences with the second conditional form of the verbs given.

1 If I .... (have) a problem, I'd call you.
2 If the bus didn't come, we .... (walk).
3 I .... (not be) happy if my parents didn't let me go out.
4 You wouldn't learn much if you .... (play) computer games all day.
5 If you .... (learn) to speak a new language, it would help you find a job.
6 If John was faster, he .... (play) football better.
7 They'd leave the restaurant immediately if they .... (not like) the food.
8 If I knew the answer, I .... (tell) you.
9 If I .... (find) money in the street, I'd try to find who it belonged to.
10 I'd buy that coat if I .... (have) enough money.
11 If I were you, I .... (ask) the teacher to explain the homework again.

Grammar extension

5 Give these people advice using *If I were you …* You can add reasons to explain your opinion.

1 I've got an exam tomorrow but it's the cup final tonight and my favourite team is playing.
....
....

2 My friends have invited me to play football tonight but my leg hurts.
....
....

3 Another student copied my answers in an exam yesterday.
....
....

4 My friends are all going to an expensive restaurant tonight but I haven't got enough money to go.
....
....

5 I can't understand the maths that we're studying at the moment but I don't want to tell anyone because I feel stupid.
....
....

6 A good friend has stopped talking to me, but I don't know why. I think he's angry with me.
....
....
....

7 I've got lots of English homework to do tonight but I forgot to bring my books home.
....
....

8 It's my mum's birthday next week but I have no idea what to buy her.
....
....

9 I'd like to learn to drive.
....
....

10 I want to be famous one day.
....
....

Asking about a job

1 Put the words in order to make polite requests.

1 me you starts Can tell job when the ?

....

2 if I need Could you any ask experience ?

....

3 you tell me apply how Could I can ?

....

4 we you do me tell to what have Can ?

....

5 Could the wages I ask what are basic ?

....

6 you me tell Can address your what is ?

....

2 Complete the dialogue with the polite requests in 1.

HOLIDAY CAMP ORGANISER: Good afternoon?

TEENAGER: Good afternoon. I'm calling about a job that was in the newspaper yesterday. Could I ask for some information?

HOLIDAY CAMP ORGANISER: Certainly.

TEENAGER: Thanks. **(a)** ....

HOLIDAY CAMP ORGANISER: Yes. It begins on 1st July and it finishes on 31st July.

TEENAGER: Oh, I see. **(b)** ....

HOLIDAY CAMP ORGANISER: Well, you have to give some sports lessons in the morning, and then in the afternoon you take groups of children on excursions or you organise games and competitions with them.

TEENAGER: I see. **(c)** ....

HOLIDAY CAMP ORGANISER: It's not essential, but we prefer people who've done similar work before.

TEENAGER: I understand. **(d)** ....

HOLIDAY CAMP ORGANISER: It's £150 a week, and lunch is included.

TEENAGER: **(e)** ....

HOLIDAY CAMP ORGANISER: It's easy. You just need to send a letter of application and CV to me and then I'll call people for interviews.

TEENAGER: That's great. **(f)** ....

HOLIDAY CAMP ORGANISER: Yes, it's …

Describing photos

3 Look at the photo and answer the questions. If you are not sure of something, use *I think* and/or *I imagine*.

1 Who can you see in the photo?

....

2 Where are they?

....

3 What are they doing?

....

4 How do you think the people are feeling? Why?

....

4 Use the questions in 3 to think of things to say about this photo. Make notes and then practise orally.

A letter of application and CV

1 Read this letter of application. What type of job do you think Benjamin Martin wants? Do you think he is a good person for the job?

....

....

12 Sefton Street
Sunderland
SU7 8BV

Ms Susan Nicholson
72 Hill Road
Birmingham
BO6 3NJ

7th February 2011

Dear Ms Nicholson,

I am writing in response to your advertisement in *The Birmingham Sun*. **I would like to** apply for the job which you advertised in this newspaper on 5th February.

I enclose a CV with information about myself, including education and work experience. **As you will see**, tennis is one of my main hobbies and interests. I have experience of giving tennis lessons and of working with children. I also think that I am patient, well-organised and hard-working.

I look forward to hearing from you.

Yours sincerely,

Benjamin Martin

Benjamin Martin

2 Look at the words and expressions in bold. Explain why they are important in letters of application.

12 Sefton Street *We write our own address in the top right corner.*

Ms ....

72 Hill Road ....

Dear ....

I am writing in response to ....

I would like to ....

As you will see ....

I look forward to hearing from you ....

Yours sincerely ....

3 Put the headings in the correct place in the CV.

1 Interests
2 Education and qualifications
3 General information
4 Work experience

CURRICULUM VITAE

Benjamin Martin

A ....

1 .... 20/7/1992
2 .... British
3 .... Single
4 .... 12 Sefton Street, Sunderland, SU7 8BV
5 .... (mobile) 0567 123 4567
6 .... (home) 651 10 11 12
7 .... benmart@binter.com

B ....

Summerfield School, Sunderland
A levels in English Literature, French and Economics

C ....

July 2010	Worked at Foxton Tennis Club giving lessons to 5–10 year olds
July 2009	Worked at Knightley Tennis Club as assistant

D ....

Tennis
Reading
Good knowledge of computers

4 Now put the specific titles in the correct place in the CV.

1 Permanent address
2 Email
3 Nationality
4 Telephone
5 Marital status
6 Telephone
7 Date of birth

5 Take a piece of paper and write out your own CV. Use the completed CV on this page as a model.

8 Good friends

Grammar	▸ Past perfect ▸ Gerunds and infinitives
Vocabulary	▸ Relationships ▸ Feelings ▸ Noun suffixes *-ness, -ship, -dom*
Speaking	▸ Reporting a past event
Writing	▸ A personal description

▸ Vocabulary

Relationships

1 Match these phrases to the pictures.

ask somebody out fall in love with somebody
get back together again get married
get on well with somebody go out with somebody
~~have an argument~~ split up with somebody

1 *have an argument* ....

2 ....

3 ....

4 ....

5 ....

6 ....

7 ....

8 ....

2 Are these stages usually at the start or the end of a relationship?

		Start	End
1	get on well with somebody	✓	☐
2	ask somebody out	☐	☐
3	have an argument	☐	☐
4	meet somebody	☐	☐
5	split up with somebody	☐	☐
6	fall in love with somebody	☐	☐
7	go out with somebody	☐	☐

Feelings

3 Complete the puzzle by writing the noun form of each adjective. Is the word in the shaded column positive or negative?

1 angry 2 bored 3 excited
4 afraid 5 happy 6 lonely

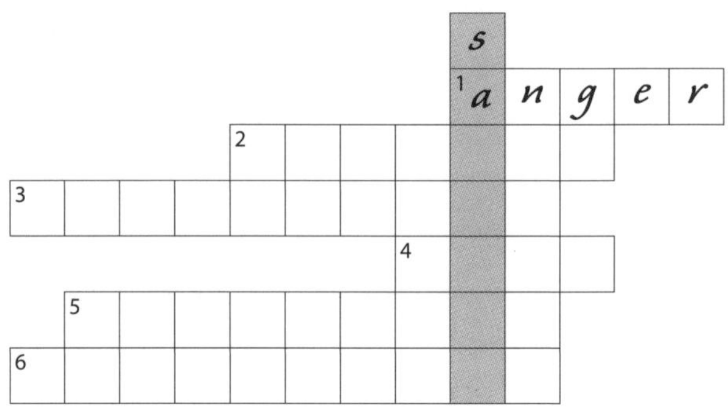

4 Write your own true answers to these questions.

1 When was the last time you were angry? What happened?

....

2 When was the last time you were bored? Why were you bored?

....

3 When you were small, what were you afraid of?

....

4 When was the last time you were very excited? What happened?

....

5 When was the last time you were lonely? What did you do?

....

1 Read the two love stories from British newspapers. Write a title for each story.

1 ....

FIVE YEARS AGO David Brown woke up with a mystery mobile phone number in his head. He couldn't stop thinking about the number. He started thinking that somebody had given him the number. In the end he decided to send a text message. The number belonged to Michelle Kitson, a 17-year-old student who was living with her parents about 100 kilometres away. She decided to answer the message. After a few more messages it became clear that they had never met before. But they continued sending messages and started calling each other on the phone. Then Michelle and David met … and fell in love. Not long after, they got married. Michelle said: 'It was a fantastic day when we got married. The weather had been awful that week but when we went to the church it was beautiful sunshine!'

2 ....

Yes, milk IS good for you. It can even find you a boyfriend or girlfriend! Just ask farmer Geraint Evans. He and four other farmers, men and women, put their photos on the side of 2,000 milk cartons with their email addresses asking people to contact them. Geraint hadn't had a girlfriend for five years because of his long days at work on the farm. He often finished at 11pm and so he had no time to go out and meet people. He was lucky. A 28-year-old American student called Laura Allison saw Geraint's photo and immediately fell in love. Laura was only in Britain on holiday. When she got back to her home in Chicago, she contacted Geraint. Six months have passed and they have sent hundreds of emails, called each other, sent letters and visited each other's homes. The couple met in person for the first time when Geraint flew to Chicago. 'After meeting and spending time together, I know this is true love and I hope we will spend the rest of our lives together,' said Laura. 'I've met the girl of my dreams and I want us to get married as soon as Laura's finished her course in America,' said Geraint.

2 Look at the information. Who does it describe – David, Michelle, Geraint or Laura? Each piece of information could describe more than one person.

1 17 years old *Michelle*
2 student ....
3 farmer ....
4 lived more than 100 kilometres from his partner ....
5 sent a lot of emails ....
6 sent a lot of text messages ....
7 met her partner when she was on holiday ....
8 got married ....
9 works many hours a day ....
10 met her partner in an unusual way ....

3 Answer the questions.

1 How did David meet Michelle?
....

2 What was special about the day when Michelle got married?
....

3 How did Geraint meet Laura?
....

4 Why did Geraint decide to look for a girlfriend in an unusual way?
....

4 Find words in the texts which have similar meanings to these words or explanations.

1 obvious, evident (*Text 1*) ....
2 one person to another person (*Texts 1 and 2*) ....
3 container for liquids, especially milk or juice (*Text 2*) ....
4 immediately after (*Text 2*) ....

5 What about *you*?

Which story do you think is more unusual and why?
....

Past perfect

1 Match the halves of the sentences. Then underline the thing which happened first in each sentence. Is the verb in the past simple or the past perfect?

1 When they had finished the exam ..c..
2 He didn't have any money that week ....
3 She started reading a new book ....
4 They hadn't eaten anything all day ....
5 When they had had their dinner ....
6 He didn't swim ....
7 They had won the competition ....

a they washed the dishes.
b so they had a party to celebrate.
c ~~they left the classroom~~.
d because he had forgotten to bring his towel.
e so they ordered a big pizza.
f because he had spent it the week before.
g because she had finished the one she was reading.

2 Which of these things had you done by half past eight this morning? Write complete sentences.

1 By 8.30am this morning *I had/hadn't had a shower.*
(have a shower)
2 ....
(read a book)
3 ....
(arrive at school)
4 ....
(have an argument)
5 ....
(speak to my parents)
6 ....
(use my mobile phone)
7 ....
(send an email)
8 ....
(watch TV)
9 ....
(spend money)

3 Write a complete sentence for each picture. Look at the example.

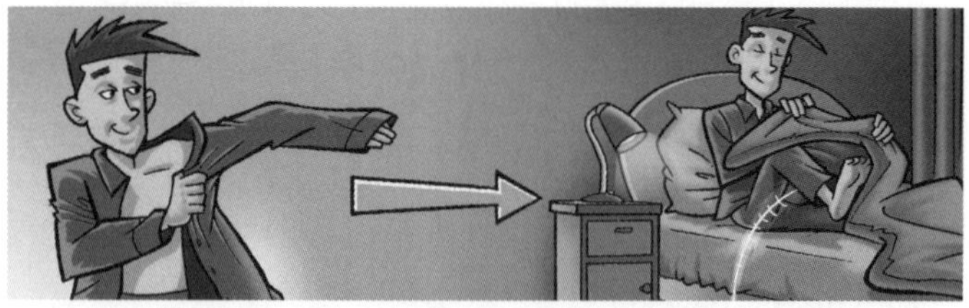

1 *When he had put his pyjamas on, he went to bed.*

2 ....

3 ....

4 ....

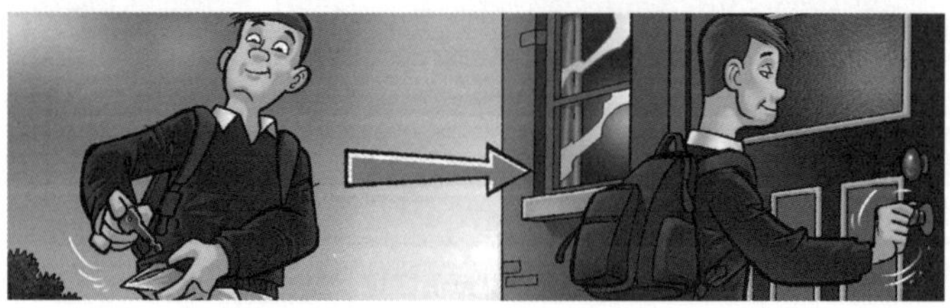

5 ....

Grammar extension

4 Look at these important dates in the history of mankind and write sentences with the past perfect. Look at the example.

1 4500 BC – invent the wheel
By 4500 BC they had invented the wheel.
2 1455 – start to print books
....
3 1796 – give the first vaccination
....
4 1800 – make the first battery
....
5 1895 – discover X-rays
....
6 1903 – fly for the first time
....
7 1928 – discover penicillin
....
8 1932 – split the atom
....
9 1953 – find the molecular structure of DNA
....
10 1969 – walk on the moon
....

Noun suffixes *-ness, -ship, -dom*

1 Put the letters in order to make nouns. Then complete the table by writing the nouns in the correct column.

~~dromfee~~ slilens moredob snakewes dessans massend redpinfish peashspin sillensone tinshiporeal

-ness	-ship	-dom
....	....	*freedom*
....	....	....
....	....	....
....	....	....
....	....	....
....	....	....
....	....	....
....	....	....
....	....	....

2 Complete the sentences with the adjective or noun form of the words in 1.

1 You don't look well. Are you ....*ill*.... ? Do you need a doctor?
2 I have a good .... with my sister. We get on well.
3 After ten years in prison they finally let him out and gave him back his ....
4 Why are you so .... ? Have you won the lottery or something?
5 She hasn't got any brothers or sisters or any good friends. I think she's .... with nobody to talk to.
6 They're quite .... They aren't strong enough to put the bags up there.
7 Can you imagine the .... of sitting around for five hours with nothing to do?
8 Your .... is really important to me. We've been friends since we were five.
9 You look like you are about to cry. Why are you so .... ?

Vocabulary extension: other nouns ending in *-ness, -ship, -dom*

3 Match the words with their definitions. Use your dictionary if necessary.

1 dark
2 wise
3 aware
4 leader
5 blind
6 king

a intelligent because you have a lot of experience
b a man who rules a country, the oldest male member of a royal family
c not able to see
d a person who is in control of other people
e black, or without much light
f knowing about a situation

4 Write the words in 3 in the correct column in the table in 1. Use your dictionary if necessary.

5 Look at the photos and answer the questions using the correct form of the words in 3.

1 What is this? The United ....

2 Why can't they see? Because of the ....

3 Why can't he see? Because he's ....

4 What is an important quality in this type of person? ....

5 What is an important quality in this type of person? ....

Click onto... A romance that made history

Cross-curricular – History
Antony and Cleopatra

INSIDE INFORMATION

- The love story between Mark Antony and Cleopatra is one of the most famous in history. William Shakespeare wrote a play about the two characters and there have been other famous books and films about them too.

1 Write three things that you <u>think</u> you know about Cleopatra.

1 ....
2 ....
3 ....

2 **Read the text and see if it mentions any of your facts in 1. The text is not in order, but that is not important at the moment.**

A
Together Mark Antony and Cleopatra had a very powerful political and romantic relationship. But Mark Antony had a rival in Rome, Octavian. Octavian declared war against Mark Antony. In a terrible battle at Actium, Mark Antony lost and, with Cleopatra, he ran away to Egypt. Mark Antony was losing the war and Roman soldiers were going to make him a prisoner. He decided to kill himself. When Cleopatra found out, she took a poisonous snake, put it next to her, and she also took her own life.

B
Cleopatra VII of Egypt is one of the most famous women in history. She was born in 69 or 68 BC. When her father died, she became the queen. Her ten-year-old brother, Ptolemy XIII, was the king. Because of an old Egyptian tradition she and her brother got married.

C
In 48 BC, Egypt became part of the conflict between Julius Caesar and Pompey. Caesar came to Egypt and he and Cleopatra began a romance. Ptolemy had exiled Cleopatra but Caesar helped Cleopatra to become queen again. In 47 BC Cleopatra had a child, possibly Julius Caesar's. Caesar went back to Rome and Cleopatra and her son followed him. But when they assassinated Caesar in Rome, Cleopatra returned to Egypt where once again she became queen.

D
Legend says that Cleopatra was incredibly beautiful. We don't know if she was, but we know that she was very clever. She spoke nine languages and was a great mathematician. While she was queen she brought prosperity and peace to Egypt.

E
In Rome some people started saying that Cleopatra had helped to kill Julius Caesar. Mark Antony, the new Emperor of Rome, wanted to discover the truth so he told her to come to see him. Cleopatra arrived in a golden boat. The legend says that Mark Antony and Cleopatra immediately fell in love. We know that they got married soon after and had three children.

WORD BOOSTER

Match the words and definitions.

1	powerful	a	kill a famous or important person
2	rival	b	strong and important
3	exile	c	make somebody leave a country
4	follow	d	go after
5	assassinate	e	somebody you compete against
6	prosperity	f	situation where people have a lot of money

3 **Read the text again and put the paragraphs in the correct order.**

1 .... 2 .... 3 ....
4 .... 5 ....

4 **Put the events into the correct chronological order.**

a Cleopatra had a relationship with Julius Caesar. ....
b Cleopatra got married to her brother. ....
c Cleopatra got married to Mark Antony. ....
d Cleopatra died. ....
e Mark Antony died. ....
f Julius Caesar died. ....
g Cleopatra went to Rome. ....

5 **Answer the questions.**

1 Why did Cleopatra marry her brother?
....
2 Why did Cleopatra go to Rome?
....
3 Why did Mark Antony want to see Cleopatra?
....
4 Why did Mark Antony kill himself?
....

6 **What about *you*?**

Do you enjoy doing history at school? Why/Why not?
....
....
....

Grammar in context

Gerunds and infinitives

1 Match the rules with the sentences.

1 We use the gerund as the subject of a sentence. *f*
2 We use the gerund with *go* to talk about physical activities. ....
3 We use the gerund after verbs of liking or disliking. ....
4 We use the gerund after prepositions. ....
5 We use the infinitive to explain why somebody does something. ....
6 We use the infinitive after adjectives. ....
7 We use the infinitive after certain verbs. ....

a I hate gett**ing** up early.
b I'm good at do**ing** maths.
c I want **to go** to Egypt.
d I go swimm**ing** three times a week.
e I went home **to see** if my mum was OK.
f Read**ing** fantasy novels is one of my hobbies.
g It's difficult **to see** when it's dark.

2 Match the halves of the sentences.

1 Professional football players should enjoy ....
2 Last week my grandfather and I went to Wembley Stadium ....
3 Scoring goals is important ....
4 It's important for football players ....
5 Professional football players don't often go ....
6 For professional football players, it usually isn't good ....

a to train hard.
b to eat lots of burgers because they aren't very healthy.
c skiing because they could have an accident.
d for football players.
e to watch a football match.
f playing football.

3 Complete the questions with the correct form of the verbs given.

1 What do you enjoy .... (do) on Saturday afternoons?
2 How often do you go .... (shop) with your friends?
3 .... (do) sport. How important is it for you?
4 What are you good at .... (do) at school?
5 How do you feel about .... (read) in English?
6 What do you want .... (do) when you finish school?
7 Do you find it easy .... (make) new friends? Why/Why not?
8 What do you hate .... (do) at the weekend?

4 Write your own true answers to the questions in 3.

1 ....
....
2 ....
....
3 ....
....
4 ....
....
5 ....
....
6 ....
....
7 ....
....
8 ....
....

Grammar extension

5 Write complete sentences about *you* using the words in bold. You cannot change the form of the words in bold. You can use verbs of liking, adjectives, *go*, prepositions or *want* just before the words. The words can come at the start of the sentence or you can explain why you do or did something.

1 *I love watching films at the weekend.* **WATCHING**
2 .... **TO SEE**
3 .... **WALKING**
4 .... **TO DO**
5 .... **TO BUY**
6 .... **LISTENING**
7 .... **LIVING**
8 .... **TO BE**
9 .... **TO READ**
10 .... **SHOPPING**

Reporting a past event – a party

1 Match the questions and answers about a party.

Questions

1 Whose party was it? ....
2 Why did they have the party? ....
3 Who did you go with? ....
4 Where was the party? ....
5 How many people were there? ....
6 Did you know all the people there? ....
7 Was there any food? What was it like? ....
8 Was there any music? What was it like? ....
9 Did you dance? ....
10 Did you meet anybody? ....
11 What time did the party end? ....

Answers

a It was his birthday.
b No, I didn't know anybody there except my cousin (and my sister of course!).
c My cousin was playing some old CDs with songs that nobody knew.
d It was in a cold, dark garage at my cousin's house.
e No, I didn't dance because I didn't know any of the songs that my cousin was playing.
f It was my cousin's.
g There was some food, but we didn't really eat anything because there were only some cakes that my cousin had made and they weren't very good.
h I met one or two people but I didn't like them much.
i The party ended at 9 pm.
j I went with my little sister.
k There weren't many because my cousin hasn't got many friends.

2 Imagine that last Saturday you went to the best party ever. Write your own answers to the questions in 1. Make it clear that it was the perfect party. Use different past tenses when necessary.

1 *It was Will Smith's.*
2 ....
3 ....
4 ....
5 ....
6 ....
7 ....
....
8 ....
9 ....
10 ....
11 ....

Describing photos

3 Look at the photo and answer the questions. If you are not sure of something, use *I think* and/or *I imagine*.

1 Who can you see in the photo?
....
....
2 Where are they?
....
....
3 What are they doing?
....
....
4 How do you think the people are feeling? Why?
....
....

4 Use the questions in 3 to think of things to say about this photo. Make notes and then practise orally.

A personal description

1 Read this description of Holly's best friend, Eleanor, and answer the questions.

1 Where did they meet?

....

2 Why was it unusual to meet there?

....

....

Get Mail | Write | Contacts | Reply | Forward | Delete | Print

Hi Alicia,

How are you? I hope you and your family are all well.

I thought I'd tell you a bit about my best friend, Eleanor. I met her two (a) .... (b) ...., my family and I were spending our holidays in Spain. Eleanor was staying at the same hotel as us. It's incredible that we met in another country because at home we actually live very close to each other but we'd never met (c) ....

(d) ...., I didn't get on with Eleanor because she didn't speak much. But (e) .... we went out one evening and we started to chat. (f) ...., we found that we had lots of things in common. For example, we both love music and we like the same singers. We also love dancing. People say we're like sisters because we're both tall, we both have long fair hair and we've both got blue eyes.

Write back and tell me about your best friend. How did you meet?

All the best,

Holly

2 Read the description again and complete it with these words and expressions of sequence and time.

at first   before   in the end   that summer   then   years ago

3 Look at this information about an imaginary best friend. Use the information and your imagination to write an email like Holly's. Remember to use expressions of sequence and time.

Name: Alfie

Met: three years ago, at a party, friend of a friend, chatting, goes to same school but had never spoken

Good friend because: like playing same sports, funny, interesting, doesn't get angry

Physical description: not very tall (like me!), long dark hair

Get Mail | Write | Contacts | Reply | Forward | Delete | Print

Dear Jake,

How are you? I hope you're well.

I thought I'd tell you a bit about my best friend, Alfie.
I met him

....

....

....

....

....

....

....

....

....

....

....

....

....

....

....

....

....

Revision: Units 7–8

Grammar

1 Complete these sentences about your school in a logical way.

1 At our school, students must ....
2 At our school, students shouldn't ....
3 At our school, students don't have to ....
....
4 At our school, students mustn't ....
5 At our school, students should ....
6 At our school, students have to ....
7 At our school, teachers don't have to ....
....

/ 7 points

2 Complete each sentence with an appropriate word.

1 If I .... a millionaire, I'd buy my parents a new car.
2 I would be really happy .... we lived in New York.
3 If it didn't rain for months, we .... have much water.
4 If I knew when his birthday was, I'd .... him a present.
5 .... you run away if you saw a ghost?
6 If it ...., we wouldn't go out because we haven't got an umbrella.

/ 6 points

3 Decide which action happened first and put one verb in the past perfect and the other in the past simple.

1 I got up/I made my breakfast.
After I had got up, I made my breakfast.
2 he finished his lunch/he wasn't hungry.
....
3 she got in the swimming pool/she swam for 20 minutes.
....
....
4 I sent the email/I wrote it.
....

/ 6 points

4 Complete the sentences with these words.

doing   to do   swimming   to swim   watching   to watch

1 .... sport is good for you.
2 It's important .... your homework every day.
3 I enjoy .... cartoons and dramas.
4 I got up early .... the news on TV.
5 Are you good at ....? Can you go under the water?
6 Do you want .... in the sea this afternoon?

/ 6 points

Total */ 25 points*

Vocabulary

1 Think of a different job for each example.

1 a job for *creative* people: ....
2 a job with a lot of *paperwork*: ....
3 a job where you need to be *calm*: ....
4 a job where you work *outdoors*: ....
5 a job for people who are *sociable*: ....

/ 5 points

2 Match these words to make compound adjectives. After each compound adjective, say if it describes a person or a job.

easy   handed   going   paid   part   ~~hard~~
~~working~~   right   looking   time   well   good

1 *hard-working* .... (person)/job
2 .... person/job
3 .... person/job
4 .... person/job
5 .... person/job
6 .... person/job

/ 10 points

3 Complete the expressions.

1 to have a good relationship with somebody = to .... on well with someone
2 to start a relationship with somebody again = to get .... together again
3 to start to love somebody = to .... in love with somebody
4 to ask somebody to go somewhere with you because you want to start a romantic relationship with them = to ask somebody ....
5 to end a relationship with somebody = to .... up with somebody

/ 5 points

4 Find the words which describe these feelings. All the words are nouns.

1 the feeling when you aren't happy = ...
2 the feeling when you want to be with other people but nobody is with you = ...
3 the feeling when you are afraid of something = ...
4 the feeling when something really good is going to happen = ...
5 the feeling when you are angry = ...

/ 5 points

Total */ 25 points*

Reading

1 Read the text. Does the photo show *child work* or *child labour*?

Work or labour?

Most teenagers in Europe have busy lives. They work hard at school, then maybe they do after-school activities or sport, they go out with their friends, and sometimes they do a Saturday job. But don't forget that there are approximately 218 million children in the world between the ages of 5 and 17 who have to work almost every day of the year.

There's a big difference between a job at the weekend in a supermarket and the type of jobs that these young people have to do. Working in a supermarket is an example of child work. Child work is an economic activity which isn't bad for a child's health or education. But the other is what we call child labour. That is when children work in dangerous conditions. Right now millions of children are working in mines, or working with chemicals and pesticides in agriculture, or working with dangerous machines in factories. These children not only work in bad conditions. They also work very long hours. Often they get no money for their work.

Of the 218 million children in child labour around the world, the majority (69%) work in agriculture. They work in very high temperatures and they use dangerous equipment like knives or machetes. Their working conditions are dirty and unhealthy. They have to work long hours and so at the end of the day they are very tired. But that's when they have to be most careful because, if not, they can suffer fatal accidents. And you should also remember that these children don't usually receive any medicine or medical treatment.

So next time you think that your life is difficult, remember that there are people of your age in worse conditions. Maybe we should all think about doing something to help them.

2 Answer the questions.

1 What examples of dangerous jobs appear in the text?

2 In typical child labour, do children work long hours? How much money do they get for their work?

3 What are the problems for children who work in agriculture?

4 What happens to these children when they have an accident?

/ 5 points

Writing

L.T. JONES NEWSPAPER SHOP

We need a hard-working teenager
to deliver newspapers this summer.

Write to Mr L.T. Jones, 36 Atlantic Drive, Bristol, B06 3LP
or ring 0123 3456789.

3 Look at the job advertisement. You need a job this summer. Write a letter to Mr L.T. Jones. Use these questions for ideas about what to write (you can invent information).

- Why are you writing?
- What other information are you sending with the letter (CV, photo, other)?
- What personal qualities do you have that could help to get the job?
- What experience do you have?

Dear Mr Jones,

/ 10 points

Total */ 15 points*

Grammar	▸ Reported speech – statements and questions
Vocabulary	▸ Fiction ▸ Non-fiction ▸ Phrasal verbs connected with reading and writing
Speaking	▸ Making offers
Writing	▸ A questionnaire

9 Read on

▸ Vocabulary

Fiction

1 Complete the puzzle with the types of fiction.

1 *Macbeth, Waiting for Godot, The Importance of Being Earnest*
2 *X-Men, Spider-man, Dragonball*
3 *Frankenstein, Dr Jekyll and Mr Hyde, The Vampire*
4 *Lord of the Rings, Harry Potter, Eragon*
5 *Love Story, Antony and Cleopatra, Women in Love*
6 *The Spy Who Came in from the Cold, The Last Assassin, The Bourne Identity*
7 *Cinderella, Snow White, Rapunzel*
8 *Murder on the Orient Express, The Adventures of Sherlock Holmes, The No.1 Ladies' Detective Agency*
9 *The Time Machine, War of the Worlds, Journey to the Centre of the Earth*
10 *Viking, Pompeii, Centurion*

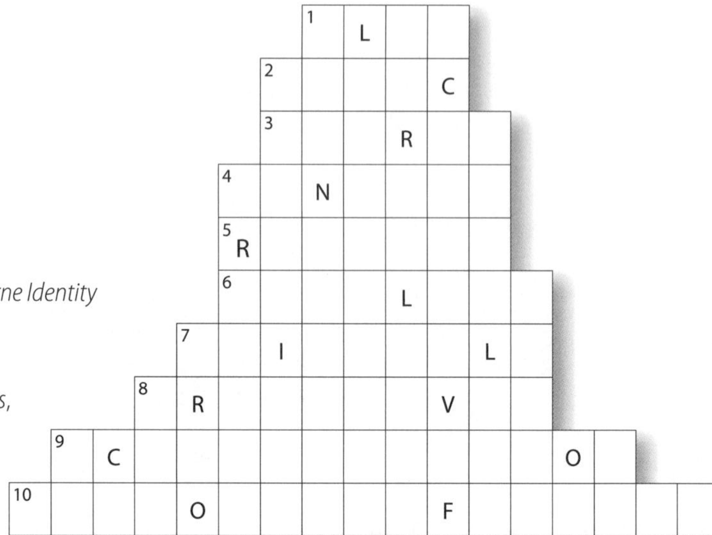

2 Look at these fictional characters. Choose the type of book in 1 that each one comes from.

1 ....

2 ....

3 ....

4 ....

5 ....

6 ....

Non-fiction

3 Match each type of non-fiction book with the type of information that it gives.

Type of non-fiction		**Information it gives**
1 atlas	....	a It tells you how to find a place and what you can do there.
2 autobiography	....	b It tells you what you need to know about a subject that you study at school.
3 biography	....	c It tells you which ingredients you need for a dish and how to prepare them.
4 cookbook	....	d It shows you the geographic location of different places.
5 dictionary	....	e It tells you what has happened very recently or what is happening now.
6 encyclopedia	....	f It tells you about somebody's life.
7 guidebook	....	g It tells you how to use or operate something.
8 manual	....	h It tells you about the writer's life.
9 newspaper	....	i It tells you about almost anything in the world.
10 textbook	....	j It tells you the meaning, form, spelling and pronunciation of words.

4 Choose one type of non-fiction that you sometimes read and one that you never read. Write a sentence for each explaining why.

1 I sometimes read ....
because ....
....
....
....

2 I never read ....
because ....
....
....
....

INSIDE INFORMATION

- Paul Auster is one of America's greatest living novelists.
- His books include *The New York Trilogy*, *Mr Vertigo* and *Moon Palace*.
- In 2006 Auster won the Prince of Asturias Prize for Letters, Spain's most important literary honour. The text you are going to read is the speech that he read out at the ceremony where he accepted the prize.

I want to tell you a story

I don't know why I do what I do. If I did know, I probably wouldn't feel the need to do it. All I can say is that I have needed to write stories since my earliest adolescence. It is an unusual way to spend your life – sitting alone in a room with a pen in your hand, hour after hour, day after day, year after year, trying to put words on pieces of paper in order to give birth to what does not exist – except in your own head. Why would anyone want to do such a thing? The only answer I have ever been able to give is: because you have to.

This need to make, to create, to invent is essential for humans. But fiction has no practical use in the real world. A book has never put food in the stomach of a hungry child. A book has never stopped a bullet from entering a murder victim's body. A book has never stopped a bomb from falling on innocent people in the middle of a war.

In other words, art is no use when you compare it, for example, to the work of a doctor or an engineer. But is that a bad thing? Does that mean that books are just a waste of our time? Many people think so. But I would say that art is what makes us different from anything else on this planet. It is what defines us as human beings.

Children love listening to stories. Why? Fairy tales are often cruel and violent. You would think this would be too frightening for a young child. But these stories allow children to meet their own fears – in a perfectly safe and protected environment. This is the magic of stories.

For years, in every country of the western world, journalists have written article after article about the fact that fewer and fewer people are reading books. This may be true, but at the same time this has not stopped the universal need for stories. Films and television and even comic books are creating vast quantities of narratives, and the public continues to read them with great passion. That is because human beings need stories. It would be impossible to imagine life without them.

1 Read the speech by the famous novelist, Paul Auster. Do you think he is happy being a writer? Why/Why not?

....

....

....

2 Read the speech again and match the halves of the sentences.

Auster thinks that

1 the life of a writer is ......
2 books are not ......
3 art makes us ......
4 fairy tales are ......
5 TV and films are ......

a useful in a practical way.
b frightening but can't hurt us.
c strange.
d different from other living things.
e popular because we all need stories.

3 Answer the questions.

1 When did Paul Auster become interested in writing stories?

....

....

2 Why does he write fiction?

....

....

3 Why does he think books and stories are important for us?

....

....

4 Match these words from the text with their definitions.

allow except innocent passion safe vast

1 let, permit ....
2 very big, enormous ....
3 apart from ....
4 not dangerous ....
5 not guilty of a crime ....
6 strong feeling of love or interest ....

5 What about *you*?

1 Do you think stories are important? Why/Why not?

....

....

....

....

2 What do you prefer – reading stories, listening to them, watching them on TV or in films? Why?

....

....

....

....

Reported speech – statements

1a Decide if the words given are necessary in the sentence or not. If they are necessary, write them in the correct place.

1 My friend said I could use his bike. (*me*)
2 They told they wanted to go home. (*us*)
3 The teacher told they had an exam on Wednesday. (*the students*)
4 He said it was his birthday. (*him*)
5 He said it wasn't his book. (*me*)
6 She told she wanted to go shopping. (*her mum*)
7 I said she was my favourite writer. (*the teacher*)
8 They told the exam was on Friday. (*James*)

1b Look at your answers in 1a. What is the difference between *say* and *tell*?

....

....

2a Complete the sentences with the correct words.

1 'I love hip-hop,' said Dylan.
Dylan said .... loved hip-hop.
2 'Those are my keys,' said Chloe.
Chloe said those were .... keys.
3 'We are the police,' said the men.
The men said .... were the police.
4 'Our parents are away,' said Ben and Amy.
Ben and Amy said .... parents were away.
5 'It's my turn to pay,' said Henry.
Henry said it was .... turn to pay.

2b Look at your answers in 2a. What words change in reported speech?

....

....

3a Complete the sentences with the correct words.

1 'I love that film,' said Megan.
Megan said .... that film.
2 'We're going by bus,' said Danny.
Danny said .... going by bus.
3 'That's my bike,' said Jacob.
Jacob said that .... bike.
4 'It isn't a problem,' Ellie told me.
Ellie .... me it .... a problem.
5 'My dad needs help,' said Olivia.
Olivia said .... dad .... help.
6 'Our lesson is about to start,' said Poppy and Freya.
Poppy and Freya said .... lesson .... about to start.

3b Look at your answers in 3a. What happens to the verbs in reported speech?

....

....

4 Rewrite the sentences in reported speech.

1 'I'm going to play basketball in July,' said Jamie.
....
2 'I want to go swimming,' said Becky.
....
3 'My friend has got a new computer game,' said Jack.
....
4 'We finish school on Friday,' said Emily and Evie.
....
5 'I think this is the answer,' said Charlotte.
....
6 'We don't need help,' said the students.
....
7 'My dad works in an office,' said Steven.
....
8 'I'm not going to the meeting,' said George.
....

Grammar extension

5a Match the people with the things they said. Then write complete sentences in reported speech.

1 Julius Caesar …

2 Nelson Mandela …

3 Oscar Wilde …

a I can resist everything except temptation.

b I came, I saw, I conquered.

c Education is the most powerful weapon which you can use to change the world.

1 ....
....
2 ....
....
3 ....
....

5b Do you know any other things that famous people said? Write them here.

Copernicus said that the earth went round the sun.

....

....

Phrasal verbs connected with reading and writing

1a Match the parts of the phrasal verbs.

1	cross	over
2	read	in
3	flick	out
4	read	out
5	fill	up
6	turn	through
7	look	on

1b Write the completed phrasal verbs next to the correct definition.

a continue reading ....
b turn a page to see the other side ....
c turn through the pages of a book quickly ....
d read so that other people can hear you ....
e try to find a particular piece of information in a book ....
f draw a line through something to show it isn't correct ....
g write information in empty spaces ....

2 Choose the correct alternative.

1 In some exercises you have to fill *in/on* the gaps.
2 He wrote *wich* but then he crossed it *out/up* and wrote *which*.
3 I don't know this word. I need to *look/read* it up in my dictionary.
4 We've finished this page. Turn *on/over* to the next one.
5 I'm going to *flick/turn* through this magazine quickly to see if I can find any good photos.
6 Read *on/out* the answer in a loud voice so that we can all hear you.
7 I really want to know how this story ends, so I'm going to read *on/out*.

3 Write sentences with the phrasal verbs in 1 and 2 saying what you should do in each situation.

1 You make a spelling mistake writing the word *which*.
You should cross it out.
2 You need to put information into boxes on an application form.
....
3 You've finished the page and want to read the next one.
....
4 The teacher wants to hear your answer to the next question.
....
5 You're reading something really interesting and you don't want to stop.
....
6 You're looking at a book in a bookshop that you possibly want to buy.
....
7 You need to find out the meaning of the word *antidisestablishmentarianism*.
....

Vocabulary extension: more phrasal verbs connected with reading and writing

4 Match these phrasal verbs with their meaning. Use your dictionary if necessary.

1	read up on	a	read only small parts (of a book, for example)
2	sum up	b	write something down to remember it
3	note down	c	give a summary of something
4	dip into	d	get information on a subject by reading a lot about it

5 Complete the sentences with the correct form of the phrasal verbs in 4.

1 Have you got a pen? Good. You can .... my address.
2 I didn't read all of the book. I just .... it to see if I liked it.
3 Next week our history teacher is going to ask us lots of questions about Ancient Rome. I don't know much about it. I need to .... it.
4 In the last paragraph of your essay, it's a good idea to .... the main ideas.
5 In our geography lesson, the teacher explains and we .... the most important points in our notebooks.
6 Finally, I would like to .... my opinion by repeating what I said at the start of this talk.
7 He never reads the whole magazine. He .... it and reads the things he finds the most interesting.
8 I've forgotten all the information on how to use that old camera. I need to .... it again.

Libraries

International cultural knowledge
Libraries in the UK

1 Write four things you can do in a library. Then read the text and check your answers.

1 ....
2 ....
3 ....
4 ....

2 Read the information for young people about using libraries in Liverpool and answer the questions.

1 You are going to go to Central Library on Saturday between 10.00 am and 2.00 pm. What special thing can you do then?
....
2 You have a three-year-old brother. Do they have books for him?
....
3 The library doesn't have a book that you want. What can you do?
....
4 You want to find out about special events at the library. What can you do?
....
5 You want a story but you're too tired to read. What can you get at the library?
....
6 You want to surf the net at the library. How much do you have to pay?
....
7 You want to relax. How can you do this at the library?
....
8 You want to do your homework at the library. How can the library help you?
....
....

File Edit View History Tools Window Help

Library services for young people

BOOKS

Liverpool Libraries have over 100,000 books for children of all ages and abilities. There are books for babies and young children and there are stories and information books for pleasure or to help with schoolwork. Look at our online catalogue to see if we have your favourite author. Why not order a copy if we don't? Apart from books, you can also find magazines for teenagers.

AUDIO/VISUAL ITEMS

Most Liverpool Libraries have a selection of 'talking books' available on CD or cassette. These are great for the times when you prefer to listen to a story instead of reading one.

Plenty of popular children's books are available as 'talking books' and we will try to get your favourite for you if we don't already have it. Videos and DVDs are also available in some libraries.

INFORMATION AND COMMUNICATION TECHNOLOGIES (ICT)

All Liverpool Libraries have public computers which you can use to surf the Internet for free – very popular with children, who can play games or look for information for their homework. There's a small charge for printing.

HOMEWORK

As well as computers with free access to the Internet, all Liverpool Libraries have collections of information books which are perfect for homework projects. Library staff can help children to start their homework. Contact your local Library or the Children's Team on 0151 233 5841 to find out more.

EVENTS, QUIZZES, ETC

Many Libraries have children's activities, especially during holiday periods. Central Library also has a Lord of the Rings Games Workshop every Saturday between 10.00 am and 2.00 pm. This is very popular with teenagers.

Central Library also has CD players and sofas to chill out on listening to your favourite music.

To find out what's available in your nearest Library check out the individual Library pages or call us on 0151 233 5841.

i INSIDE INFORMATION

- An investigation by the National Literacy Trust in 2008 discovered that 58% of young people in Britain said that they enjoyed reading very much or quite a lot.
- In 2004 people borrowed 341 million books from UK libraries.

WORD BOOSTER

Match the words and definitions.

1	available	a	people who work in a place
2	charge	b	lots of
3	staff	c	money to pay for a service or product
4	printing	d	making a paper copy of a document
5	plenty of	e	that you can find, take or use

3 What about *you*?

1 Would you be interested in using Liverpool Libraries? Why/Why not?
....
....
2 What are libraries like in your country?
....
....
....

Reported speech – questions

1 Look at the direct and reported questions and decide if the rules are true (T) or false (F).

a 1 'When did you arrive?' Aaron asked Ben.
  2 Aaron asked Ben when he had arrived.

b 1 'Why do you want to go?' Ruby asked Isaac.
  2 Ruby asked Isaac why he wanted to go.

c 1 'Are you hungry?' Sylvia asked Helen.
  2 Sylvia asked Helen if she was hungry.

1 We don't change tenses and pronouns in the same way in reported statements and reported questions. ....
2 We don't use question marks in reported questions. ....
3 We use the auxiliary verb *do* in reported questions. ....
4 We don't put the verb before the subject in reported questions. ....
5 We use *if* or *whether* in reported questions when there is no question word (*who, what, why*, etc) in the original question. ....

2 Rewrite the questions in reported speech.

1 'Are you sure about this answer?' the teacher asked the boy.
The teacher ....

2 'Why are you crying?' the girl asked the boy.
The girl ....

3 'Is it your birthday today?' Beth asked Nathan.
Beth ....

4 'Do you know the time?' Adam asked Mia.
Adam ....

5 'Where have you put my glasses?' Eric asked his granddaughter.
Eric ....

6 'How did you know my name?' William asked the girl.
William ....

7 'Have you read this book?' Sophie asked Tom.
Sophie ....

8 'Do you like crime novels?' Mark asked Sally.
Mark ....

3 Rewrite the jokes in reported speech.

1 Customer: *What is this fly doing in my soup?*
Waiter: *I think it's swimming.*
The customer ....
....
The waiter ....

2 Customer: *There's a dead fly in this salad.*
Waiter: *Oh no! Who's going to take care of its family?*
The customer ....
The waiter ....

3 Customer: *I can't eat this meat.*
Waiter: *Why can't you eat it?*
Customer: *You haven't brought me a knife and fork.*
The customer ....
The waiter ....
The customer ....

4 Customer: *Why is there a little spider in my ice cream?*
Waiter: *I wasn't able to find a big one.*
The customer ....
....
The waiter ....

Grammar extension

4 Look at the direct question. Is the reported question correct or not? If it isn't, correct it.

1 'Do you like vanilla ice cream?' Jamie asked Becky.
Jamie asked Becky whether she liked vanilla ice cream.

2 'Are you listening to this programme?' my mum asked me.
My mum asked me if you're listening to this programme.

3 'Where does Daisy live?' asked Isabel.
Isabel asked where Daisy did live.

4 'Why isn't your mobile phone working?' Jack asked Emma.
Jack asked Emma why her mobile phone wasn't working.

5 'Do we need our books today?' the students asked the teacher.
The students asked the teacher if they needed their books that day.

6 'Why are you looking at me?' Amanda asked Pete.
Amanda asked Pete why was he looking at her.

7 'Did you enjoy the meal?' the waiter asked the customers.
The waiter asked the customers if they had enjoyed the meal?

8 'Have you finished your ice cream?' Sam asked Joe.
Sam asked Joe if he had finished his ice cream.

At a bookshop

1a Look at the customer's side of this dialogue.

SHOP ASSISTANT: (**a**) ....

CUSTOMER: Yes, please. I'm looking for a book called *Dragon Horse*. It's a novel. They told me that it would be in the fantasy section.

SHOP ASSISTANT: (**b**) ....

CUSTOMER: Yes, I have, but I can't see it.

SHOP ASSISTANT: OK, I'll just check on the computer. (**c**) ....

....

CUSTOMER: Yes, it's Peter Ward.

SHOP ASSISTANT: Let me see. No, I'm sorry. We don't have it at the moment. (**d**) ....

....

CUSTOMER: How long will it take?

SHOP ASSISTANT: (**e**) ....

....

CUSTOMER: That's great.

SHOP ASSISTANT: (**f**) ....

....

CUSTOMER: Yes, please. Do you want me to give you my name and telephone number?

SHOP ASSISTANT: (**g**) ....

CUSTOMER: My name is Philip Reeve and my number is 0123 4567890.

SHOP ASSISTANT: Thank you. We'll call you when the book arrives. Bye!

1b Answer the questions.

1 What book does the customer want?

....

2 What type of book is it?

....

3 Who is the author?

....

4 Does the customer find, buy, order or leave the book?

....

2 Put the shop assistant's questions and answers in the correct place in the dialogue.

1 Have you looked there?
2 Yes, please.
3 Shall I order it for you?
4 Can I help you?
5 It should be here in a week.
6 Do you know the name of the author?
7 Would you like me to call you when the book gets here?

3 Look at the complete dialogue and underline four ways of making offers.

Describing photos

4 Look at the photo and answer the questions. If you are not sure of something, use *I think* and/or *I imagine*.

1 Who can you see in the photo?

....

....

2 Where are they?

....

....

3 What are they doing?

....

....

4 How do you think the people are feeling? Why?

....

....

5 Use the questions in 4 to think of things to say about this photo. Make notes and then practise orally.

A questionnaire

1 Choose the correct alternative in these questions from a questionnaire about free time.

1 How/Who do you usually spend your free time?

I read, listen to music and go out with my friends.

2 Which/Who is your favourite hobby of all?

I don't know. Maybe reading.

3 Why/What do you like it?

Because I find it relaxing. I can 'escape'.

4 How/Who often do you go out during the school week?

Never. I only go out at the weekend.

5 Who does spend/spends more time with you at the weekend, your family or your friends?

It depends, but probably my friends.

6 Where/When do you like going with your friends?

We like going to the cinema or going to the park to play football and basketball or go skateboarding.

7 How much/many money do you spend on your hobbies?

I don't spend much. The most expensive thing is going out at the weekends.

2 Write your own true answers to the questions in 1.

1 ....

2 ....

3 ....

4 ....

5 ....

6 ....

7 ....

3 You are going to write questions for a questionnaire about what you do in the holidays. Before you write the questions, brainstorm ideas.

HOLIDAYS
- Destinations
- Months
- Transport
- People
- Money
- Things to take

4 Now write your questionnaire by completing these questions.

1 Where .... ?

2 How long .... ?

3 How much .... ?

4 What .... ?

5 Who .... ?

6 When .... ?

7 How often .... ?

8 Do you usually .... ?

9 Have you ever .... ?

10 Cyberspace

Grammar ▸ The passive – present simple and other tenses
Vocabulary ▸ Computers and computing ▸ The Internet ▸ Collocations with *ema*
Speaking ▸ Talking about photos
Writing ▸ Text messages

▸ Vocabulary

Computers and computing

1 Join these words or parts of words and write them under the correct picture. You can use some words more than once.

1 ....

2 ....

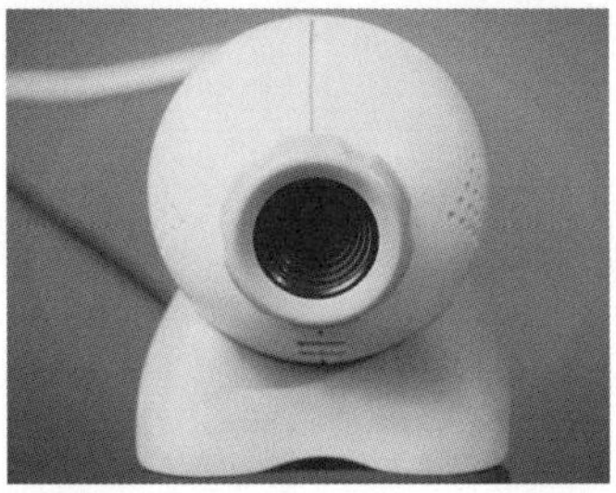

3 ....

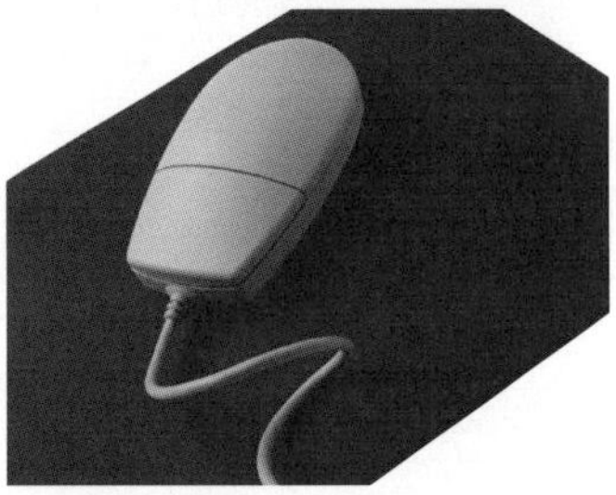

4 ....

5 ....

6 ....

7 ....

8 ....

2 Which part of the computer do you …

1 use to click on things? ....
2 use to connect cameras, etc? ....
3 listen to music with? ....
4 write with? ....
5 make videos with? ....

The Internet

3 Match the halves to form questions.

1	Have you got a broad	a	load films from the Internet?
2	Do you ever chat	b	site do you visit the most?
3	Which search	c	online with friends?
4	How long do you spend surfing	d	the Internet at the weekend?
5	How often do you down	e	engine do you usually use?
6	Which web	f	band connection to the Internet?
7	Do you read or write	g	a blog?

4 Write your own true answers to the questions in 3. Write complete sentences and decide if you need to write the two halves of the words together (e.g. *download*).

1 ....
2 ....
3 ....
4 ....
5 ....
6 ....
7 ....

1 Before you read the text, answer the questions.

1 Do you have an MP3 player?

....

2 What can you do with an MP3 player?

....

2 Read the text. Apart from listening to music, find one positive and one negative use of MP3 players by school students.

....

....

MP3 players at school – yes or no?

A ....

And of course it's one of the teachers' jobs to stop this cheating. To do this, they have to keep up to date with new technology. That's because students who cheat are always looking for new ways to cheat without their teachers realising.

B ....

Students were writing answers inside the caps. Then came the mobile phone. Schools also stopped these. It was just too easy for students to send each other text messages or even connect to the Internet.

C ....

Lots of students take MP3 players to school to listen to music at break times. And usually with new MP3 players, you can watch music videos or films too. But some uses of MP3 players are not quite so innocent. Some students download formulas and other information onto their players. Others use them to record answers before an exam and then listen to them during the exam. Others download their own notes onto their MP3 player and then put them in the 'song lyrics' text files.

D ....

Some students say no. They're angry because they say that they used to listen to their MP3 players to listen to music and relax before exams, not to cheat. They don't see why they should suffer just because some students use them for the wrong reasons. Others say that the students who cheat are always going to cheat, with or without an MP3 player.

E ....

That isn't because they want students to be able to use them for listening to music. They want them to use MP3 players to learn. Some schools have started preparing educational material for MP3 players. Students can read, watch and listen to this material in any place and at any time. This helps them and motivates them too. It's clear that technology is not always bad. It can be used in highly productive ways too.

3 Read the text again and put the sentences in the correct place (A–E) in the text.

1 So, are schools right to stop students taking MP3 players to school?
2 Not long ago, US schools stopped students from wearing baseball caps in exams.
3 Some students just can't stop trying to cheat in exams.
4 There are also some schools that disagree with stopping the use of MP3 players.
5 The latest type of technology to be banned is the MP3 player.

4 Answer the questions.

1 How exactly did students cheat in exams with baseball caps and mobile phones?

....

....

2 In what different ways do students use MP3 players to cheat in exams?

....

....

....

3 Why do some students think that it's wrong to stop them taking MP3 players to school?

....

....

4 Why do some schools want students to take MP3 players to school?

....

....

5 Find words in the text which have similar meanings to these words or explanations.

1 a hat with a part to keep the sun from your eyes (*paragraph B*) ....
2 put sounds or images onto a CD, DVD, MP3, etc (*paragraph C*) ....
3 groups of letters or numbers that represent rules in science or maths (*paragraph C*) ....
4 the words to a song (*paragraph C*) ....
5 places where you keep papers and documents together (*paragraph C*) ....
6 makes people interested and excited about doing something (*paragraph E*) ....
7 positive, with good results (*paragraph E*) ....

6 What about *you*?

How do you use new technology to learn better?

....

....

....

....

....

The passive – present simple

1a **Complete the sentences with an appropriate word.**

1 Dictionaries .... used by many students who are learning English.
2 Football is .... on TV by thousands of people every weekend.
3 Coffee .... drunk by babies.
4 The Wii™ is made .... Nintendo®.
5 This television programme .... watched by people in many different countries.
6 The French language is .... by people in France, Belgium, Switzerland, Senegal and other countries.

1b **Look at the completed sentences in 1a and choose the correct alternative.**

1 To make the passive we use the verb *to be* and the past simple/past participle.
2 To introduce the person who does the action we use by/for.

2 **Choose the correct alternative.**

1 These computers is/are made in China.
2 A lot of mineral water is drank/drunk in the summer.
3 Portuguese is speak/spoken in Brazil.
4 The students in my class are written/write essays once a month.
5 Christmas presents are gave/given on 25th December in Britain.
6 A lot of rice is/are eaten every day.
7 My sister does/is done the shopping on Saturday.
8 German teaches/is taught at my school.
9 That song sings/is sung on special occasions.
10 New roads is/are built each year.
11 My friends send/are sent emails to each other every day.
12 Thousands of miles are flew/flown by pilots every year.

3 **Complete the sentences with the present passive form of these verbs.**

check drink drive make play sell
speak teach wear write

1 Jeans .... by people all over the world.
2 This sport .... by many people every weekend.
3 Spanish .... in many South American countries.
4 On computers, many documents .... by using Microsoft® Word.
5 Paella .... with rice.
6 Thousands of litres of orange juice .... every day.
7 Maths .... in almost all schools.
8 Your passport .... at the airport before you get on the plane.
9 Buses .... by bus drivers.
10 Bread .... in a bakery

4 **Rewrite these active sentences in the present passive form. Only use *by* plus the agent if you know exactly who does the action.**

1 BMW make the new MINI.
....
2 Sometimes they find gold in this river.
....
3 They don't stop football matches if it rains.
....
4 The waiter brings your meal to the table.
....
5 They give a prize to the best actor.
....
6 In this hotel they take your bags to your room.
....
7 They don't grow tea in Britain.
....
8 In Japan students clean the classrooms.
....
9 A lot of people use public transport.
....
10 In this song my brother plays the guitar.
....

Grammar extension

5 **Each sentence contains a mistake. Find the mistake and rewrite the sentence correctly.**

1 The song *Jingle Bells* is sang at Christmas in Britain.
....
2 The city of Florence is visited for hundreds of people every day.
....
....
3 Tennis played by two or four players.
....
4 Many products made in China nowadays.
....
5 More manga comics are drawing in Japan than in any other country.
....
....
6 That book is wrote by a famous novelist.
....
7 Sometimes spectacular eclipses is seen in this part of the world.
....
....
8 More ice creams eaten in the summer than in the winter.
....

Collocations with *email*

1 Find eight words which frequently go with *email*.

f	a	d	e	r	e	p	l	y
o	d	w	v	n	u	f	d	a
r	d	l	p	b	n	c	e	d
w	r	t	a	o	s	r	y	e
a	e	l	m	u	p	i	u	l
r	s	e	r	n	d	f	w	e
d	s	a	c	c	o	u	n	t
q	w	b	v	e	k	l	b	e
a	s	e	n	d	a	c	c	o
f	o	r	d	c	h	e	c	k

2 Complete these sentences with a word in 1.

1 Could you give me your email .... so that I can .... you an email?
2 My inbox is full. I need to .... some emails.
3 I have sent him an email but I am still waiting for him to .... to it.
4 Didn't you receive her email? I still have it and will .... it to you.
5 If you type in the wrong address, the email will ....
6 I want to open a new email .... with a different provider.
7 I am looking for an Internet café. I need to .... my emails.

3 Match the definitions with the words in 1. Note that the definitions give the general meaning of the words.

1 when something hits a surface and then immediately moves away ....
2 an arrangement where a bank looks after your money ....
3 examine something to get information, or to see if it is good or correct ....
4 arrange for something (for example a letter) to arrive for someone in another place ....
5 take something away, for example from a computer ....
6 the name of the place where you live ....

4 Complete these sentences with the correct form of the words in 1.

1 My .... is 167 Rothfuss Road, Leeds.
2 When you finish an exam, you should .... your answers carefully.
3 I wrote him a letter inviting him to the party and then I .... it by post but he didn't .... so I don't know if he's coming or not.
4 I haven't got any money in my bank ....
5 In basketball when you have the ball you have to .... it when you run.
6 I don't need that document on this computer. I'm going to .... it.
7 I received this letter but it's for the person who lived in this house before. I'll .... it to him at his new house.

Vocabulary extension

5 With new technology such as the Internet we often use abbreviations to name things more easily and quickly. Find the full names in the box for the abbreviations below. Use your dictionary if necessary. You can use some words more than once.

asked compact digital disc frequently global identification memory message number only personal positioning questions read recordable rewritable service short system versatile ~~web~~ ~~wide~~ ~~world~~

1 WWW = *world* *wide* *web*
2 DVD = ... - ....
3 CD-ROM = ... - ....
4 CD-R = ... - ....
5 CD-RW = ... - ....
6 SMS = ...
7 GPS = ...
8 FAQ = ...
9 PIN = ...

6 Match the abbreviations with these explanations.

1 a secret number you need to operate a mobile phone, for example ....
2 a disc that people usually use to watch films ....
3 a disc that you can use to record data once ....
4 a disc that you can use to record data more than once ....
5 typical questions that people ask on a website ....
6 a large collection of documents, pictures and sounds kept on computers in many different places and connected through the Internet ....
7 a disc that computers can read, containing text, image and sound ....
8 a system for finding exactly where you are in the world using satellites ....
9 a way of sending a text message to a mobile phone ....

Click onto... Global communication

Cross-curricular – Geography/Science
A real web around the world

1 Look at the map and headline from a newspaper. It is from an article about a real incident. What do you think happened?

....

....

....

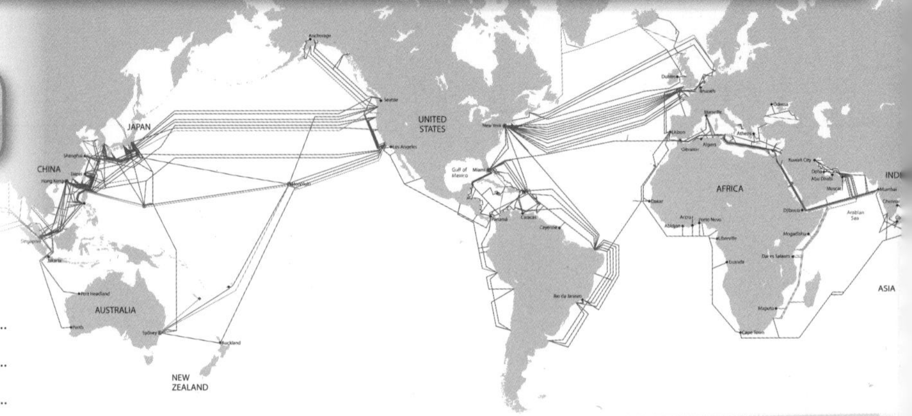

How one ship cut off the web for 75 million people

Just one ship was responsible for breaking an essential submarine cable that connects the Middle East and India with the rest of the world via the Internet. This has left 75 million people with only limited access to the Internet.

The accident was caused on Wednesday by a ship in bad weather near the coast of Egypt, close to Alexandria. Since then, there have been terrible problems with phones and the Internet in countries including India, Egypt and the United Arab Emirates. It has been a problem for approximately 70% of users there.

Tens of millions of people have had problems with phones and the Net. It has also made a big difference to economies across Asia and the Middle East. Governments have started to take direct action. To help businesses, the Egyptian Communications Ministry has asked surfers not to connect to the Internet. 'People who download music and films are going to make problems for businesses who have more important things to do.'

Experts say that this shows that our global communications network is very fragile. 'People don't know that all these things go through cables under the sea,' said Alan Mauldin, an expert in communications. 'In general, the Internet uses real, physical connections, not satellites.'

People think the Internet always works by satellite. But a big part of the world needs real, physical connections. It was not easy to create these connections. The expensive cables go in long lines around the world, carrying millions of conversations all at the same time from one country to another.

One expert said that this week's accident should make governments understand that they must spend more time and energy to protect essential communications such as mobile phones and the Net. We must protect them from natural disasters or from terrorists. 'It would be very easy to attack global communications,' said Mustafa Alani, head of security and terrorism at the Gulf Research Centre in Dubai. 'The important thing isn't building great new technology. The important thing is to protect it.'

One of the cables that was broken this week is called the Sea-Me-We 4. It is one of the most important information lines between Europe and the East. It goes in a continuous line from Germany to Singapore. It covers a total of 39,000 kilometres and connects 32 different countries. It took three years and cost an incredible £500m to put the line in place.

2 Read the newspaper article and check your ideas in 1. What are the bold lines on the map?

....

....

▸ WORD BOOSTER

Match the words and definitions.

1 submarine	a strong, thick metal rope
2 cable	b easy to break
3 businesses	c under the water
4 fragile	d organisations that buy or sell products or services

3 Choose the most important message in the text: 1, 2 or 3.

1 It is important to create Internet connections by satellite.
2 It is important to defend existing cables because something or somebody could break them again.
3 It is important to learn better ways of creating new technology.

4 Read the text again and decide if these sentences are true (T) or false (F). Write the line(s) in the text where you found the answer.

1 An accident at sea on Wednesday made it difficult for people to access the Internet. ....
2 Since Wednesday it has been impossible for anyone in India to connect to the Internet. ....
3 The incident has caused problems in the financial markets of some of these countries. ....
4 Without cables under the sea, the Internet would not work in many parts of the world. ....
5 It is quite cheap and easy to install submarine cables. ....

5 What about *you*?

How important is the Internet in your daily life and would you survive without it?

....

....

....

....

....

The passive – other tenses

1a Choose the correct alternative.

1. Radioactivity is/was discovered by Henri Becquerel in 1896.
2. Thousands of silicon chips are/are being made at this very moment.
3. Oscars are/have been given to actors since 1927.
4. The book *One Hundred Years of Solitude* was/has been written by Gabriel Garcia Marquez in 1967.
5. Many useful things have been/were invented since the start of the 20th century.
6. 741 burgers are/were eaten by Don Gorske in 2003. In total he's already eaten over 20,000 in his lifetime!

1b Look at the sentences in 1a and choose the correct alternative in the rule below.

To change the tense in passive sentences, we change to be/the past participle.

2 Complete the sentences with the present simple or past simple passive form of these verbs.

make paint ~~see~~ send wash win write

1. The film *was seen* by 6,000 spectators last week.
2. Yesterday's prize .... by a 16-year-old boy.
3. 3,000 cars .... in this factory every week.
4. The towels in this hotel .... every day.
5. Those novels .... in 1962.
6. Thousands of Valentine's Day cards .... every 14th February in the UK.
7. Those pictures .... by Picasso about 50 years ago.

3 Complete the sentences with the correct passive form of the verbs given.

1. That cartoon .... (create) in 1985.
2. Listen! That song .... (sing) in Japanese.
3. That film .... (see) for the first time in 1919.
4. The pictures .... (draw) in prehistoric times.
5. The criminal .... (follow) by the police right now.
6. The first cheap cars .... (produce) nearly 100 years ago in the USA.
7. Look! The window .... (break) by the wind.

4 Write passive sentences using the words given.

1. The novel *Animal Farm*/write/by George Orwell in 1944.
....
2. The race/organise/by the school each year.
....
3. Dynamite/invent/by Alfred Nobel in the 19th century.
....
4. Cartoons/watch/by thousands of children around the world at this very minute.
....
5. The FA World Cup/win/by Brazil five times since 1958.
....
6. The planet Uranus/find/by William Herschel in 1781.
....
7. The men's 100-metre world record/break/by Usain Bolt in August 2009.
....

Grammar extension

5 Make the passive sentences in 4 into questions.

1. *Was Animal Farm written by George Orwell in 1944?*
2. ....
3. ....
4. ....
5. ....
6. ....
7. ....

A conversation based on a photo

1 Look at the photos and make speculations to complete the sentences.

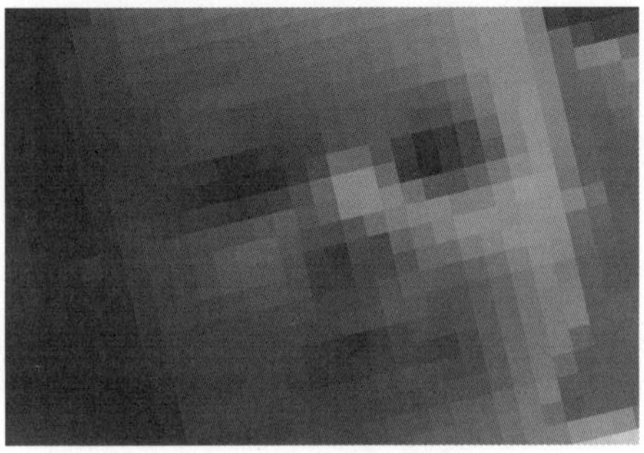

1 I'm not sure, but I think that it's ....

2 It looks like ....

3 I imagine that ....

4 It's probably .... or ....

5 It might be ....

6 It looks as if ....

2 Look at photo A. Write five questions to ask about it.

1 ....
2 ....
3 ....
4 ....
5 ....

3 Write answers to your questions in 2. Use the different ways of speculating in 1 when you aren't sure.

1 ....
2 ....
3 ....
4 ....
5 ....

4 Use your questions in 2 to think of things to say about photo B. Make notes and then practise orally.

Writing text messages

1 The text message abbreviations for the words below are just one letter or number. Write the abbreviation for each one. Think about the pronunciation.

1 for ....
2 you ....
3 are ....
4 to/too ....
5 see ....
6 be ....

2 These text message abbreviations all use numbers. Think about how we pronounce the numbers and write the complete words with normal spelling.

1 2day ....
2 2nite ....
3 2moro ....
4 B4 ....
5 L8 ....
6 GR8 ....
7 W8 ....
8 L8R ....

3 In these text message abbreviations some letters (especially vowels) are missing or have been changed. Write the complete words with normal spelling.

1 YR ....
2 PLS ....
3 WOT ....
4 BCZ ....
5 SPK ....
6 WKND ....
7 THX ....
8 XLNT ....
9 MSG ....
10 HMWK ....

4 Write these text messages as complete sentences.

1 Can U PLS come 2 C me L8R?

....

2 I'll C U 2moro B4 school.

....

3 I'll W8 4 YR next MSG.

....

4 Wot R U doing at the WKND?

....

5 Will U B at home L8R 2day?

....

6 THX 4 the presents. They R GR8.

....

7 I can C U @ 6 BCZ I haven't got any HMWK.

....

5 Write these sentences using text message abbreviations.

1 What are you doing tonight?

....
....

2 Amy and I are going to eat out because it's her birthday today. Do you want to come?

....
....
....

3 OK. Thanks. What time are you meeting?

....
....

4 At eight because before that I have to study for an exam tomorrow.

....
....

5 What time is your exam?

....
....

6 At ten. I have to go now. I'll speak to you later.

....
....

7 Great!

....

Revision: Units 9–10

Grammar

1 Rewrite the underlined words as they would appear in reported speech.

1 'It's my birthday,' said Katie. ....
2 'I was in London last week,' said Cameron. ....
3 'Today is going to be a good day,' said Owen. ....
4 'She's been to Africa twice,' said the TV presenter. ....
5 'I wanted to go out last weekend,' said Lucy. ....
6 'The exam is tomorrow,' said the teacher. ....
7 'I'll come to your house,' Alex said to his friend. ....

/7 points

2 Choose the correct alternative.

1 Ella asked the boy what *your/his/her* name was.
2 The teacher asked her students *that/whether/how* they wanted to see the concert.
3 Ava asked Henry where *is he/was he/he was* going.
4 The doctor asked him if he *has ever had/had ever have/had ever had* a serious accident.
5 Jack asked Isabella if she *liked/does like/did like* that music.
6 Harry asked who *saw/did see/had seen* the film.

/6 points

3 Rewrite the active sentences in the passive form and the passive sentences in the active form. All the sentences are present simple.

1 British children eat a lot of chocolate.

....

2 The TV programme is presented by Stephanie Zimmerman.

....

3 The race is organised by a school.

....

4 David Spencer writes these books.

....

5 Robots build many different products.

....

6 The tickets are sold by members of the club.

....

/6 points

4 Correct the passive sentences if necessary.

1 The new film is be made in Australia now.
2 *The Four Seasons* was written by Vivaldi.
3 When did the Euro Cup won by Spain?
4 My grandmother is being helped across the road with a policeman.
5 Five cats has been rescued by firefighters today.
6 The DVD has been bought by thousands of people.

/6 points

Total /25 points

Vocabulary

1 Choose the best type of book for each person.

1 Sam wants to learn how to make a new pasta dish.

....

2 Sophia likes stories about robots. ....
3 Ryan wants to learn how to use his new digital camera.

....

4 Jasmine is four years old and she likes stories about princes and princesses. ....
5 Edward likes reading about the lives of famous people, written by the person him- or herself. ....
6 Ben loves the theatre and he loves reading the story again at home. ....

/6 points

2 Choose the correct alternative.

1 When a story is good, you want to read *on/out* to the end.
2 When you make a mistake, you cross it *on/out*.
3 When you want to get a quick idea of a book, you *flick/turn* through it.
4 At the end of an essay it's a good idea to sum *on/up* your ideas and opinions.

/4 points

3 Make nine words connected with computers or the Internet from these words or parts of words.

band board broad cam down drive
engine hard key line lap load
on port search top USB web

1 .... 6 ....
2 .... 7 ....
3 .... 8 ....
4 .... 9 ....
5 ....

/9 points

4 Complete the text with these words.

address bounces delete receive reply send

A simple guide to email

First find out the email **(a)** .... of the person you are writing to. Write the email, then **(b)** .... it. When you **(c)** .... an email, **(d)** .... to it quite quickly. When you have a lot of old emails, **(e)** .... them if you don't want to keep them. If an email **(f)** .... back, it's probably because you made some type of mistake.

/6 points

Total /25 points

Reading

1 Read this interview with the inventor of mobile phones, Martin Cooper, and choose a, b or c to complete the sentences.

BBC: Tell us how you created the mobile phone.
MARTIN: The time was the late 1960s. AT&T were the largest telephone company in the world and they had invented car telephones. Can you imagine? We believed people didn't want to talk to cars and that people wanted to talk to other people. So at Motorola, a small company at the time, we decided to build a mobile telephone.
BBC: What about that first call on the streets of Manhattan? Who did you call and what did you say?
MARTIN: Who do you think I called? I called my rival at another phone company and said: 'I'm calling you from a 'real' mobile telephone.'
BBC: Do you agree that your first mobile phone looks big now?
MARTIN: Yes! Between 1973, when we made that phone, and 1983, when the first commercial mobile phone service started, we actually built five different phones. Each one got smaller and smaller and by 1983 we had gone from one kilo to 450 grams. The phone which I carry with me today weighs just 85 grams!
BBC: Did you really think your invention would become so popular, with millions of people using them around the world?
MARTIN: Well, not at the time because in 1983 those first phones cost $3,500. That was a lot of money! But we did think that phones would get really small.
BBC: How do you feel when you see so many people walking down the street talking into your invention?
MARTIN: It makes me really happy. I've made a small difference to people's lives because these phones do make people's lives better. They make people more comfortable, they make them feel safe. It makes me feel good to know that I made a small contribution there.

BBC: Do you like people calling you the father of the mobile phone?
MARTIN: It was my idea but we needed teamwork and hundreds of people to create the mobile phone as it is today. We're still working on it and we're still trying to make it better.
BBC: How will phone technology change in the future?
MARTIN: In the future, the Internet will be everywhere you go.
BBC: As the inventor of the personal mobile phone, are you very rich?
MARTIN: I'm extremely rich in satisfaction and in happiness.
BBC: But not in dollars and cents?
MARTIN: Not necessarily.

1 The company which invented mobile phones
  a was one of the most important telephone companies in the USA.
  b began by inventing telephones for cars.
  c wanted to do more than make phones for cars.

2 Martin Cooper and his team couldn't
  a make smaller mobile phones.
  b imagine a very small mobile phone.
  c sell a very small mobile phone.

3 Martin Cooper knew
  a mobile phones would be popular because they were very useful.
  b mobile phones were very useful but didn't think many people would buy them.
  c people only wanted to buy small mobile phones.

4 Martin Cooper thinks that
  a he made the modern mobile phone and has made a big change to the world.
  b he helped to create the modern mobile phone and this has been a good thing for the world.
  c when the mobile phone is finished it will make the world better.

5 The mobile phone has made Martin Cooper
  a feel good.
  b a lot of money.
  c important for many people.

/ 5 points

Writing

2 Write a questionnaire with ten questions to ask people about the Internet. Use these question words and the words given below for ideas about what to write.

- What?
- Which?
- When?
- Why?
- How?
- How often?
- How long?
- Where?
- Who?
- Do/Did?

blog broadband chat connect download online search engine surf the Net website

1 ....
2 ....
3 ....
4 ....
5 ....
6 ....
7 ....
8 ....
9 ....
10 ....

/ 10 points

Total */ 15 points*

Progress Test: Units 1–2

Grammar

1 Complete the sentences with the present simple or present continuous form of the verbs given.

1 What programme .... they .... (watch) now?
2 What programme .... she .... (watch) on Mondays.
3 I .... (not do) my homework after 9pm usually.
4 She .... (go) to yoga classes three times a week.
5 We .... (study) grammar at the moment.
6 Do you want to use the computer? I .... (not use) it now.
7 Why .... you .... (speak) in French? My friend here understands English.

/ 7 points

2 Complete the text with *a, an, the* or *0* (no article).

'When **(a)** .... teenagers have **(b)** .... problem, it can be **(c)** .... good idea for them to talk about **(d)** .... problem with **(e)** .... friend. In general, **(f)** .... people always need to talk.'

/ 6 points

3 Complete the sentences with the past simple or past continuous form of the verbs given.

1 While I was walking home, I .... (meet) my friend.
2 My parents .... (have) an argument when I walked into the room.
3 The students were talking all the time while the teacher .... (explain) the exercise.
4 What were you doing when you .... (hear) the news?
5 The students .... (write) an essay when the teacher told them to stop.
6 My mum .... (drive) when her mobile phone started to ring.
7 The birds .... (sing) when we left home this morning.

/ 7 points

Total */ 20 points*

Vocabulary

1 Find the words.

1 the period of life when you are a child ....
2 the brother of your husband or wife .... - .... - ....
3 an old adult ....
4 the period of life when you stop working ....
5 a child with no brothers or sisters ....
6 not married ....

/ 6 points

2 Complete the nouns. They all contain the suffixes *-ment* or *-ence*.

1 You don't need much .... q u .... p m .... to go running.
2 What an i .... p r .... v ....! Before you weren't a very good guitarist but now you're great.
3 That state wants i .... p ...... d ....They don't want any other state or country to control them.
4 There's no big d .... f .... e .... between him and his brother. They're very similar.

/ 4 points

3 Choose the correct alternative.

'Last night a man tried to **(a)** steal/burgle a lot of money from a bank. While he was **(b)** robbing/stealing the bank, the police came and arrested the **(c)** theft/thief. At the police station, when they started investigating, they found out the man was also a **(d)** mugger/murder because a victim recognised him. They discovered that the criminal often attacked people in the park and **(e)** stole/robbed their money. He's going to go to prison for quite a long time!'

/ 5 points

4 Match the parts of the phrasal verbs. Then match the phrasal verbs to their meanings.

1 look	for	a investigate
2 look	across	b discover
3 turn	into	c appear or arrive unexpectedly
4 come	out	d find by accident
5 find	up	e try to find

/ 5 points

Total */ 20 points*

Progress Test: Units 1–4

Grammar

1 Correct the sentences if necessary.

1 We haven't got many bread.

....

2 We've got a little apples in the fridge – two or three, I think.

....

3 There's a little shampoo in the bottle, but not much.

....

4 We've got a few CDs here but not many.

....

5 We don't need much books to do this project.

....

6 Have we got any paper in the classroom? Yes, there's a lot of.

....

7 We haven't got some milk.

....

/ 7 points

2 Complete the sentences in a logical way using these words. Use each word once.

when where which who whose

1 Summer is the time of year ....
2 Japan is a country ....
3 Hip hop is a type of music ....
4 Madonna is a singer ....
5 Beethoven was a composer ....

/ 5 points

3 Complete the text by choosing the correct option to fill each gap: A, B, C or D.

'My father usually **(1)** .... a lot because he has **(2)** .... translations of a lot of famous novels. He has **(3)** .... come back (yesterday, in fact) from a trip to Italy. He **(4)** .... talking at a conference for translators there. He has **(5)** .... translated a lot of famous books from Italian into English, but he has **(6)** .... translated any books by Umberto Eco. Now he's **(7)** .... on a book by a new writer. He **(8)** .... started work on it last year.'

	A	B	C	D
1	A travelled	B travel	C travelling	D travels
2	A writing	B writes	C written	D wrote
3	A just	B been	C not	D wanted
4	A is	B was	C has	D have
5	A already	B yet	C just	D ever
6	A ever	B never	C yet	D always
7	A working	B worked	C work	D works
8	A has	B hasn't	C –	D is

/ 8 points

Total */ 20 points*

Vocabulary

1 Correct the sentences if necessary.

1 I did three mistakes in the exam.

....

2 In Brazil they speak Spanish.

....

3 In Germany they speak Dutch.

....

4 My sister took three exams last week.

....

5 Have you made that English exercise yet?

....

6 I need to make a lot of those exercises.

....

/ 6 points

2 Complete the sentences with the correct word.

1 He can't talk because he's got a very sore ....
2 He had a .... attack and died.
3 I didn't just have a cold. It was much worse. I think it was ....
4 We ate something bad at the weekend and now we've got food ....
5 I need an aspirin. I've got a ....
6 On each foot we have five ....

/ 6 points

3 Match the correct words with the definitions. There are 16 words but only eight definitions.

burglary cousin death equipment illegal
impractical improvement invisible look into
nephew niece robber senior citizen
stepfather theft work out

1 when you steal from somebody's house ....
2 the daughter of your brother or sister ....
3 solve a problem by considering the facts ....
4 when something goes from bad to good, or from good to very good ....
5 something that is not practical ....
6 something you cannot see ....
7 the objects or things you need for a particular activity ....
8 someone who is more than 60 years old ....

/ 8 points

Total */ 20 points*

Progress Test: Units 1–6

Grammar

1 Complete the sentences with the correct word.

1 This computer is much faster .... that one.
2 The film isn't as good .... the book.
3 A mobile phone is .... expensive than a computer.
4 When you are 15, you aren't old .... to drive a car.
5 When you're 17, you're .... young to vote in a general election.
6 I think it's the best country .... the world.

/ 6 points

2 Each sentence contains a mistake. Find the mistake and rewrite the sentence correctly.

1 The teacher and the students going to go on an excursion.
....
2 What do you do tomorrow?
....
3 They say it's raining next week.
....
4 The Prime Minister will make a decision today?
....
5 I can't meet you tomorrow because I'll do an exam.
....
6 If scientists don't find a solution for this problem, the planet gets much hotter.
....
....
7 I may definitely arrive at the station at six o'clock.
....

/ 7 points

3 Choose the correct alternative.

On Sundays I always **(a)** watch/am watching a TV documentary series about nature. I **(b)** saw/have seen every programme in the series since it **(c)** started/has started in 2008. The presenter is a really interesting man **(d)** who/whose name is Jack Wild. He doesn't always give **(e)** many/much information about the different things they show but there are **(f)** any/some cool scenes with animals that you **(g)** aren't usually seeing/don't usually see on TV.

/ 7 points

Total / 20 points

Vocabulary

1 Complete the sentences with the correct word.

adverts bored boring comedies informative interested interesting relaxed relaxing soaps

1 .... are programmes that are funny and make you laugh.
2 A good documentary needs to be .... and ....
3 People often feel .... when they listen to soft, slow music.
4 A lot of people think .... for soap or toothpaste are .... so they switch the TV off.
5 The stories in .... are usually about romance, family relationships, money and health problems.

/ 7 points

2 Label the pictures.

1 ....

2 ....

3 ....

4 ....

5 ....

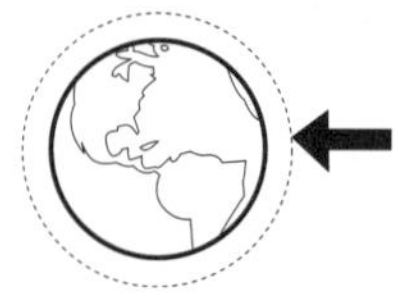
6 ....

/ 6 points

3 Answer the questions.

1 What prefix do we need to make the opposite of *correct*? ....
2 What is a synonym for *get* in this sentence? *I got home at ten o'clock.* ....
3 What crime does a thief commit? ....
4 What word do we need to complete the compound noun meaning *a place to go when we are ill? health* ....
5 What noun do we make from the verb *improve*? ....
6 What word do we need to complete this phrasal verb which means *find by accident? come* ....
7 What is a synonym for *get* in this sentence? *Can you get the bread when you go out?* ....

/ 7 points

Total / 20 points

Progress Test: Units 1–8

Grammar

1 Complete the sentences with the correct word.

1 My father .... to wear a uniform – he's a police officer.
2 You're always tired in the morning. You .... go to bed earlier.
3 If I .... you, I'd go to bed earlier.
4 You .... smoke here. It's illegal.
5 My mum .... go to the gym every day if she had time.
6 You don't .... to do the essay this week. You can do it next week if you like.
7 You .... eat chocolate just before you go to bed. It's bad for your teeth.

/ 7 points

2 Correct the sentences if necessary.

1 Are you interested in go to Cambridge next week?
....
2 Dancing is my favourite hobby.
....
3 I don't enjoy to play basketball.
....
4 My friends and I go swimming every day in the summer.
....
5 I went to Liz's house yesterday for seeing if she was OK.
....
6 He found the answer by using a calculator.
....

/ 6 points

3 Match the sentences with their explanations.

1 When I'd eaten my lunch, I watched a film on TV. ....
2 When I ate my lunch, I watched a film on TV. ....
3 When I had watched a film on TV, I ate my lunch. ....
4 While I was having my lunch, my phone rang. ....
5 When I eat my lunch, I watch a film on TV. ....
6 I've just had my lunch. ....
7 Tomorrow I'm going to have lunch and then I'm going to watch a film on TV. ....

a a plan for two actions in the future
b an action that finished very recently
c an action that came in the middle of another action in the past
d two actions in the past that happened at the same time
e two actions that happened in the past, one after the other – first eating lunch, then watching a film
f two actions that happened in the past, one after the other – first watching a film, then eating lunch
g two actions that are part of a routine

/ 7 points

Total */ 20 points*

Vocabulary

1 Join the words to find two jobs, three personal qualities and two adjectives to describe jobs. Then complete the table by writing them in the correct column.

1 well — a time
2 hard — b assistant
3 fashion — c paid
4 full — d minded
5 shop — e organised
6 open — f working
7 badly — g designer

Jobs	Personal qualities	Describing jobs
....	....	....
....	....	....
....	....	....

/ 7 points

2 Answer the questions.

1 What is the noun which we make from *excited*?
....
2 How do we complete this phrase which means *end a relationship with somebody*? *split* .... *somebody*
3 What is the noun which we make from *bored*? ....
4 How do we complete this phrase which means *have a good relationship with somebody*? .... *well with somebody*
5 How can you explain *get back together again* in other words?
....
6 What is the adjective for the noun *fear*? ....
7 What noun can we make from *friend*? ....

/ 7 points

3 Complete the words.

1 .... *father* = your mother's new husband
2 .... *throat* = when your throat hurts and you can't speak, for example
3 *shop* .... = stealing from a shop
4 .... *show* = a TV programme with a competition, often to win money
5 *mountain* .... = a line of mountains like the Andes
6 *global* .... = the change in the temperature around the world

/ 6 points

Total */ 20 points*

Progress Test: Units 1–10

Grammar

1 Rewrite the sentences in reported speech.

1 'I bought a computer in this shop,' said Lily.
Lily said ....

2 'We've got an exam today,' Jessica said to her mum.
Jessica told ....

3 'Where is your jacket?' Sam's mum asked him.
Sam's mum asked ....

4 'Has Thomas seen this film?' they asked Jim.
They asked ....

5 'I'm going to London tomorrow,' said Helen.
Helen said ....

6 'My sister is doing her homework,' Jack said to Chloe.
Jack told ....

7 'Why are you here today?' the teacher asked the students.
The teacher asked ....

/7 points

2 Rewrite the active sentences in the passive form and the passive sentences in the active form.

1 Grandparents play computer games too.
Computer games ....

2 Arthur Wynne invented crosswords in 1913.
Crosswords ....

3 A museum is being opened by the Queen tomorrow.
The Queen ....

4 The concert was seen by 40,000 people.
40,000 people ....

5 Alex Smith has won the competition.
The competition ....

6 They design Honda motorbikes in Japan.
Honda motorbikes ....

/6 points

3 Complete the sentences with the correct form of the verbs given, or find the correct word.

1 If I .... (be) the Prime Minister, I .... (build) more hospitals.

2 This is the city .... I was born.

3 Yesterday I .... (have) an accident when I .... (play) tennis.

4 Emma .... come to the party tonight but she hasn't decided yet.

5 .... (surf) the Net is my favourite hobby.

/7 points

Total /20 points

Vocabulary

1 Complete the words with the missing letters and then complete the table by writing them in the correct column.

re ... d ... n = *read on*

1 m ... nu ... l
2 thr ... l ... r
3 f ... nt ... y
4 r ... ad ... t
5 lo ... k ... p
6 b ... gr ... phy
7 f ... ry t ... le

Fiction	Non-fiction	Phrasal verbs connected with reading
....	....	*read on*
....	....	....
....	....	....

/7 points

2 Complete the sentences with the correct words.

1 Google is a popular search ....

2 The hard .... is the part of the computer which has the information that the computer needs to work.

3 The USB .... is where you can connect a keyboard or a camera, for example.

4 Emails .... back if the email address isn't correct.

5 Yesterday I received an email from my cousin so I decided to .... to it quickly.

6 You move the mouse on the mouse ....

7 A broad.................................. Internet connection is faster than a normal connection.

/7 points

3 Match the words or parts of words and then write a simple definition or explanation for each.

			Definition/explanation
1 have	into something	1	....
2 ice	hood	2	....
3 look	an argument	3	....
4 first	somebody out	4	....
5 child	aid	5	....
6 ask	cap	6	....

/6 points

Total /20 points

Gateway B1 Dictionary

INTRODUCTION

This Macmillan Dictionary has been especially designed to meet the needs of Gateway students who are at B1 level. The words have been selected from the B1 student's book and this workbook. Other words that often appear in school-leaving exams have also been included.

The most common and useful words are marked according to the Macmillan Dictionary 'star rating'. This is so that you can easily recognise the vocabulary you need to know especially well.

★★★ = very common words
★★ = common words
★ = fairly common words

GRAMMAR CODES

Nouns

- **[C]** countable nouns that are used with *a* or *an* or a number and have a plural: *car, soldier*
- **[U]** uncountable nouns that cannot be used with *a* or *an* or a number and have no plural: *happiness, pasta*
- **[singular]** nouns that are used with *a*, *an*, or *the* but are never used in the plural: *heat, mess*
- **[plural]** nouns that are used only in the plural and always take a plural verb: *congratulations, surroundings*

Verbs

- **[I]** intransitive verbs that have no direct object: *He **paused** for a moment.* ♦ *Could you **speak up** please?*
- **[T]** transitive verbs that have a direct object: *I ate my lunch.* ♦ *She **handed** the note over to me.*
- **[linking verb]** verbs that are followed by a noun or adjective complement describing the subject: *They **looked** happy.* ♦ *I **feel** better now.*

WORD CLASSES USED IN THIS DICTIONARY

adj (=adjective)	**phrase**
adv (=adverb)	**phr vb** (=phrasal verb)
conj (=conjunction)	**prep** (=preposition)
det (=determiner)	**pron** (=pronoun)
noun	**verb**

A a

absence /'æbs(ə)ns/ noun [C/U] ★ a time when someone is not where they should be or where they usually are: *We are concerned about your child's frequent absences from school.*

academic /,ækə'demɪk/ adj ★ **1** relating to education, especially in colleges and universities: *We expect our students to meet high academic standards.* **2** based on learning from study rather than practical skills and experience: *The college offers both academic and vocational qualifications.* noun [C] a teacher at a college or university

accept /ək'sept/ verb [T] ★★★ to take something that someone gives you: *It gives me great pleasure to accept this award.* verb [I/T] ★★★ to say yes to an invitation, offer, or suggestion: *Our clients will never accept this proposal.*

accident /'æksɪd(ə)nt/ noun [C] ★★★ **1** an unexpected event that causes injury or damage: *He was killed in a climbing accident.* **2** something that happens without being planned: *I didn't mean to do it! It was an accident.*

accidentally /,æksɪ'dent(ə)li/ adv ★ **1** by chance, as the result of an accident: *Police believe the fire was started accidentally.* **2** by mistake rather than deliberate intention: *The program prevents files from being accidentally erased.*

accommodation /ə,kɒmə'deɪʃ(ə)n/ noun [U] ★★ a place for someone to stay, live or work in: *The hotel provides accommodation for up to 100 people.*

according to /ə'kɔːdɪŋ ,tuː/ prep ★★★ **1** used for stating where information or ideas have come from: *According to newspaper reports, fighting has broken out in the northern provinces.* **2** in a way that agrees with or obeys a particular plan, system, or set of rules: *The game was played according to the rules.*

account /ə'kaʊnt/ noun [C] ★★ **1** an arrangement in which a bank looks after your money: *There was only £50 in his bank account.* **2** an arrangement with a company or Internet provider to use a service they provide: *an email account.*

accuse /ə'kjuːz/ verb [T] ★★ to say that someone has done something wrong or illegal: *Her employers accused her of theft.*

ache /eɪk/ noun [C] a pain that is continuous but usually not very strong verb [I] to feel a continuous but not very strong pain in part of your body

achievement /ə'tʃiːvmənt/ noun [C] ★★ a particular thing that someone has achieved: *Winning the gold medal was a remarkable achievement.*

acupuncture /'ækjʊ,pʌŋktʃə/ noun [U] a medical treatment that involves putting needles into particular parts of someone's body

adaptation /,ædæp'teɪʃ(ə)n/ noun [C] a film or TV programme made from a book or play

addict /'ædɪkt/ noun [C] someone who cannot stop taking illegal or harmful drugs: *a heroin addict*

addicted /ə'dɪktɪd/ adj unable to stop taking an illegal or harmful drug: *He was addicted to cocaine.*

addictive /ə'dɪktɪv/ adj an addictive drug is difficult to stop taking

adjust /ə'dʒʌst/ verb [T] to change or move something slightly so that it works or fits better: *She stopped to adjust the strap on her sandal.* verb [I] to get used to a new situation by changing your ideas or the way you do things: *It took her two years to adjust to life in England.*

admit /əd'mɪt/ verb [I/T] ★★★ to agree that something bad is true, or to agree that you have done something wrong: *Davis admitted causing death by careless driving.*

adolescence /,ædə'les(ə)ns/ noun [U] the period of your life when you are changing from being a child to being an adult, especially when you are a young teenager: *He spent his adolescence in a children's home.*

adult /'ædʌlt, ə'dʌlt/ noun [C] ★★★ someone who is no longer a child and is legally responsible for their actions: *Tickets are £2.50 for adults and £1.50 for children.*

advantage /əd'vɑːntɪdʒ/ noun [C/U] ★★ something that makes one person or thing more likely to succeed than others: *the advantages of a good education* noun [C] ★★ a good feature or quality that something has: *Having children when you're older has both advantages and disadvantages.*

advertisement /əd'vɜːtɪsmənt/ noun [C] an announcement in a newspaper, on television, on the Internet etc that is designed to persuade people to buy a product or service, go to an event, or apply for a job

advice /əd'vaɪs/ noun [U] ★★★ an opinion that someone gives you about the best thing to do in a particular situation: *Ask your father for advice.*

advise /əd'vaɪz/ verb [I/T] ★★ to give your opinion to someone about the best thing to do in a particular situation: *Her doctor advised her to rest.*

aerial /'eəriəl/ noun [C] a piece of equipment made of wire or thin metal, used for receiving radio or television signals

affect /ə'fekt/ verb [T] ★★★ to change or influence something, often in a negative way: *Did the newspapers really affect the outcome of the election?*

afraid /ə'freɪd/ adj ★★★ **1** worried that something bad might happen: *I was afraid that you'd miss the flight.* **2** frightened: *Don't be afraid – I won't hurt you.*

A

afterwards /ˈɑːftəwədz/ adv ★★ after something else that you have already mentioned: *Let's go and see a film and afterwards we could go for a meal.*

agony aunt /ˈæɡəni ˌɑːnt/ noun [C] a woman who gives advice about personal problems in a newspaper or magazine by answering readers' letters

agree /əˈɡriː/ verb [I/T] ★★★ to have the same opinion as someone else: *Doreen thought that the house was too small, and Jim agreed.* verb [I] ★★★ to say that you will do something that someone else wants or suggests: *I asked her to marry me, and she agreed.*

ahead /əˈhed/ adv ★★★ **1** in the direction in front of you: *There's a motel just a few miles ahead.* **2** used for saying what will happen in the future: *Where will the money come from in the years ahead?*

airline /ˈeəˌlaɪn/ noun [C] ★ a company that owns aircraft and takes people or goods by plane from one place to another

alien /ˈeɪliən/ noun [C] a creature from another planet

allow /əˈlaʊ/ verb [T] ★★★ to give someone permission to do something or have something: *I'm sorry, sir, but smoking is not allowed.*

almost /ˈɔːlməʊst/ adv ★★★ nearly but not completely: *'Are you ready?' 'Almost! I'm just putting my shoes on.'*

alone /əˈləʊn/ adj, adv ★★ if you are alone, no one else is with you: *Shelley is divorced and lives alone.*

alternative /ɔːlˈtɜːnətɪv/ noun [C] ★★ something that you can choose to do instead of something else: *There was no alternative – we had to close the bridge.*

amateur /ˈæmətə, ˈæmətʃʊə/ adj done for pleasure instead of as a job: *amateur photography* noun [C] someone who does something because they enjoy it, instead of as a job

amazed /əˈmeɪzd/ adj very surprised: *Frankly, I was amazed that he was interested.*

amazing /əˈmeɪzɪŋ/ adj ★ very good, surprising, or impressive: *Her story was quite amazing.*

ambitious /æmˈbɪʃəs/ adj determined to become successful, rich, or famous: *an ambitious young lawyer*

among /əˈmʌŋ/ prep ★★★ **1** included in a particular group of people or things: *Robert was the only one among them who had ever ridden a horse.* **2** with other people or things all around: *It was pleasant strolling among the olive trees.*

amusement park /əˈmjuːzmənt ˌpɑːk/ noun [C] a place where people pay money to go on rides

analyse /ˈænəˌlaɪz/ verb [T] to examine something in detail in order to understand or explain it: *Scientists analysed samples of leaves taken from the area.*

anatomy /əˈnætəmi/ noun [C] the body of a human or animal, or the structure of a plant

ancient /ˈeɪnʃ(ə)nt/ adj ★★ **1** very old: *an ancient city/book/tradition* **2** relating to a period of history a very long time ago: *the ancient Greeks/Britons/Egyptians*

anger /ˈæŋɡə/ noun [U] ★★ the strong feeling you get that makes you want to hurt someone or shout at them: *Some people express their anger through violence.*

angry /ˈæŋɡri/ adj ★★★ very annoyed: *There's no point in getting angry.*

ankle /ˈæŋk(ə)l/ noun [C] the part at the bottom of your leg where your foot joins your leg

anniversary /ˌænɪˈvɜːs(ə)ri/ noun [C] a date when you celebrate something that happened in a previous year that is important to you: *a wedding anniversary*

annual /ˈænjuəl/ adj ★★ **1** happening once a year: *an annual conference/festival/holiday* **2** calculated over a period of one year: *an annual salary*

anorak /ˈænəˌræk/ noun [C] a short coat with a hood

ant /ænt/ noun [C] a small insect that lives under the ground in large organised groups

apart from /əˈpɑːt ˌfrəm/ phrase in addition to someone or something: *Apart from providing humanitarian aid, the UN is also supposed to enforce agreements.*

apologise /əˈpɒləˌdʒaɪz/ verb [I] ★★ to tell someone that you are sorry for doing something wrong: *I apologise for taking so long to reply.*

apparent /əˈpærənt/ adj ★ easy to see or understand: *It was apparent that the two women knew each other.*

appeal /əˈpiːl/ noun [C] ★ an urgent request for people to do something or give something: *There have been several appeals for an end to the fighting.* noun [U] ★ a quality that something has that makes people like it or want it: *How do you explain the appeal of horror films?* verb [I] ★ **1** to make an urgent request for people to do something or give something: *She appealed to her former husband to return their baby son.* **2** if something appeals to you, you like it or want it: *The show's mixture of comedy and songs will appeal to children.*

appear /əˈpɪə/ verb [linking verb] ★★★ to make other people think that you are something, or that you feel something: *Matt appears unaffected by all the media attention.* verb [I] ★★★ **1** if someone or something appears somewhere, you see them suddenly or for the first time: *Cracks began to appear in the ceiling.* **2** to start to exist, or to start to be available for the first time: *the latest Internet guide to appear on the market*

appearance /əˈpɪərəns/ noun [U] ★★★ **1** the way that someone or something looks: *The twins are almost identical in appearance.* **2** the time when something starts to exist, or starts to be seen: *the appearance of fast food restaurants on every high street* **3** the fact that someone arrives somewhere: *She was startled by Julie's sudden appearance in the doorway.*

application form /ˌæplɪˈkeɪʃ(ə)n fɔː(r)m/ noun ★★ a printed list of questions that you answer in order to try to get a job, borrow money, get a place at university etc

apply /əˈplaɪ/ verb [I] ★★★ to make a formal request to do something or have something: *Students can apply for money to help with their living costs.* verb [T] ★★★ to put a layer of something such as paint onto a surface

appointment /əˈpɔɪntmənt/ noun [C] ★★★ an arrangement to see someone, for example a doctor, at a particular time: *Why don't you make an appointment with one of our doctors?*

appropriate /əˈprəʊpriət/ adj ★★ suitable for a particular situation: *This isn't the appropriate time to discuss the problem.*

approximately /əˈprɒksɪmətli/ adv ★ used for showing that an amount or number is not exact: *Approximately 60,000 people filled the stadium.*

archeologist /ˌɑːkiˈɒlədʒɪst/ noun [C] someone who studies archeology

archer /ˈɑː(r)tʃə(r)/ noun [C] someone who shoots arrows from a bow

architect /ˈɑːkɪˌtekt/ noun [C] someone whose job is to design buildings

argue /ˈɑːɡjuː/ verb [I] ★★★ to discuss something that you disagree about, usually in an angry way: *Those girls are always arguing!*

argument /ˈɑːɡjʊmənt/ noun [C] ★★★ an angry disagreement between people: *The decision led to a heated argument.*

arm /ɑːm/ noun [C] ★★★ one of the two long parts of your body with your hands at the end: *I put my arm around his shoulders.*

armband /ˈɑːmˌbænd/ noun [C] **1** a plastic ring that is filled with air, worn around each arm by people learning to swim **2** a small piece of cloth that you wear around one arm

armchair /ˈɑːmˌtʃeə/ noun [C] a large comfortable chair with parts for you to rest your arms on

army /ˈɑːmi/ noun [C] ★★★ a large organisation of soldiers who are trained to fight wars on land: *an army officer/colonel*

arrangement /əˈreɪndʒmənt/ noun [plural] ★★★ arrangements: practical plans for organising and managing the details of something: *sleeping/seating arrangements* noun [C] ★★★ an agreement or plan that you make with someone else: *They have an arrangement with Pepsi-Cola to share distribution facilities.*

arrest /əˈrest/ verb [T] ★★ if the police arrest someone, they take that person to a police station because they think that he or she has committed a crime: *Police raided the building and arrested six men.*

arsonist /ˈɑː(r)s(ə)nɪst/ noun [C] someone who deliberately starts fires, especially in buildings

art /ɑːt/ noun [U] ★★★ paintings, drawings, and other objects that are created in order to be beautiful or interesting: *the art of ancient Mexico*

artificial /ˌɑːtɪˈfɪʃ(ə)l/ adj ★ not natural or real, but made by people: *The growers use both natural and artificial light.*

artist /ˈɑːtɪst/ noun [C] ★★ someone who creates paintings or other objects that are beautiful or interesting

ask somebody out /ˌɑːsk sʌmbədi ˈaʊt/ phr vb to invite someone to go somewhere with you because you want to start a romantic relationship with them

assassination /əˌsæsɪˈneɪʃ(ə)n/ noun [C/U] ★ the murder of a famous or important person, especially for political reasons: *an assassination attempt*

assess /əˈses/ verb [T] to think about something carefully and make a judgment about it: *We tried to assess his suitability for the job.*

assessment /əˈsesmənt/ noun [U] ★★ the process of making a judgment or forming an opinion, after considering something or someone carefully: *The investigation was reopened after careful assessment of new evidence.*

assistant /əˈsɪst(ə)nt/ noun [C] ★★ someone whose job is to help another person in their work, for example by doing the easier parts of it: *a personal assistant*

atlas /ˈætləs/ noun [C] a book of maps

atmosphere /ˈætməsˌfɪə/ noun [singular] ★★ **1** the mood that exists in a place and affects the people there: *There is an atmosphere of tension in the city today.* **2** the air round the Earth or round another planet: *The Earth's atmosphere is getting warmer.*

attraction /əˈtrækʃ(ə)n/ noun [C] an interesting place or object that people come to see noun [C/U] a reason for liking something or someone or being interested in it/them

attractive /əˈtræktɪv/ adj ★★ nice to look at: *a stunningly attractive woman*

au pair /əʊ ˈpeə/ noun [C] a young woman who lives with a family in a foreign country and helps to look after their children

audience /ˈɔːdiəns/ noun [C] ★★★ the people who watch or listen to a performance: *Chaplin's films were loved by audiences throughout the world.*

aunt /ɑːnt/ noun [C] ★★ the sister of your mother or father, or the wife of your uncle: *I loved visiting my aunt and uncle.*

authentic /ɔːˈθentɪk/ adj real, not false or copied: *The letter is certainly authentic.*

author /ˈɔːθə/ noun [C] ★★ **1** someone who writes books or articles as their job **2** the person who wrote a particular document or other piece of writing: *the author of the report*

authority /ɔːˈθɒrəti/ noun [U] ★★ **1** the power to make decisions and make people do what you want: *The president's authority is being questioned in the press.* **2** official permission to do something: *We do not release the names of our customers without their authority.* noun [plural] ★★ the authorities: the police or other organisations with legal power to make people obey laws: *The French authorities have refused to issue him a visa.*

autobiography /ˌɔːtəʊbaɪˈɒgrəfi/ noun [C] a book about your life that you write yourself

autograph /ˈɔːtəˌgrɑːf/ noun [C] a famous person's name that they sign on something

available /əˈveɪləb(ə)l/ adj ★★ **1** able to be obtained, taken, or used: *We'll notify you as soon as tickets become available.* **2** not too busy to do something: *I'm available next Tuesday if you want to meet then.*

avalanche /ˈævəˌlɑːntʃ/ noun [C] a large amount of snow that suddenly falls down a mountain

average /ˈæv(ə)rɪdʒ/ noun [C/U] ★ the typical amount or level: *Unemployment here is twice the national average.*

avoid /əˈvɔɪd/ verb [T] ★★★ **1** to try to prevent something from happening: *Try to avoid confrontation.* **2** to stay away from someone or something: *We went early to avoid the crowds.*

aware /əˈweə/ adj ★★★ knowing about a situation or fact: *As far as I'm aware, he didn't tell her anything.*

awareness /əˈweə(r)nəs/ noun [singular/U] ★★ knowledge or understanding of a subject, issue, or situation: *There was a general lack of awareness about safety issues.*

awful /ˈɔːf(ə)l/ adj ★★ extremely bad: *This wine tastes awful.*

Bb

B

baby /ˈbeɪbi/ noun [C] ★★★ a very young child who cannot yet talk or walk: *their new baby daughter*

bachelor /ˈbætʃələ/ noun [C] a man who has never been married

bachelor's degree /ˈbætʃələz dɪˌgriː/ noun [C] a first university degree

back /bæk/ noun [C] ★★★ **1** the part of your body between your neck and your bottom, on the opposite side to your chest and stomach: *I have a pain in my back.* **2** the part or side of something that is furthest from the front: *Get in the back of the car.*

background /ˈbækˌgraʊnd/ noun [C] ★★ **1** the general experiences and influences that have formed someone's character, or the type of education and training they have had: *students from very different backgrounds* **2** the part of a picture or pattern that is behind the main people or things in it: *a picture of palm trees with mountains in the background*

backup /ˈbækʌp/ noun [U] people or equipment that can be used when extra help is needed: *The gang was armed, so the police called for backup.* noun [C] a copy of information on your computer that you make in case you lose the original information

baddy /ˈbædi/ noun [C] someone in a film or book who does unkind or illegal things

badge /bædʒ/ noun [C] **1** a small round object with words or symbols on it. You fasten it onto your clothes with a pin, for example to show that you support an idea or a political party. **2** a special piece of metal, cloth, or plastic with words or symbols on it. You wear it or carry it to show your official position: *a police badge*

badly-paid /ˈbædli peɪd/ phrase if someone is badly-paid, they do not earn much money, or they earn less money than is fair for the work they do

bad-tempered /ˌbæd ˈtempəd/ adj made annoyed or angry very easily

balcony /ˈbælkəni/ noun [C] a place sticking out from the outside of a building where you can sit or stand

bald /bɔːld/ adj with little or no hair on your head

ban /bæn/ noun [C] an official statement ordering people not to do something: *There is a total ban on smoking anywhere in the college.* verb [T] ★ to say officially that someone is not allowed to do something: *She was banned from competing for two years after failing a drugs test.*

bank /bæŋk/ noun [C] ★★★ **1** a financial institution where people can keep their money, or can borrow money: *I need to go to the bank this morning.* **2** a large collection or store of something: *a blood bank*

bargain /ˈbɑːgɪn/ noun [C] something you buy that costs much less than normal: *Her dress was a real bargain.*

basic /ˈbeɪsɪk/ adj ★★★ **1** forming the main or most important part or aspect of something: *Rice is the basic ingredient of the dish.* **2** simple, with nothing special or extra: *The state provides only basic health care.*

beach /biːtʃ/ noun [C] ★★ an area of sand or small stones beside the sea or a lake

bean /biːn/ noun [C] **1** a seed of various plants that is cooked and eaten, or a plant that produces these seeds **2** a dried bean that you grind and use to make drinks such as coffee and cocoa

beard /bɪəd/ noun [C] hair that grows on a man's chin and cheeks

beat /biːt/ verb [T] ★★★ **1** to defeat someone in a game, competition, election, or battle: *England needed to beat Germany to get to the final.* **2** to hit someone violently several times: *They were arrested for beating their children.*

beautician /bjuːˈtɪʃ(ə)n/ noun [C] someone whose job is to give people beauty treatments

behave /bɪˈheɪv/ verb [I] ★★ to do things in a particular way: *The children behaved very badly.* verb [I/T] ★★ to be polite and not cause trouble: *Mum's always telling me to behave when we go out.*

behaviour /bɪˈheɪvjə/ noun [U] ★★★ the way that someone behaves: *Anna was sick of her brother's behaviour.*

B

behind /bɪ'haɪnd/ adv, prep ★★★ **1** at the back of someone or something: *The teacher was standing behind me, looking over my shoulder.* **2** used for saying what causes something or who is responsible for making it happen, especially when this is not obvious: *Police believe that a racist group is behind the attacks.* **3** late or too slow in doing things that you have to do: *The project is already a month behind schedule.*

belong to /bɪ'lɒŋ tə/ phr vb to be owned by someone: *The car belongs to the woman next door.*

best-seller /ˌbest'selə/ noun [C] a book that many people buy

big-headed /ˌbɪg'hedɪd/ adj behaving in a way that shows that you think you are very important or intelligent

bill /bɪl/ noun [C] ★★★ a written statement that shows how much money you owe for goods or services that you have received: *a telephone bill*

biodegradable /ˌbaɪəʊdɪ'greɪdəb(ə)l/ adj decaying naturally in a way that is not harmful to the environment

biography /baɪ'ɒgrəfi/ noun [C] a book that someone writes about someone else's life

birth /bɜːθ/ noun [C/U] ★★ the occasion when a baby is born: *We are happy to announce the birth of our son, Andrew.*

biscuit /'bɪskɪt/ noun [C] a small flat dry cake that is usually sweet: *a packet of chocolate biscuits*

a bit /ə 'bɪt/ phrase slightly, or a little: *I'm feeling a bit tired.*

blame /bleɪm/ noun [U] ★ responsibility for an accident, problem, or bad situation: *Why do I always get the blame for everything?* verb [T] ★★★ to say or think that someone or something is responsible for an accident, problem, or bad situation: *If it all goes wrong, don't blame me.*

bleed /bliːd/ verb [I] to have blood flowing from your body, for example from a cut: *He was bleeding from a wound in his shoulder.*

blind /blaɪnd/ adj ★ unable to see: *Blind and sighted children attend the same school.*

block /blɒk/ noun [C] ★★ **1** a large building with a lot of different levels: *an apartment/office block* **2** a solid piece of wood, stone, ice etc with straight sides: *a block of marble* **3** an area of buildings in a town or city with streets on all four sides: *I was early, so I walked around the block a couple of times.* verb [T] ★ to stop something from moving along or passing through something: *A car was blocking the road.*

blog /blɒg/ noun [C] a biographical web log: a type of diary on a website that is changed regularly, to give the latest news.

blood /blʌd/ noun [U] ★★★ the red liquid that flows around inside your body: *Oxygen is carried in the blood.*

blow /bləʊ/ verb [I] ★★ **1** if wind or air blows, the air moves: *A strong wind was blowing across the island.* **2** to push out air from your mouth: *He bent towards the candle and blew gently.*

board /bɔːd/ noun [C] ★★★ **1** a thin flat piece of wood or other material that is used for a particular purpose: *a chopping/ironing board* **2** a flat wide surface such as a noticeboard or blackboard that is used for showing information: *The exam results were pinned up on the board.* verb [I/T] to get onto a ship, aircraft, train, or bus

board game /'bɔːd ˌgeɪm/ noun [C] any game in which you move objects around on a special board

boarding school /'bɔːdɪŋ skuːl/ noun [C] a school in which the students live during the part of the year that they go to lessons

boat /bəʊt/ noun [C] ★★★ a vehicle for travelling on water: *The only way to get there was by boat.*

boil /bɔɪl/ verb [I/T] ★ **1** if a liquid boils, or if you boil it, it becomes so hot that bubbles rise to the surface: *When the water boils, add the rice.* **2** to cook something in boiling water, or to be cooked in this way: *How long does it take to boil an egg?*

book /bʊk/ noun [C] ★★★ a written work that is printed on pages fastened together inside a cover: *Please open your books at page 25.* verb [I/T] ★ to arrange to have or use something at a particular time in the future: *Shall I book a room for you?*

boost /buːst/ noun [singular] something that helps something to increase or improve: *The festival has been a major boost for the local economy.* verb [T] to help something to increase or improve: *The cold weather boosted demand for electricity.*

bored /bɔːd/ adj ★★ feeling impatient and annoyed because nothing is interesting: *The waiter looked very bored.*

boredom /'bɔːdəm/ noun [U] the feeling of being bored

boring /'bɔːrɪŋ/ adj ★★ not at all interesting: *a boring, badly-paid job*

born /bɔːn/ adj ★★★ **1** when a baby is born, it comes out of its mother's body and starts its life: *Her grandfather died before she was born.* **2** if something such as a new organisation or idea is born, it begins to exist

borrow /'bɒrəʊ/ verb [T] ★★ to receive and use something that belongs to someone else, and promise to give it back: *Can I borrow your calculator?*

bossy /'bɒsi/ adj someone who is bossy is annoying because they keep telling other people what to do

bounce /baʊns/ verb [I/T] **1** if a ball or other object bounces, or if you bounce it, it hits a surface then immediately moves away: *The ball bounced twice before hitting the net.* **2** if an email message bounces, it is sent back to you without reaching the person you sent it to

bowl /bəʊl/ noun [C] ★★ **1** a round container that you use for eating, serving, or preparing food: *In a large bowl, mix together the eggs, sugar, and butter.* **2** a large container without a lid, used for holding liquids: *a washing-up bowl*

bowling /'bəʊlɪŋ/ noun [U] an indoor game in which players roll heavy balls along a track and try to knock down a group of pins

box /bɒks/ noun [C] ★★★ **1** a container with straight sides and a flat base: *a cardboard box* **2** a space for writing information on a printed form, or a space on a computer screen with information in it: *a dialogue box*

boxer /'bɒksə/ noun [C] someone who takes part in the sport of boxing

brain /breɪn/ noun [C] ★★ the organ inside your head that allows you to think and feel, and controls your body: *The illness had affected his brain.*

branch /brɑːntʃ/ noun [C] ★★ **1** one of the parts of a tree that grows out of its trunk **2** a shop or office representing a large company or organisation in a particular area: *The store has branches in over 50 cities.*

brave /breɪv/ adj ★★ able to deal with danger, pain, or trouble without being frightened or worried: *the brave soldiers who fought and died for their country*

break /breɪk/ verb [I/T] ★★★ **1** if something breaks, or if you break it, it separates into two or more pieces when it is hit, dropped etc: *I broke two dishes this morning.* **2** if a piece of equipment breaks, or if you break it, it stops working correctly: *Don't play with the camera – you'll break it.* verb [T] ★★★ to fail to obey a rule or law: *Students who break these rules will be punished.*

bride /braɪd/ noun [C] a woman who is getting married, or one who has recently married

bright /braɪt/ adj ★★★ **1** bright colours are strong but not dark: *She was wearing a bright red scarf.* **2** full of strong shining light: *It was a bright sunny day.* **3** intelligent: *one of the brightest students in the class*

bring /brɪŋ/ verb [T] ★★★ to take someone or something with you from one place to another: *Bring a coat in case it turns cold.*

broadband /'brɔːdˌbænd/ noun [U] a type of connection between a computer and the Internet that allows you to send or receive a large amount of information in a short time

broadcast /'brɔːdˌkɑːst/ noun [C] a programme that is broadcast: *Channel 5's main news broadcast* verb [I/T] to send out messages or programmes to be received by radios or televisions: *The BBC will be broadcasting the match live from Paris.*

broken /'brəʊkən/ adj ★★★ **1** a broken object has been damaged with the result that it is in two or more pieces: *Nearly all the houses had broken windows.* **2** if a piece of equipment is broken, it is not working correctly: *You can't use the microwave – it's broken.*

broken-hearted /ˌbrəʊkən 'hɑːtɪd/ adj extremely sad

brother /'brʌðə/ noun [C] ★★★ a boy or man who has the same parents as you: *his younger/older/little/big brother*

brother-in-law /ˈbrʌðə(r)ɪnˌlɔː/ noun [C] **1** your sister's husband **2** the brother of your husband or wife

browser /ˈbraʊzə/ noun [C] a computer program that allows you to use the Internet

builder /ˈbɪldə/ noun [C] someone whose job is to build and repair houses

building /ˈbɪldɪŋ/ noun [C] ★★★ a structure such as a house that has a roof and walls: *The town hall was a large, impressive building.*

bully /ˈbʊli/ noun [C] someone who uses their strength or status to threaten or frighten people verb [T] to frighten or hurt someone who is smaller or weaker than you

bunker /ˈbʌŋkə/ noun [C] a room with very strong walls that is built underground as a shelter against bombs

burglar /ˈbɜːglə/ noun [C] someone who enters a building illegally in order to steal things

burglary /ˈbɜːgləri/ noun [C/U] the crime of entering a building illegally in order to steal things

burgle /ˈbɜːg(ə)l/ verb [T] to enter a building illegally and steal things

burn /bɜːn/ verb [T] ★★★ **1** to damage or destroy something with fire: *Demonstrators burned flags outside the embassy.* **2** to injure someone or a part of your body with something hot: *The sand was so hot it burnt my feet.* **3** to put information onto a CD-ROM

bury /ˈberi/ verb [T] ★ to put something in the ground and cover it with earth: *There's supposed to be treasure buried around here.*

bush /bʊʃ/ noun [C] ★★ a plant that is smaller than a tree and has a lot of thin branches: *a holly/rose/currant bush*

business /ˈbɪznəs/ noun [U] ★★★ **1** the work of buying or selling products or services: *the music/fashion business* **2** the work that you do as your job: *a business trip*

busy /ˈbɪzi/ adj ★★★ **1** having a lot of things to do: *He is an extremely busy man.* **2** full of people or vehicles: *a busy main road*

butcher /ˈbʊtʃə/ noun [C] someone whose job is to sell meat. The shop they work in is called a butcher's or a butcher's shop.

butterfly /ˈbʌtəˌflaɪ/ noun [C] an insect with large colourful wings

button /ˈbʌt(ə)n/ noun [C] ★★ **1** a small object that you press to make a machine do something: *Press this button to start the computer.* **2** a small round object that is used for fastening clothes by pushing it through a hole: *He had undone the top button of his shirt.*

Cc

cable /ˈkeɪb(ə)l/ noun [C/U] **1** thick wire used for carrying electricity or electronic signals **2** strong thick metal rope

calculate /ˈkælkjʊˌleɪt/ verb [T] ★★ to discover a number or amount by using mathematics: *Calculate the size of the angle.*

calm /kɑːm/ adj ★★ **1** not affected by strong emotions: *a calm voice* **2** peaceful: *The city appears calm after last night's missile attack.*

camera /ˈkæm(ə)rə/ noun [C] ★★★ **1** a piece of equipment for taking photographs **2** a piece of equipment for making television programmes, films, or videos

camp /kæmp/ noun [C/U] ★★ a place where people go for a holiday that often has tents or other temporary shelters: *music camp*

cancer /ˈkænsə/ noun [U] ★ a serious illness that is caused when cells in the body increase in an uncontrolled way: *He died of lung cancer.*

candidate /ˈkændɪˌdeɪt, ˈkændɪdət/ noun [C] ★ one of the people who is competing in an election or competing for a job: *the Labour/Liberal/Conservative candidate*

canteen /kænˈtiːn/ noun [C] a room in a factory, school, or hospital where meals are served

capture /ˈkæptʃə/ verb [T] ★★ to catch a person or animal and stop them from escaping: *Most of the men had been either killed or captured.*

carbon dioxide /ˌkɑːbən daɪˈɒksaɪd/ noun [U] the gas that is produced when you breathe out

care /keə/ verb [I/T] ★★★ to be interested in someone or something and think that they are important: *Her son didn't care enough to come and visit her.*

career /kəˈrɪə/ noun [C] ★★ a job or profession that you work at for some time: *the problems of combining a career and a family*

caring /ˈkeərɪŋ/ adj kind, helpful and sympathetic towards other people

carpenter /ˈkɑːpɪntə/ noun [C] someone whose job is to make or repair wooden things

cartoon /kɑːˈtuːn/ noun [C] **1** a film or TV programme made by photographing a series of drawings so that things in them seem to move **2** a humorous drawing or series of drawings in a newspaper or magazine

case /keɪs/ noun [C] ★★★ a situation that involves a particular person or thing: *In the majority of cases, it's easy to keep costs down.*

cashier /kæˈʃɪə/ noun [C] someone whose job is to receive or give money to customers in a shop, bank etc

cast /kɑːst/ noun [C] **1** all the performers in a film, play etc **2** a hard cover for protecting a broken part of your body while it is getting better

catastrophic /ˌkætəˈstrɒfɪk/ adj causing a lot of damage, or making a lot of people suffer: *catastrophic floods*

catch /kætʃ/ verb [I/T] ★★★ **1** to stop something that is falling or moving through the air, and hold it: *Stewart caught the ball with one hand.* **2** to get on a train, bus, plane, or boat that is travelling somewhere: *I caught the next train to London.* verb [T] ★★★ **1** if the police catch someone, they find them and arrest them **2** to get a disease or illness: *Brian caught chickenpox from his nephew.*

catwalk /ˈkætˌwɔːk/ noun [C] the raised area at a fashion show that the models walk along

celebrate /ˈseləˌbreɪt/ verb [I/T] ★★ to do something enjoyable in order to show that an occasion or event is special: *Let's have a party to celebrate.*

celebrity /səˈlebrəti/ noun [C] ★ a famous entertainer or sports personality: *TV/sports celebrities*

century /ˈsentʃəri/ noun [C] ★★★ a period of 100 years, usually counted from a year ending in –00: *16th century paintings*

certainly /ˈsɜːt(ə)nli/ adv ★★★ **1** used for emphasising that something is definitely true or will definitely happen: *There certainly wasn't any point in going now.* **2** used for expressing agreement or for giving permission: *'We'd like you to explain your proposal to us in greater detail.' 'Certainly.'*

challenge /ˈtʃælɪndʒ/ noun [C/U] ★★ something that needs a lot of skill, energy, and determination to deal with or achieve: *I felt I needed a new challenge at work.* verb [T] to invite someone to compete or fight: *The girls challenged the boys to a cricket match.*

champion /ˈtʃæmpiən/ noun [C] ★ someone who has won an important competition, especially in sport: *the world heavyweight boxing champion*

chance /tʃɑːns/ noun [C] ★★★ an opportunity to do something, especially something that you want to do: *Students are given the chance to learn another language.*

channel /ˈtʃæn(ə)l/ noun [C] ★★ a television station and the programmes that it broadcasts: *What's on the other channel?*

chapter /ˈtʃæptə/ noun [C] ★★★ one of the sections of a book: *See Chapter Three for more details.*

character /ˈkærɪktə/ noun [C] ★★★ a person in a book, play, film etc: *The film's main character is played by George Clooney.*

charity /ˈtʃærəti/ noun [C/U] ★★ an organisation that gives money and help to people who need it: *a registered charity*

chart /tʃɑːt/ noun [C] a list, drawing, or graph that shows information

chat /tʃæt/ verb [I] ★ **1** to talk in a friendly way: *They sat waiting, chatting about their families.* **2** to exchange messages with someone using computers, in a way that lets you see each other's messages immediately

chat show /ˈtʃæt ˌʃəʊ/ noun [C] a television or radio programme in which famous people talk about themselves and their work

C

C

cheap /tʃiːp/ adj ★★★ **1** not expensive: *People should have access to cheap, fresh food.* **2** not expensive and not of good quality: *cheap wine*

cheat /tʃiːt/ verb [I] ★ to behave dishonestly, or to not obey rules: *Kids have always found ways of cheating in school exams.*

check /tʃek/ verb [I/T] ★★★ to examine something in order to get information, or to find out whether it is good or correct: *Always check your spelling.* verb [T] ★★★ to give your bags and cases to an official at an airport so that they can be put on a plane: *How many bags do you have to check?*

checkout /ˈtʃekaʊt/ noun [C] the place where you pay in a supermarket or other large shop

cheek /tʃiːk/ noun [C] ★★ the soft part on each side of your face below your eyes: *Sarah kissed him on the cheek.*

cheer up /ˌtʃɪə(r) ˈʌp/ phr vb to become less sad, or to make someone feel less sad: *I tried to cheer him up, but he just kept staring out of the window.*

chef /ʃef/ noun [C] someone whose job is to cook food in a restaurant

chemical /ˈkemɪk(ə)l/ noun [C] ★★★ a substance used in chemistry, or one produced by a process that involves chemistry: *toxic chemicals*

chemist /ˈkemɪst/ noun [C] **1** a shop that sells medicines, beauty products, and toiletries **2** someone whose job is preparing and selling medicines in a chemist's shop **3** a scientist who studies chemistry

cheque /tʃek/ noun [C] ★ a piece of printed paper that you can use instead of money: *a cheque for £50*

chess /tʃes/ noun [U] a game that two people play on a board with black and white squares. The pieces that you use have different shapes and move in different ways.

chest /tʃest/ noun [C] ★★★ the upper front part of your body between your neck and your stomach: *a broad/hairy chest*

chewing gum /ˈtʃuːɪŋ ˌɡʌm/ noun [U] a type of sweet that you chew for a long time but do not swallow

child /tʃaɪld/ noun [C] ★★★ **1** a young person from the time when they are born until they are about 14 years old: *The nursery has places for 30 children.* **2** someone's son or daughter of any age: *All of our children are grown and married.*

childhood /ˈtʃaɪldˌhʊd/ noun [C/U] the time of your life when you are a child: *We spent our childhood in a small town in the mountains.*

childish /ˈtʃaɪldɪʃ/ adj behaving in a silly and annoying way, like a small child

chilly /ˈtʃɪli/ adj cold enough to be unpleasant: *The evenings are getting chilly.*

chip /tʃɪp/ noun [C] ★★ **1** a long thin piece of potato cooked in hot oil: *fish and chips* **2** a very small piece of silicon that is marked with electronic connections. It is used in computers and other machines **3** a small piece of something such as wood or glass that has broken off something: *wood chips*

choice /tʃɔɪs/ noun [singular/U] ★★★ the opportunity or right to choose between different things: *We try to provide greater choice for our customers.* noun [C] ★★★ a decision to choose someone or something: *He was facing a difficult choice between staying with his family or working abroad.*

choke /tʃəʊk/ verb [I/T] if you choke, or if something chokes you, you cannot breathe because there is not enough air, or because something is blocking your throat: *Joe took a bite of the steak and started to choke.* verb [T] to squeeze someone's neck so that they cannot breathe

chop /tʃɒp/ noun [C] a small piece of meat with a bone in it: *lamb/pork chops* verb [T] to cut something such as food or wood into pieces: *Chop the meat into small cubes.*

christening /ˈkrɪs(ə)nɪŋ/ noun [C] a religious ceremony during which a baby is made a member of the Christian religion and is given a name

citizen /ˈsɪtɪz(ə)n/ noun [C] ★★ someone who lives in a particular country, town or city: *the citizens of Edinburgh*

clear /klɪə/ adj ★★★ **1** obvious and certain to be true: *It appears to be a clear case of discrimination.* **2** easy to understand: *Clear instructions are provided.* **3** transparent: *a clear glass bottle*

clever /ˈklevə/ adj ★★ good at learning or understanding things: *I'd like to be a doctor but I'm not clever enough.*

cliff /klɪf/ noun [C] the steep side of an area of high land

climb /klaɪm/ verb [I/T] ★★★ to use your hands and feet to move up, over, down, or across something: *He climbed onto the roof.*

close /kləʊs/ adj ★★★ **1** only a short distance away: *We can walk to the swimming pool – it's quite close.* **2** giving careful attention to every detail: *I'll take a closer look at it tomorrow.* **3** connected by shared feelings such as love and respect: *My brother and I are very close.*

clothing /ˈkləʊðɪŋ/ noun [U] ★ clothes: *a piece/item/article of clothing*

coach /kəʊtʃ/ noun [C] ★ **1** someone who trains a sports player or team: *a baseball coach* **2** a comfortable bus for long journeys verb [T] to train a sports player or team

coast /kəʊst/ noun [C] ★★ an area of land along the edge of a sea: *the east coast of England*

coin /kɔɪn/ noun [C] ★★★ a flat round piece of metal used as money: *Put a coin into the slot.*

cold /kəʊld/ adj ★★★ with a low temperature, or a temperature that is lower than normal: *The water was too cold for a shower.* noun [C] ★★ a minor illness that blocks your nose and makes you cough: *I didn't go to the game because I had a cold.*

combine /kəmˈbaɪn/ verb [I/T] ★★ if you combine things, or if they combine, they are used, done, or put together: *an attempt to combine the advantages of two systems*

come across /ˌkʌm əˈkrɒs/ phr vb to meet someone or find something by chance: *I came across a word I'd never seen before.*

comedy /ˈkɒmədi/ noun [C] ★ a funny film, play or television programme

comic /ˈkɒmɪk/ noun [C] a magazine that contains stories told in a series of drawings

commercial /kəˈmɜːʃ(ə)l/ adj ★ relating to the business of buying and selling goods and services: *One of their first commercial products was an electronic typewriter.* noun [C] an advertisement on television or radio

commit /kəˈmɪt/ verb [T] ★★★ to do something that is illegal or morally wrong: *The study aims to find out what makes people commit crimes.*

common /ˈkɒmən/ adj ★★★ happening frequently, or existing in large amounts or numbers: *Today smog is a common occurrence in many major cities.*

community /kəˈmjuːnəti/ noun [C] ★★★ the people who live in an area: *small rural communities*

company /ˈkʌmp(ə)ni/ noun [C] ★★★ an organisation that sells services or goods: *Max works for a large oil company.*

compartment /kəmˈpɑːtmənt/ noun [C] one of the separate parts of a container or place where things are stored

competition /ˌkɒmpəˈtɪʃ(ə)n/ noun [C] ★★★ **1** an organised event in which people try to win prizes by being better than other people: *He'd entered a competition in the local newspaper.* **2** the competition: the person, company, or thing that someone is competing with: *Let's look at what the competition is doing and do it better.*

complicated /ˈkɒmplɪˌkeɪtɪd/ adj ★★ difficult to do, deal with, or understand

compliment /ˈkɒmplɪmənt/ noun [C] something nice that you say to praise someone: *He kept paying me compliments on my cooking.* verb [T] to say something nice to or about someone: *Everybody complimented her on the way she handled the emergency.*

component /kəmˈpəʊnənt/ noun [C] ★ a part of a machine or piece of equipment

composer /kəmˈpəʊzə/ noun [C] someone who writes music

compulsory /kəmˈpʌlsəri/ adj ★ something that is compulsory must be done or used because of a rule or law: *compulsory exams*

concentrate /ˈkɒns(ə)nˌtreɪt/ verb [I/T] ★★★ to give all your attention to the thing that you are doing: *Shh! I'm trying to concentrate.*

condition /kənˈdɪʃ(ə)n/ noun [singular/U] ★★★ the physical state of something or someone: *Engineers will examine the condition of the damaged buildings.* noun [C] ★★★ an illness or health problem that lasts a long time and affects the way you live: *a heart condition*

conference /ˈkɒnf(ə)rəns/ noun [C] ★★ a large meeting where people who are interested in a particular subject discuss ideas: *a conference hall/room/centre*

confident /ˈkɒnfɪd(ə)nt/ adj ★★★ certain about your abilities and not nervous or frightened: *a confident mood/smile/manner*

confused /kənˈfjuːzd/ adj ★ unable to understand something or think clearly about it: *She was completely confused.*

confusing /kənˈfjuːzɪŋ/ adj ★ not easy to understand: *She left a very confusing message.*

confusion /kənˈfjuːʒ(ə)n/ noun [U] ★ a feeling that you do not understand something or cannot decide what to do: *There seems to be some confusion about who actually won.*

congratulation /kənˌɡrætʃʊˈleɪʃ(ə)n/ noun [plural] ★ congratulations: used for telling someone that you are pleased about their success, good luck, or happiness on a special occasion: *'I've passed my driving test.' 'Congratulations!'* noun [U] ★ an expression of pleasure to someone for their success, good luck, or happiness on a special occasion: *We had thousands of letters of congratulation.*

connected /kəˈnektɪd/ adj **1** related to each other: *Were the two deaths connected?* **2** joined to each other or to something else: *connected underground tunnels*

connection /kəˈnekʃ(ə)n/ noun [C] ★★★ **1** a relationship between things or people: *I don't see a connection between the two cases.* **2** a train, bus, or plane that allows you to continue a journey: *My train was late and I missed my connection.*

consequence /ˈkɒnsɪkwəns/ noun [C] ★★★ a result or effect of something: *Climate change could have disastrous consequences.*

conservative /kənˈsɜːvətɪv/ adj ★ **1** not willing to accept much change: *The small farming communities tend to be very conservative.* **2** conservative clothing or styles are traditional

consider /kənˈsɪdə/ verb [I/T] ★★★ to think about something carefully before you make a decision: *The jury went out to consider its verdict.* verb [T] ★★★ to have a particular opinion about someone or something: *We all considered him a hero.*

consist of /kənˈsɪstəv/ verb to be made of particular parts or things: *Breakfast consisted of dry bread and a cup of tea.*

consonant /ˈkɒnsənənt/ noun [C] ★ any letter of the English alphabet except for 'a', 'e', 'i', 'o', and 'u'

constant /ˈkɒnstənt/ adj ★★ **1** continuous or regular over a long period of time: *the constant noise of traffic* **2** continuing at the same rate, level, or amount over a particular period of time: *Maintain a constant speed.*

contain /kənˈteɪn/ verb [T] ★★★ to have something inside: *boxes containing toys and books*

contest /ˈkɒntest/ noun [C] a competition: *a writing contest*

convenient /kənˈviːniənt/ adj ★★ easy for you to do, or suitable for your needs: *If it's convenient, call me tomorrow.*

convention /kənˈvenʃ(ə)n/ noun [C/U] ★★ a way of behaving that is generally accepted as normal and right: *social conventions* noun [C] ★★ a large meeting of people from a particular profession or organisation

convict /ˈkɒnvɪkt/ noun [C] someone who is in prison because they have committed a crime

convict /kənˈvɪkt/ verb [T] ★ to prove in a court of law that someone is guilty of a crime: *There wasn't enough evidence to convict her.*

cook /kʊk/ verb [I/T] ★★★ to prepare and heat food so that it is ready to eat: *What's the best way to cook fish?* noun [C] someone who cooks food, either as their job or for pleasure

cookbook /ˈkʊkˌbʊk/ noun [C] a cookery book

cookery /ˈkʊk(ə)ri/ noun [U] the skill or activity of preparing or cooking food

cool /kuːl/ adj ★★★ fairly cold: *The water was wonderfully cool and refreshing.* **2** fashionable and attractive: *one of Britain's coolest young designers* **3** good or enjoyable: *The restaurant was really cool.*

corner /ˈkɔːnə/ noun [C] ★★★ **1** the part of an object, space, or room where two edges or sides meet: *The baby banged his head on the corner of the table.* **2** a place where two roads meet, or where there is a sharp bend in the road: *I get my newspaper from the shop on the corner.*

cost /kɒst/ noun [C/U] ★★★ the amount of money that you need in order to buy something or to do something: *The cost of basic foods has risen dramatically.*

cosy /ˈkəʊzi/ adj warm and comfortable, relaxing or friendly

cough /kɒf/ noun [C] an illness in which you cough a lot and your throat hurts verb [I] ★ to force air up through your throat with a sudden noise, especially when you have a cold or when you want to get someone's attention: *My chest felt painful, and I was coughing uncontrollably.*

count /kaʊnt/ verb [I/T] ★★★ to calculate how many people or things there are in a group: *All the votes have been counted.* verb [I] ★★★ to say numbers one after another in order: *I can count up to ten in German.*

country /ˈkʌntri/ noun [C] ★★★ an area of land that has its own government and official borders: *We have offices in 15 European countries.* noun [singular] ★★★ the country: areas away from towns and cities, consisting of fields, farms, villages etc: *We went for a picnic in the country.*

countryside /ˈkʌntriˌsaɪd/ noun [U] ★★ areas away from towns and cities, with farms, fields and trees

couple /ˈkʌp(ə)l/ noun [singular] ★★★ two things or people of the same type: *'Has he had any serious girlfriends?' 'A couple.'* noun [C] ★★★ two people who are married to each other, or who have a romantic relationship with each other

course /kɔːs/ noun [C] ★★★ a series of lessons or lectures in an academic subject or a practical skill: *a drama/secretarial/Spanish course* **2** one of the parts of a meal: *We both chose fish as our main course.* **3** an area where a race or sport takes place: *a golf/race course*

cousin /ˈkʌz(ə)n/ noun [C] ★★ a child of your uncle or aunt

cover /ˈkʌvə/ noun [C] ★★★ **1** something that you put over something else in order to hide it, protect it, or close it: *She put plastic covers on all the furniture.* **2** the outside page on the front or back of a book or magazine: *Her face was once on the cover of Vogue magazine.* verb [T] ★★★ to put one thing over another in order to protect or hide it: *Cover the food until you are ready to eat it.*

cowboy /ˈkaʊˌbɔɪ/ noun [C] a man whose job is to look after cows on a ranch in the US

crash /kræʃ/ noun [C] ★ an accident that happens when a vehicle hits something: *He was seriously injured in a car crash.* **2** a loud noise like the sound of things hitting each other and breaking **3** an occasion when a computer or a computer program suddenly stops working

creative /kriˈeɪtɪv/ adj ★ having a lot of imagination and new ideas: *The programme offers children the chance to be creative.*

credit /ˈkredɪt/ noun [U] ★★ an arrangement to receive money from a bank, or receive goods from a shop, and to pay for them later: *I don't like buying things on credit.* noun [plural] ★★ the credits: a list at the beginning or end of a film or television programme that shows the people who were involved in making it

credit card /ˈkredɪt ˌkɑːd/ noun [C] a small plastic card that you use to buy things now and pay for them later

critic /ˈkrɪtɪk/ noun [C] ★ someone whose job is to give their opinions about things such as books, films or plays

criticise /ˈkrɪtɪˌsaɪz/ verb [I/T] ★★ to say what you think is wrong or bad about something: *We were told not to criticise the policy publicly.*

cross /krɒs/ adj angry

cross out /ˌkrɒs ˈaʊt/ phr vb to draw an X or a line through writing because it is wrong, or because you want to write something else

crossroads /ˈkrɒsˌrəʊdz/ noun [C] a place where one road crosses another

crossword /ˈkrɒsˌwɜːd/ noun [C] a word game in which the answers to questions are written in rows of squares that cross each other

cruelty /ˈkruːəlti/ noun [C/U] cruel behaviour: *cruelty to children/animals*

cruise /kruːz/ noun [C] a journey on a ship for pleasure, often visiting a series of places

cup /kʌp/ noun [C] ★★★ a small round container for a drink, usually with a handle: *She filled my cup with hot tea.*

cure /kjʊə/ noun [C] ★ **1** a medicine or treatment that makes someone who is ill become healthy: *Doctors say there are several possible cures.* **2** a solution to a problem: *It's the only possible cure for high unemployment.*

curly /ˈkɜːli/ adj forming curves: *curly hair*

D

customer /ˈkʌstəmə/ noun [C] ★★★ a person or company that buys goods or services: *Supermarkets use a variety of tactics to attract customers.*

cut down /ˌkʌt ˈdaʊn/ phr vb to cut through a tree and make it fall to the ground

cutlery /ˈkʌtləri/ noun [U] the knives, forks, and spoons that you use for eating food

cutting-edge /ˌkʌtɪŋˈedʒ/ adj extremely modern and advanced: *cutting-edge technology*

CV /ˌsiː ˈviː/ noun [C] curriculum vitae: a document that gives details of your qualifications and the jobs you have had

cycle /ˈsaɪk(ə)l/ verb [I] to go somewhere on a bicycle

cyclist /ˈsaɪklɪst/ noun [C] someone who rides a bicycle

Dd

daffodil /ˈdæfədɪl/ noun [C] a tall yellow flower that grows in spring

damage /ˈdæmɪdʒ/ noun [U] ★★★ negative effects on someone or something: *The damage to the bank's image is extremely serious.* verb [T] ★★★ to harm something physically: *Many buildings had been damaged in the blast.*

dangerous /ˈdeɪndʒərəs/ adj ★★★ likely to cause serious harm, or to have a bad effect: *a dangerous dog*

dark /dɑːk/ adj ★★★ **1** with very little or no light: *a dark and stormy night* **2** close to black in colour: *He was dressed in a dark suit.*

darkness /ˈdɑːknəs/ noun [U] the lack of light: *The front rooms were all in darkness.*

data /ˈdeɪtə, ˈdɑːtə/ noun [U] ★★★ information that is used for making calculations or decisions: *The document contained data from tests of biological weapons.*

database /ˈdeɪtəˌbeɪs/ noun [C] a large amount of information that is stored in a computer in an organised way

daughter /ˈdɔːtə/ noun [C] ★★★ your female child

deadly /ˈdedli/ adj capable of killing people: *This is a potentially deadly disease.*

death /deθ/ noun [C/U] ★★★ the end of someone's life: *Sandra was very close to death.*

decision /dɪˈsɪʒ(ə)n/ noun [C] ★★★ a choice that you make after you have thought carefully about something: *The committee will make a decision by the end of the week.*

defend /dɪˈfend/ verb [T] ★★ **1** to protect someone or something from attack: *Can the military defend the city against attack?* **2** to try to prevent your team's opponents from scoring

definitely /ˈdef(ə)nətli/ adv ★★ **1** without any doubt: *I'm definitely going to Ben's party.* **2** used for emphasising that you mean 'yes': *'So we'll see you on Sunday at 7 o'clock?' 'Definitely!'*

deforestation /diːˌfɒrɪˈsteɪʃ(ə)n/ noun [U] the process of removing the trees from an area of land

delay /dɪˈleɪ/ noun [C/U] ★★ a situation in which something happens later or more slowly than you expected: *After a long delay, the plane finally took off.* verb [I/T] ★ to do something later than is planned or expected: *They delayed the decision for as long as possible.*

delete /dɪˈliːt/ verb [T] to remove something that has been written, recorded, or stored in a computer: *I deleted the file by mistake.*

deliberately /dɪˈlɪb(ə)rət(ə)li/ adv ★ with a definite intention, and not by chance or by accident: *Police believe the fire was started deliberately.*

delivery /dɪˈlɪv(ə)ri/ noun [C/U] ★★ **1** the process of bringing goods, letters or a service to a place or person: *Please allow ten days for delivery.* **2** the process of giving birth to a baby

demonstration /ˌdemənˈstreɪʃ(ə)n/ noun [C] ★★ an occasion when people protest about something in public: *Angry students held demonstrations.* noun [C/U] ★★ an occasion when someone shows how something works or how to do something: *cookery demonstrations*

department store /dɪˈpɑːtmənt ˌstɔː/ noun [C] a large shop that is divided into separate sections, with each section selling a different type of thing

depend on /dɪˈpend ˌɒn/ phr vb **1** if one thing depends on another, it is changed or affected by the other thing: *Their future depends on how well they do in these exams.* **2** to need someone or something in order to continue to exist or to be successful: *The project's success depends on the support of everyone concerned.* **3** if you can depend on someone to do something, you can trust them to do it: *I knew I could depend on you.*

depressing /dɪˈpresɪŋ/ adj making you feel very unhappy and without any feelings of hope or enthusiasm

description /dɪˈskrɪpʃ(ə)n/ noun [C] ★★★ a statement about what someone or something is like: *a brief description of the area*

desert /ˈdezət/ noun [C/U] ★★ a large area of land with few plants and dry weather

desert island /ˌdezət ˈaɪlənd/ noun [C] a small tropical island with no people living on it

design /dɪˈzaɪn/ noun [C/U] ★★★ the way that something is made so that it works and looks a certain way, or a drawing that shows what it will look like: *The car has a new design.* noun [C] ★★★ a pattern that decorates something: *simple geometric designs* verb [T] ★★★ to decide how something will be made, how it will work, or what it will look like, and often to make drawings of it: *The bride wore a dress that she designed herself.*

designer /dɪˈzaɪnə/ noun [C] ★ someone whose job is to decide how to make things, how they will work, and what they will look like: *a fashion designer*

dessert /dɪˈzɜːt/ noun [C/U] ★ sweet food that you eat after the main part of a meal

destination /ˌdestɪˈneɪʃ(ə)n/ noun [C] ★ the place where someone or something is going

destroy /dɪˈstrɔɪ/ verb [T] ★★★ to damage or harm something so severely that it cannot exist as it was before: *An earthquake destroyed the town.*

destruction /dɪˈstrʌkʃ(ə)n/ noun [U] ★ damage that is so severe that something cannot exist as it was before: *the destruction of the environment*

destructive /dɪˈstrʌktɪv/ adj causing severe damage or harm

detail /ˈdiːteɪl/ noun [C/U] ★★★ one of many small facts or pieces of information relating to a situation: *No details of the offer were revealed.* noun [U] ★★★ all the small aspects or features that something has, especially when they are difficult to notice: *Attention to detail is important in this job.*

develop /dɪˈveləp/ verb [I/T] ★★★ **1** to change, grow or improve, or to make something grow, change or improve: *All children develop at different rates.* verb [T] ★★★ **2** to create a new product or method: *We've recently developed new communications software.* **3** to treat a film with chemicals in order to make photographs

dial /ˈdaɪəl/ noun [C] **1** the round part of a clock, watch or machine that has numbers on it **2** a round control on a piece of equipment that you turn to change something verb [I/T] to press the buttons or turn the dial on a telephone in order to call someone

diameter /daɪˈæmɪtə/ noun [C/U] a straight line that crosses a circle through the centre, or the length of this line

dictionary /ˈdɪkʃən(ə)ri/ noun [C] a book that gives an alphabetical list of words with their meanings or their translations

difference /ˈdɪfrəns/ noun [C/U] ★★★ something that makes one person or thing not the same as another person or thing: *cultural/social/political differences* noun [C] ★★★ the amount by which one thing is different from another thing: *The same car costs £500 less here which is quite a difference!*

difficult /ˈdɪfɪk(ə)lt/ adj ★★★ not easy to do, deal with, or understand: *Choosing the winner was a difficult task.*

difficulty /ˈdɪfɪk(ə)lti/ noun [C] ★★★ a problem: *Many students have serious financial difficulties.* noun [U] ★★★ the degree to which something is difficult: *The courses vary in content and difficulty.*

dimension /daɪˈmenʃ(ə)n/ noun [C] length, height or width

dip into /ˌdɪp ˈɪntuː/ phr vb to read different parts of a book, but not the whole book

director /dəˈrektə, daɪˈrektə/ noun [C] ★★★ **1** someone whose job is to tell the actors and technical staff who are involved in a film, play or programme what to do **2** someone whose job is to manage all or part of a company, organisation or institution: *the finance/marketing/personnel director*

disability /ˌdɪsəˈbɪləti/ noun [C/U] a condition in which someone is not able to use a part of their body or brain normally: *children with learning disabilities*

disadvantage /ˌdɪsədˈvɑːntɪdʒ/ noun [C] ★ something that makes someone or something less effective, successful or attractive: *One of the disadvantages of the job is the long hours I work.*

disagree /ˌdɪsəˈgriː/ verb [I] ★ to have a different opinion from someone else: *Teenagers and their parents often disagree.*

disagreement /ˌdɪsəˈgriːmənt/ noun [C/U] ★ a situation in which people do not agree: *Bowen resigned from the club following a disagreement with the head coach.*

disappear /ˌdɪsəˈpɪə/ verb [I] ★★★ to no longer happen or exist: *The symptoms should disappear within a few days.*

disappointed /ˌdɪsəˈpɔɪntɪd/ adj ★ unhappy because something did not happen or because someone or something was not as good as you expected: *She was disappointed that he never replied to her letter.*

disappointing /ˌdɪsəˈpɔɪntɪŋ/ adj not as good as you had hoped or expected: *This year's sales figures were very disappointing.*

disaster /dɪˈzɑːstə/ noun [C/U] ★ **1** something very bad that happens and causes a lot of damage or kills a lot of people: *A series of disasters forced the company to close down.* **2** a very bad or annoying situation, or a complete failure: *Our party was a complete disaster.*

disastrous /dɪˈzɑːstrəs/ adj very bad, harmful or unsuccessful: *The spending cuts would be disastrous for schools.*

discipline /ˈdɪsəˌplɪn/ noun [U] ★★ the practice of making people obey rules and punishing them if they do not: *He believes in strict discipline.*

discourse /ˈdɪskɔːs/ noun [C] a long serious speech or piece of writing on a particular subject

discover /dɪˈskʌvə/ verb [T] ★★★ to find something that was hidden or that no one knew about before: *William Herschel discovered Uranus in 1781.*

discovery /dɪˈskʌv(ə)ri/ noun [C] ★★ something that is found, or something new that is learned: *This is one of the most important archeological discoveries of the century.*

discuss /dɪˈskʌs/ verb [T] ★★★ to write or talk about a subject in detail: *The causes of stress have already been discussed in Chapter 3.*

disgusted /dɪsˈgʌstɪd/ adj **1** feeling very angry and upset about something that you do not approve of: *I was disgusted by the way he treated those women.* **2** feeling physically ill because something is extremely unpleasant to see, smell or taste

disgusting /dɪsˈgʌstɪŋ/ adj **1** extremely unpleasant **2** very bad or shocking

dishonest /dɪsˈɒnɪst/ adj willing to do things that are not honest

dislike /dɪsˈlaɪk/ verb [T] ★ to not like someone or something: *She knew Philip disliked her.*

disobey /ˌdɪsəˈbeɪ/ verb [I/T] to deliberately not pay attention to a rule or an order from someone in authority

disorganised /dɪsˈɔː(r)gənaɪzd/ adj **1** not arranged according to a clear plan or system **2** someone who is disorganised does not deal with things in a clear or sensible way

display /dɪˈspleɪ/ noun [C] ★★ **1** an arrangement of things for people to look at: *a window display* **2** a performance for people to look at: *a firework display* verb [T] ★★ to put something in a particular place so that people can see it easily: *She displayed some of her paintings at the local arts festival.*

disqualify /dɪsˈkwɒlɪˌfaɪ/ verb [T] to not allow someone to take part in something, usually because they have done something wrong

dissatisfied /dɪsˈsætɪsˌfaɪd/ adj annoyed because something is not as good as you expected it to be: *a dissatisfied customer*

distance /ˈdɪstəns/ noun [C/U] ★★★ the amount of space between two people or things: *the distance from the Earth to the sun*

distant /ˈdɪstənt/ adj ★ far away from the place where you are: *the distant sound of traffic*

divide /dɪˈvaɪd/ verb [I/T] ★★★ to separate into groups or parts, or to make people or things separate into groups or parts: *Divide the class into three groups.*

diving /ˈdaɪvɪŋ/ noun [U] **1** the activity or sport of swimming deep under water **2** the activity or sport of jumping into water with your head first and your arms stretched out in front of you

divorce /dɪˈvɔːs/ noun [C/U] ★ a legal way of ending a marriage: *I want a divorce.*

divorced /dɪˈvɔːst/ adj ★ no longer married because your marriage has been legally ended: *a divorced mother of three*

dizzy /ˈdɪzi/ adj feeling that the things around you are spinning and that you are going to fall

document /ˈdɒkjʊmənt/ noun [C] ★★★ **1** a piece of paper or a set of papers containing official information: *He refused to sign the documents.* **2** a computer file that you can write in: *The program will automatically save any documents you have open.*

documentary /ˌdɒkjʊˈment(ə)ri/ noun [C] a film or television programme that deals with real people and events

doll /dɒl/ noun [C] a children's toy in the shape of a small person

download /ˌdaʊnˈləʊd/ verb [I/T] to move information to your computer from a computer system or from the Internet

drag /dræg/ verb [T] ★ **1** to pull something along with difficulty, especially something heavy: *She dragged her suitcase down the path.* **2** to move something across a computer screen using the mouse

dragon /ˈdrægən/ noun [C] in stories, an imaginary large animal that breathes out fire

drama /ˈdrɑːmə/ noun [C] ★ a play for the theatre, television, or radio noun [U] ★ plays in general or as a subject that you study: *He teaches drama.*

dress up /ˌdres ˈʌp/ phr vb to put on clothes that make you look like someone else, for fun: *They had dressed up as princes and princesses.*

driver /ˈdraɪvə/ noun [C] ★★★ someone who drives a vehicle, especially as their job: *a taxi driver*

drought /draʊt/ noun [C/U] a long period of time when there is little or no rain

drug /drʌg/ noun [C] ★★★ **1** an illegal substance that affects someone physically or mentally when they put it into their body: *drug smuggling* **2** a substance that a doctor gives you in order to treat a disease or medical problem: *Your doctor may prescribe drugs for this condition.*

dry /draɪ/ adj ★★★ **1** something that is dry has little or no water or other liquid inside or on it: *Are your hands dry?* **2** with no rain: *warm dry places like southern Spain* verb [T] ★★ to remove the water from something by wiping it, heating it, or blowing air onto it: *We washed and dried all the sheets.*

dub /dʌb/ verb [T] to change the sound in a film by replacing the original speech with words spoken in a different language

Dutch /dʌtʃ/ adj **1** someone who is Dutch is from the Netherlands **2** relating to the Netherlands, or to the language and culture of the Netherlands

DVD /ˌdiː viː ˈdiː/ noun [C] an object like a CD that has a film or television programme recorded on it

dynamic /daɪˈnæmɪk/ adj very lively and enthusiastic, with a lot of energy and determination: *dynamic leadership*

D

Ee

ear /ɪə/ noun [C] ★★★ one of the two parts at the sides of your head that you hear with

earache /ˈɪəreɪk/ noun [C/U] pain in your ear

earthquake /ˈɜːθˌkweɪk/ noun [C] a sudden shaking movement of the ground

E

east /iːst/ noun [U] ★★★ the direction that is in front of you when you are facing the rising sun: *driving from east to west* noun [singular] the East: the eastern part of the world, especially China and Japan

easygoing /ˌiːziˈɡəʊɪŋ/ adj relaxed, calm, and not easy to upset

eclipse /ɪˈklɪps/ noun [C] a short period when all or part of the Sun or Moon becomes dark: *a total eclipse of the Sun is when all of the Sun is dark*

economist /ɪˈkɒnəmɪst/ noun [C] an expert in economics

effective /ɪˈfektɪv/ adj ★★★ working well and producing the result that was intended: *You need more effective communication within the organisation.*

efficient /ɪˈfɪʃ(ə)nt/ adj ★★ working well and producing good results by using the available time, money, supplies etc in the most effective way: *The new machine is far more efficient than the old one.*

effort /ˈefət/ noun [singular/U] ★★★ physical or mental energy needed to do something: *Writing a book takes a lot of time and effort.*

elbow /ˈelbəʊ/ noun [C] ★★ the part in the middle of your arm, where it bends: *She sat with her elbows on the table.*

electronic /ˌelekˈtrɒnɪk/ adj ★★ using electricity and extremely small electrical parts such as microchips: *an electronic calculator*

elf /elf/ noun [C] a small imaginary person with magic powers

email address /ˈiːmeɪl əˌdres/ noun [C] an individual name that you use to receive email on the Internet

embarrassed /ɪmˈbærəst/ adj ★ feeling slightly ashamed, and worried about what other people will think of you: *She looked embarrassed when we asked her about her boyfriend.*

embarrassing /ɪmˈbærəsɪŋ/ adj ★ making you feel nervous, ashamed or stupid: *an embarrassing situation*

emergency /ɪˈmɜːdʒ(ə)nsi/ noun [C] ★★ an unexpected situation in which immediate action is necessary, often because there is danger: *The club is now facing a financial emergency.*

employer /ɪmˈplɔɪə/ noun [C] ★★ a person or organisation that pays workers to work for them: *The factory is the largest single employer in the area.*

enclose /ɪnˈkləʊz/ verb [T] to send something such as a document with a letter: *Please enclose a copy of your birth certificate with your application.*

encyclopedia /ɪnˌsaɪkləˈpiːdiə/ noun [C] a book or set of books that gives information about a lot of different subjects or one particular subject

end up /end ˈʌp/ phr vb to be in a place or state after doing something, or because of doing something: *Somehow they all ended up at my house.*

endangered species /ɪnˌdeɪndʒəd ˈspiːʃiːz/ noun [C] a type of animal or plant that may soon stop existing because not many of them are left in the world

enemy /ˈenəmi/ noun [C] ★★ someone who is opposed to someone else and tries to harm them: *They searched for information on political enemies.*

energy /ˈenədʒi/ noun [U] ★★★ **1** the power that your body needs in order to do physical things: *She didn't even have the energy to get out of bed.* **2** electricity and other forms of power used for making things work: *energy sources/supplies*

engaged /ɪnˈɡeɪdʒd/ adj ★ if two people are engaged, they have formally agreed to get married: *She's engaged to someone she met at work.*

engineer /ˌendʒɪˈnɪə/ noun [C] ★ someone who designs things such as roads, railways or machines

enjoyable /ɪnˈdʒɔɪəb(ə)l/ adj something that is enjoyable gives you pleasure: *an enjoyable evening*

enormous /ɪˈnɔːməs/ adj ★★ very large in size or quantity: *an enormous birthday cake*

enquire /ɪnˈkwaɪə/ verb [I/T] to ask someone for information about something: *I am writing to enquire whether you have any positions available.*

enter /ˈentə/ verb [I/T] ★★★ **1** to go or come into a place: *The man had entered through the back door.* **2** to arrange to be in a race or competition, or to arrange for someone else to do this: *The competition is free, and anyone over the age of 18 can enter.*

entertainment /ˌentəˈteɪnmənt/ noun [C/U] ★★ performances that people enjoy: *A jazz band provided entertainment for the evening.*

environment /ɪnˈvaɪrənmənt/ noun [C] ★★★ the place in which people live and work, including all the physical conditions that affect them: *Parents are responsible for providing the right environment for their children to learn in.* noun [singular] ★★★ the environment: the natural world, including the land, water, air, plants and animals: *Industrial development is causing widespread damage to the environment.*

environmental /ɪnˌvaɪrənˈment(ə)l/ adj ★★★ relating to the natural world and the effect that human activity has on it: *The Minister discussed environmental issues.*

environmentally friendly /ɪnvaɪrənˌmentəli ˈfrendli/ adj not harming the natural environment

episode /ˈepɪsəʊd/ noun [C] one part of a series in a television or radio story

equally /ˈiːkwəli/ adv ★★ in equal amounts or quantities: *The money raised will be divided equally among the charities.*

equipment /ɪˈkwɪpmənt/ noun [U] ★★★ the tools, machines or other things that you need for a particular job or activity: *camping equipment*

escape /ɪˈskeɪp/ verb [I] ★★ to get away from a dangerous or unpleasant place: *Three people died in the fire, but John escaped through the bedroom window.*

essential /ɪˈsenʃ(ə)l/ adj ★★★ basic and important: *food, fuel, and other essential supplies*

estate agent /ɪˈsteɪt ˌeɪdʒənt/ noun [C] someone whose job is to help people to buy, sell or rent property

everywhere /ˈevriˌweə(r)/ adv, conj, pron ★★★ used for talking about a very large area such as a region, a country or the whole world: *I'd like to thank all my fans everywhere for their support.*

evidence /ˈevɪd(ə)ns/ noun [U] ★★★ facts or physical signs that help to prove something: *The study found no evidence that fish feel pain.*

evil /ˈiːv(ə)l/ adj very bad or cruel: *a dangerous and evil dictator*

exactly /ɪɡˈzæk(t)li/ adv ★★★ no more and no less than a particular amount or time: *It's exactly three o'clock.*

except /ɪkˈsept/ conj, prep ★★★ used for introducing the only person, thing or fact that is not included in your main statement: *All the team were there except Eddie Stratton, who was ill.*

excited /ɪkˈsaɪtɪd/ adj ★★ very happy and enthusiastic because something good is going to happen: *I was so excited I couldn't sleep.*

excitement /ɪkˈsaɪtmənt/ noun [U] ★★ the feeling of being excited: *The long wait only added to our excitement.*

excursion /ɪkˈskɜːʃ(ə)n/ noun [C] a short journey that you make for pleasure

exhausted /ɪɡˈzɔːstɪd/ adj extremely tired and without enough energy to do anything else: *After two days of travel the children were completely exhausted.*

exhausting /ɪɡˈzɔːstɪŋ/ adj extremely tiring

exhibition /ˌeksɪˈbɪʃ(ə)n/ noun [C] ★★ a public show where art or other interesting things are put so that people can go and look at them: *an exhibition hall/centre/space*

exotic /ɪɡˈzɒtɪk/ adj interesting or exciting because of being unusual or not familiar

expect /ɪkˈspekt/ verb [T] ★★★ **1** to think that something will happen: *We're expecting good weather at the weekend.* **2** to think that it is right or reasonable that something should happen: *Our customers expect good service.*

expensive /ɪkˈspensɪv/ adj ★★★ something that is expensive costs a lot of money: *He always wears expensive clothes.*

experience /ɪkˈspɪəriəns/ noun [U] ★★★ knowledge and skill that you get by doing a particular job or activity: *You don't need any experience to work here.* noun [C] ★★★ something that happens to you, or a situation that you are involved in: *our childhood experiences*

experiment /ɪkˈsperɪmənt/ noun [C] ★★ a scientific test to find out what happens to someone or something in particular conditions: *laboratory experiments*

exploration /ˌekspləˈreɪʃ(ə)n/ noun [C/U] a journey around an area in order to learn about it or in order to search for something valuable such as oil

explore /ɪkˈsplɔː/ verb [I/T] ★★ to travel around an area in order to learn about it, or in order to search for something valuable such as oil: *The town is a good base from which to explore this part of Italy.*

export /ˈekspɔːt/ noun [C] ★★ a product that is sold to another country: *Agricultural produce is the country's largest export.*

export /ɪkˈspɔːt/ verb [I/T] ★ to send a product to another country so that it can be sold there: *Their flowers are exported around the world.*

expression /ɪkˈspreʃ(ə)n/ noun [C] ★★★ a word or phrase: *He uses childish expressions like 'easy-peasy'.*

extinct /ɪkˈstɪŋkt/ adj if something such as a type of animal or plant is extinct, it no longer exists

extra /ˈekstrə/ noun [C] something that is added to a basic service, product etc: *A virus checker is available as an optional extra for your computer.*

extracurricular /ˌekstrəkəˈrɪkjʊlə/ adj extracurricular activities are things that you do at school or college that are not part of your usual classes

F f

factor /ˈfæktə/ noun [C] ★★★ one of the things that influence whether an event happens or the way that it happens: *Several factors have contributed to the increase in the number of road accidents.*

factory /ˈfæktri/ noun [C] ★★★ a building where large quantities of goods are produced using machines: *She works in a factory.*

faint /feɪnt/ verb [I] to suddenly become unconscious for a short time

fair /feə/ adj ★★★ **1** if a situation is fair, everyone is treated equally and in a reasonable way: *free and fair elections* **2** fair hair is blonde or very light brown in colour

fairy tale /ˈfeəri ˌteɪl/ noun [C] a traditional children's story in which magic things happen

fall /fɔːl/ verb [I] ★★★ **1** to move quickly downwards from a higher position by accident: *I keep falling off my bike.* **2** to come down to the ground from the sky: *Snow began to quietly fall.*

fall in love /ˌfɔːl ɪn ˈlʌv/ phrase to start to love someone: *Why do we fall in love with one person rather than another?*

fall asleep /ˌfɔːl əˈsliːp/ phrase to start to go to sleep

familiar /fəˈmɪliə/ adj ★★ well known to you, or easily recognised by you: *People are more relaxed in familiar surroundings.*

famine /ˈfæmɪn/ noun [C/U] a serious lack of food that causes many people to become ill or to die

fantasy /ˈfæntəsi/ noun [C] a pleasant, exciting or unusual experience that you imagine is happening to you

FAQ /ˌef eɪ ˈkjuː/ noun [C] frequently asked questions: a list of typical questions that people ask and their answers

far /fɑː/ adj, adv ★★★ **1** used for talking about a long distance, or for asking or stating how great a distance is: *You can go outside and play, but don't go far.* **2** used for emphasising a difference when you are making a comparison: *The situation is bad in England, but it is far worse in Scotland.* **3** used for talking about the degree to which something happens or how extreme an action is: *The opinion polls show how far his popularity has fallen.*

F

farmer /ˈfɑːmə/ noun [C] someone who owns or manages a farm

fascinated /ˈfæsɪneɪtɪd/ adj very interested in, or attracted by, someone or something

fashion /ˈfæʃ(ə)n/ noun [U] ★★ **1** the activity or business that involves styles of clothes and people's appearance: *the world of fashion* **2** the state of being popular at a particular time: *High heels are back in fashion.*

fashion designer /ˈfæʃən dɪˌzaɪnə/ noun someone whose job is to decide how to make clothes or to decide their shape or appearance

fashionable /ˈfæʃ(ə)nəb(ə)l/ adj ★★ popular at a particular time: *fashionable clothes*

fast /fɑːst/ adj ★★★ moving, happening or doing something quickly: *Simon loves fast cars.*

fat /fæt/ adj ★★ a person or animal that is fat has too much flesh on their body and weighs too much: *She can eat whatever she likes and she never gets fat.* noun [U] ★ a soft white substance that you store in a layer under your skin

father-in-law /ˈfɑːðə(r)ɪnˌlɔː/ noun [C] the father of your husband or wife

fault /fɔːlt/ noun [C] ★★ **1** a feature that makes someone or something less good: *She has her faults, but on the whole she's very nice.* **2** a problem with a machine or piece of equipment that stops it from working correctly: *The fire was caused by an electrical fault.*

faulty /ˈfɔːlti/ adj not working correctly, or not made correctly: *faulty brakes*

fear /fɪə/ noun [U] ★★★ the feeling that you have when you are frightened: *She eventually managed to overcome her fear of the dark.* noun [C] ★★★ something bad or unpleasant that you are afraid might happen: *He expressed fears for his missing wife's safety.*

feature /ˈfiːtʃə/ noun [C] ★★★ an important part or aspect of something: *The latest model has a lot of new safety features.* verb [T] ★★ if something features a particular person or thing, they are an important part of it: *a concert featuring music by Haydn and Mozart*

fed up /ˌfed ˈʌp/ adj annoyed or bored with something that you feel you have accepted for too long: *I'm fed up with this job.*

fee /fiː/ noun [C] ★★ an amount of money that you pay to be allowed to do something such as join an organisation: *The gallery charges a small entrance fee.*

fever /ˈfiːvə/ noun [C/U] a medical condition in which the temperature of your body is very high

fiancé /fiˈɒnseɪ/ noun [C] the man that a woman is going to marry

fiancée /fiˈɒnseɪ/ noun [C] the woman that a man is going to marry

fiction /ˈfɪkʃ(ə)n/ noun [U] ★★ books and stories about imaginary events and people: *Hardy wrote poetry as well as fiction.*

fight /faɪt/ noun [C] ★★★ **1** a situation in which people hit each other: *He had a fight with a man in the pub.* **2** a situation in which people disagree or argue with each other: *All teenagers have fights with their parents.*

fill in /ˌfɪl ˈɪn/ phr vb to add information in the empty spaces on an official document: *Please fill in the application form.*

film /fɪlm/ noun [C] ★★★ moving pictures that tell a story: *Have you seen the new James Bond film?*

find out /ˌfaɪnd ˈaʊt/ phr vb to discover a fact or piece of information: *I don't want Jerry to find out about this.*

fine /faɪn/ noun [C] an amount of money that you must pay because you have broken the law: *I had to pay a $40 fine for parking on the street overnight.*

finger /ˈfɪŋgə/ noun [C] ★★★ the long thin parts on the end of your hands

fire /faɪə/ noun [C/U] ★★★ flames and heat from something that is burning in an uncontrolled way: *Lightning may have started the fire.* verb [I/T] ★★ if a weapon fires, or if someone fires it, someone uses it to shoot something: *The rebels fired their machine guns into the air.* verb [T] ★★ to make someone leave their job as a punishment: *She was fired for refusing to include the information in her report.*

firefighter /ˈfaɪəˌfaɪtə/ noun [C] someone whose job is to put out fires and help people to escape from other dangerous situations

fireplace /ˈfaɪəˌpleɪs/ noun [C] a place in a room where a fire burns

first aid /ˌfɜːst ˈeɪd/ noun [U] basic medical treatment that is given as soon as someone is injured or ill

fit /fɪt/ adj ★ healthy, strong and able to do physical exercise: *Running around after the kids keeps me fit.*

fitness /ˈfɪtnəs/ noun [U] the state of being physically healthy and strong: *a high level of physical fitness*

fizzy /ˈfɪzi/ adj a fizzy drink is a sweet drink without alcohol that has bubbles

flat /flæt/ adj ★★★ smooth and level on the surface, with no lumps or slopes: *The farmland is very flat.*

flatmate /ˈflætˌmeɪt/ noun [C] someone you share a flat with

flavour /ˈfleɪvə/ noun [C] ★ the particular taste that food or drink has: *The drink has a very strong citrus flavour.*

flick through /ˌflɪk ˈθruː/ phr vb to look quickly at the pages of a magazine or book.

flirt /flɜːt/ verb [I] to behave towards someone in a way that shows that you are sexually attracted to them

flood /flʌd/ noun [C/U] ★ a large amount of water that covers an area that was dry before: *The southwest of England has been badly hit by floods.*

floor /flɔː/ noun [C] ★★★ **1** the flat area that you walk on inside a building or room: *The house has polished wooden floors.* **2** one of the levels in a building: *a first-floor flat*

florist /ˈflɒrɪst/ noun [C] someone whose job is to arrange and sell flowers

flower /ˈflaʊə/ noun [C] ★★★ the coloured part of a plant from which the plant's seeds develop: *The plant has small white flowers.*

flu /fluː/ noun [U] a very common infectious disease that lasts for a short time and makes you feel weak and tired

fluent /ˈfluːənt/ adj able to speak a foreign language very well: *I'm fluent in three languages.*

fog /fɒg/ noun [U] thick clouds that form close to the ground and are difficult to see through

folder /ˈfəʊldə/ noun [C] **1** a thin flat container for sheets of paper **2** a group of programs or documents that are stored in a computer

following /ˈfɒləʊɪŋ/ noun [C] a group of people who support or admire another person or group

food poisoning /ˈfuːd ˌpɔɪzənɪŋ/ noun [U] an illness caused by eating food that contains harmful bacteria

foot /fʊt/ noun [C] ★★★ **1** the part of your body at the end of your leg, on which you stand: *He wiped his feet on the mat.* **2** a unit used for measuring length that is equal to 12 inches or about 30 centimetres: *We had over two feet of snow last night.*

football /ˈfʊtbɔːl/ noun [U] ★★ a game in which two teams of 11 players kick a ball and try to score goals noun [C] ★★ a ball used for playing football

footprint /ˈfʊtˌprɪnt/ noun [C] a mark made by a human or animal foot in a soft surface such as earth, snow or sand

footstep /ˈfʊtstep/ noun [C] the sound of a foot touching the ground as someone walks

force /fɔːs/ noun [U] ★★★ physical strength, violence or energy: *The force of the bomb blast shattered windows in 15 buildings.* verb [T] ★★★ to make something happen: *Opposition to the plans forced a rapid change of policy.*

forecast /ˈfɔːkɑːst/ verb [T] to make a statement about what is likely to happen, usually relating to the weather business, or the economy

foreign /ˈfɒrɪn/ adj ★★★ from another country, or in another country: *Working in a foreign country takes some getting used to.*

forest /ˈfɒrɪst/ noun [C/U] ★★★ a large area of land that is covered by trees and other plants growing close together

forgive /fəˈgɪv/ verb [T] ★ to decide to stop being angry with someone who has done something that is bad: *John has never forgiven himself for the accident.*

fortunate /ˈfɔːtʃənət/ adj lucky: *Not everyone is as fortunate as we are.*

forward /ˈfɔːwəd/ verb [T] to send a letter, parcel, email etc that has been sent to your address to someone else at another address

franc /fræŋk/ noun [C] the unit of money used in France and Belgium before the Euro replaced it and still used in Switzerland and some other countries

free /friː/ adj ★★★ **1** something that is free does not cost anything: *There is plenty of free parking.* **2** not held, tied or fixed somewhere: *Hand me the free end of the rope.* **3** not a prisoner or a slave: *He'll soon be a free man.* **4** available to see someone or do something: *I'm busy at the moment, but I'll be free this afternoon.*

freedom /ˈfriːdəm/ noun [U] ★★★ the right or opportunity to do what you want: *a law that restricts religious freedom*

frequent /ˈfriːkwənt/ adj ★ happening often: *Their arguments were becoming more and more frequent.*

fresh /freʃ/ adj ★★★ **1** clearly new and different: *We need a completely fresh approach to the problem.* **2** fresh food has not been preserved in any way: *You can use fresh or tinned tomatoes for this recipe.* **3** food that is fresh is still good to eat because it was prepared or produced recently: *Cooked meat will keep fresh for several days in the fridge.* **4** fresh water is water in lakes and rivers that does not contain any salt

fridge /frɪdʒ/ noun [C] ★ a piece of equipment that is used for storing food at low temperatures

friendship /ˈfren(d)ʃɪp/ noun [C/U] ★ a relationship between people who are friends: *Whatever happened, I did not want to lose Sarah's friendship.*

frightened /ˈfraɪt(ə)nd/ adj ★ feeling or showing fear: *The puppy looked cold and frightened.*

frightening /ˈfraɪt(ə)nɪŋ/ adj ★ making you feel afraid, nervous, or worried: *a frightening noise/thought/experience*

frustrating /ˈfrʌˌstreɪtɪŋ/ adj making you feel annoyed and impatient because you are prevented from achieving something: *It's frustrating to wait all day for a repairman who doesn't show up.*

full-time /ˌfʊlˈtaɪm/ adj done or doing something for the number of hours that people normally work or study in a complete week: *a full-time student*

fumes /fjuːmz/ noun [plural] smoke or gas that has an unpleasant smell and that may be harmful: *traffic/petrol fumes*

funeral /ˈfjuːn(ə)rəl/ noun [C] ★ a ceremony that takes place after someone dies, and the formal process of taking the body to the place where it is buried or cremated: *He flew home to arrange for his father's funeral.*

funny /ˈfʌni/ adj ★★★ **1** someone or something that is funny makes you laugh: *a funny story* **2** strange or unusual: *This tea tastes funny.*

fur /fɜː/ noun [U] the soft hair that covers the body of some animals

furious /ˈfjʊəriəs/ adj extremely angry: *Rosie was absolutely furious that I'd borrowed her car without asking.*

fussy /ˈfʌsi/ adj only satisfied if things are exactly as you want them to be

Gg

gadget /ˈgædʒɪt/ noun [C] a small tool or piece of equipment that does something that is useful or impressive

game show /ˈgeɪm ˌʃəʊ/ noun [C] a television programme in which people play games or answer questions in order to win prizes

gang /gæŋ/ noun [C] **1** a group of young people who spend time together and often cause trouble: *a study of Chicago street gangs* **2** a group of criminals working together: *a gang of thieves* **3** a group of friends

garage /ˈgærɑːʒ, ˈgærɪdʒ/ noun [C] ★ **1** a building for keeping a car in **2** a place that repairs or sells cars **3** a place where you go to buy petrol

gardener /ˈgɑː(r)d(ə)nə(r)/ noun [C] ★★ **1** someone whose job is to look after a garden: *the head gardener on an estate* **2** someone who enjoys growing plants and is good at it

general election /ˌdʒenrəl ɪˈlekʃən/ noun [C] an election in which every adult in the country can vote for the people who will represent them

generate /ˈdʒenəˌreɪt/ verb [T] ★★ to produce something, or to cause something to exist: *The food processing industry generates billions of dollars a year.*

generous /ˈdʒenərəs/ adj ★ giving people more of your time or money than is usual or expected: *She is a warm and generous human being.*

get /get/ verb [T] ★★★ **1** to obtain, receive, or be given something: *Ross's father got a new job.* **2** to buy something: *They had to stop and get some petrol.* **3** to go and bring something back from somewhere else: *She went and got a photograph from the desk.* **4** to start to have an idea or feeling: *I got a strange feeling as we walked towards the house.* **5** to start to have an illness or a medical condition: *I hope I don't get the flu this winter.* **6** to answer the door or phone: *It's OK, I'll get it.* verb [I] ★★★ to arrive at a place: *What time did you get home last night?*

get back /ˌget ˈbæk/ phr vb **1** to return to a place: *It's late, I ought to get back.* **2** to receive or have something again after a time when it was taken away from you or lost: *She left her briefcase on the train and she doesn't know how to get it back.*

get back together /ˌget bæk təˈgeðə/ phr vb [I] if two people who ended their sexual or romantic relationship get back together, they start having a relationship with each other again: *I kept hoping we would get back together.*

get behind /ˌget bɪˈhaɪnd/ phr vb if you get behind with work or payments, you have not done as much work or made as many payments as you should have done

get off /ˌget ˈɒf/ phr vb **1** to leave a bus, plane, or train **2** to have a particular period of time as a holiday: *Do you get much time off at Christmas?*

get on /ˌget ˈɒn/ phr vb **1** to continue doing something with more effort or more quickly than before: *Can we please get on, because there are a lot of things still to discuss.* **2** used for asking about or talking about how well someone has done a particular activity: *How did you get on in your exams?*

get out /ˌget ˈaʊt/ phr vb used for telling someone to leave: *The teacher screamed at him to get out.*

get (someone) ready /ˌget ˈredi/ phrase to prepare yourself or someone else to do something: *She's upstairs getting ready to go out.*

get rid of /ˌget ˈrɪd əv/ phrase to throw away, give away, or sell something that you no longer want or need: *We're moving, so we have to get rid of a lot of our furniture.*

get together /ˌget təˈgeðə/ phr vb if people get together, they meet in order to do something or in order to spend time together: *The whole family usually gets together at Christmas.*

get up /ˌget ˈʌp/ phr vb to get out of bed after sleeping: *He never gets up before nine.*

get well (soon) /ˌget ˈwel/ phrase used for giving good wishes to someone who is ill

ghost /gəʊst/ noun [C] the spirit of a dead person that someone believes that they can see or hear

giant /ˈdʒaɪənt/ adj extremely large: *a giant bronze statue*

give up /ˌgɪv ˈʌp/ phr vb **1** to stop trying to do something because it is too difficult: *I give up. Tell me the answer.* **2** to stop doing something that you do regularly: *I'm trying to give up smoking.* **3** to allow someone to have something that was yours: *The new arrangement would mean giving up some of their political independence.*

glass /glɑːs/ noun [U] ★★★ a hard clear substance that is used for making objects such as windows or bottles: *the sound of breaking glass* noun [C] ★★★ a small container made of glass that you use for drinking from, or the drink in it: *a wine/brandy/beer glass*

global warming /ˌgləʊbəl ˈwɔːmɪŋ/ noun [U] the increase in the temperature of the Earth that is caused partly by increasing amounts of carbon dioxide in the atmosphere

GM /ˌdʒiː ˈem/ adj genetically modified: used for describing crops whose genes have been changed, or for describing foods made from these crops

go out /ˌgəʊ ˈaʊt/ verb **1** to leave your house and go somewhere, especially to do something enjoyable: *I wanted the evenings free for going out with friends* **2** to have a relationship with someone and spend a lot of time with them: *How long have Rob and Sue been going out?*

goal /gəʊl/ noun [C] ★★★ **1** in games such as football, the net or structure that you try to get the ball into in order to score points **2** the action of putting a ball into a goal: *Nielsen scored two goals in the last ten minutes.*

good-looking /ˌgʊd ˈlʊkɪŋ/ adj physically attractive

government /ˈgʌv(ə)nmənt/ noun [C/U] ★★★ the people who control a country or area and make decisions about its laws and taxes: *The government has announced plans to raise the minimum wage next year.*

GPS /ˌdʒiː piː ˈes/ noun [U] global positioning system: a system for finding exactly where you are anywhere in the world using satellites

grade /greɪd/ noun [C] ★ **1** a level of quality or importance: *Their wool is suitable for finer grades of cloth.* **2** a letter or number that shows the quality of a student's work: *You need to improve your grades.*

graduate /ˈgrædʒuət/ noun [C] ★ someone who has a degree from a university: *careers for history graduates*

granddaughter /ˈgræn(d)ˌdɔːtə/ noun [C] the daughter of one of your children

grandfather /ˈgræn(d)ˌfɑːðə/ noun [C] ★ the father of one of your parents

grandmother /ˈgræn(d)ˌmʌðə/ noun [C] ★ the mother of one of your parents

grandson /ˈgræn(d)ˌsʌn/ noun [C] the son of one of your children

grant /grɑːnt/ noun [C] ★★ an amount of money that the government or an organisation gives you for a specific purpose and does not ask you to pay back: *a research grant*

grape /greɪp/ noun [C] a small green or purple fruit that grows in bunches on a vine and that is often used for making wine

graphic novel /ˌgræfɪk ˈnɒvəl/ noun [C] a novel that uses drawings to tell the story

grave /greɪv/ noun [C] ★ the place where a dead body is buried in a deep hole in the ground: *He's never even visited his mother's grave.*

greengrocer /ˈgriːnˌgrəʊsə/ noun [C] **1** greengrocer's: a shop that sells fruit and vegetables **2** someone whose job is to sell fruit and vegetables in a shop

greenhouse /ˈgriːnˌhaʊs/ noun [C] a building made of glass that is used for growing plants that need protection from the weather

greenhouse effect, the /ðə ˈgriːnhaʊs ɪˌfekt/ noun [singular] the situation in which heat is unable to escape from the atmosphere, which causes the temperature of the Earth to rise

gripping /ˈgrɪpɪŋ/ adj very exciting and interesting

groom /gruːm/ noun [C] a bridegroom

grow up /ˌgrəʊ ˈʌp/ phr vb to change from being a child to being an adult: *She's really starting to grow up now.*

G

guarantee /ˌgærən'tiː/ noun [C] ★ a promise that something will definitely happen: *I can't give you any guarantees at the moment.*

guard /gɑːd/ noun [C] ★★ **1** someone whose job is to protect a place or person: *a prison guard* **2** an official on a train whose job is to check tickets

guess /ges/ verb [I/T] ★★ to say or decide what you think is true, without being certain about it: *a competition to guess the weight of the pig*

guide /gaɪd/ noun [C] ★★ **1** a book that gives information: *It is worth buying a good travel guide.* **2** someone whose job is to give information to people who are visiting a place: *a tour guide* verb [T] ★ **1** to show someone where to go by going with them: *He guided them through the forest.* **2** to help someone to do something or make a decision: *There was no research to guide them.*

guidebook /'gaɪdˌbʊk/ noun [C] a book for tourists that provides information about a place

guilty /'gɪlti/ adj ★★ **1** ashamed and sorry because you have done something wrong: *a guilty look/expression* **2** someone who is guilty has committed a crime or has done something wrong: *Patrick knew that he was guilty of lying.*

H

gun /gʌn/ noun [C] ★★★ a weapon that shoots bullets or large shells: *Enemy guns fired a shell every two or three minutes.*

gym /dʒɪm/ noun [C] a room or club with equipment for doing physical exercises

Hh

habit /'hæbɪt/ noun [C/U] ★★ something that you do often: *healthy eating habits*

habitat /'hæbɪˌtæt/ noun [C] the type of place that an animal normally lives in or that a plant normally grows in

hairdresser /'heəˌdresə/ noun [C] someone whose job is to cut people's hair

half brother /'hɑːf ˌbrʌðə/ noun [C] a brother who has either the same mother or the same father as you have

half sister /'hɑːf ˌsɪstə/ noun [C] a sister who has either the same mother or the same father as you have

hand /hænd/ noun [C] ★★★ **1** the part of your body at the end of each arm that you use for holding things: *Mrs Bennet put her hands over her ears to shut out the noise.* **2** the hands on a clock are the long parts that move round and show the time

handbag /'hæn(d)ˌbæg/ noun [C] a small bag that women use for carrying personal things such as money and keys

handle /'hænd(ə)l/ noun [C] ★ the part of something that you use for holding it: *knives with plastic handles*

handsome /'hæns(ə)m/ adj ★★ a handsome man or boy has a very attractive face

handwriting /'hændˌraɪtɪŋ/ noun [U] the particular way that someone writes when they use a pen or pencil

hang out /ˌhæŋ 'aʊt/ phr vb to spend time in a particular place or with particular people: *She knew all the clubs where he usually hung out.*

happen /'hæpən/ verb [I] ★★★ to take place, usually without being planned: *The accident happened at 4.30 pm yesterday.*

happiness /'hæpinəs/ noun [U] the feeling of being happy

happy /'hæpi/ adj ★★★ feeling pleased and relaxed, with no worries: *The children seem very happy at school.*

harbour /'hɑːbə/ noun [C] an area of water next to the land where boats can stop

hard /hɑːd/ adj ★★★ **1** stiff, firm, and not easy to bend or break: *hard wooden benches* **2** difficult to do: *Some of the questions were very hard.* **3** strong and not easily frightened: *He likes to pretend he's hard, but he's really soft underneath.*

hard copy /'hɑːd ˌkɒpi/ noun [U] a printed copy of information that is held on a computer

hard drive /'hɑːd ˌdraɪv/ noun [C] a hard disk

hard hat /'hɑːd ˌhæt/ noun [C] a hat made of metal or hard plastic worn by workers to protect their heads

hardware /'hɑːdˌweə/ noun [U] computer equipment

hard-working /ˌhɑːd'wɜːkɪŋ/ adj putting a lot of effort into your work

harm /hɑːm/ verb [T] to injure, damage or have a bad effect on someone or something: *chemicals that harm the environment*

hay fever /'heɪˌfiːvə/ noun [U] a medical condition that affects your nose and eyes. It is caused by pollen.

head /hed/ noun [C] ★★★ **1** the top part of your body that has your brain, eyes, mouth etc in it: *Lynn had a bruise on the side of her head.* **2** the leader or most important person in a group: *the head waiter* **3** the teacher who is in charge of a school

headache /'hedeɪk/ noun [C] ★ a pain in your head: *I had a bad headache yesterday.*

headband /'hedˌbænd/ noun [C] a narrow piece of cloth that you wear around your head to keep hair or sweat out of your eyes

headlight /'hedˌlaɪt/ noun [C] one of the two lights on the front of a vehicle

headline /'hedˌlaɪn/ noun [C] the title of a newspaper story, printed in large letters

headphones /'hedˌfəʊnz/ noun [plural] a piece of equipment that you wear over your ears in order to listen to the radio or recorded sound

headquarters /ˌhed'kwɔːtez/ noun [plural] the place where a company, organisation or military unit has its main offices or its main centre of control

headteacher /ˌhed'tiːtʃə/ noun [C] a teacher who is in charge of a school

health /helθ/ noun [U] ★★★ the condition of your body, especially whether or not you are ill: *His health improved once he stopped working.*

health centre /'helθ ˌsentə/ noun [C] a building where people can go to see a doctor or nurse

healthy /'helθi/ adj ★★ **1** physically strong and not ill: *a healthy baby* **2** working well and likely to continue to be successful: *The country still has a healthy economy.*

heart attack /'hɑːt əˌtæk/ noun [C] an occasion when someone suddenly has a lot of pain because their heart stops working normally

heat /hiːt/ noun [singular/U] ★★★ the quality of being hot, or how hot something is: *We felt the intense heat from the fire.* verb [I/T] ★ to make something hot, or to become hot: *Heat the oil gently in a large frying pan.*

helmet /'helmɪt/ noun [C] a hard hat that you wear to protect your head

hide /haɪd/ verb [T] ★★★ to put something in a place so that no one can find it or see it: *She hid the key in the drawer.* verb [I] ★★★ to go somewhere or be somewhere where no one can find you or see you: *He ran and hid behind a bush.*

hill /hɪl/ noun [C] ★★★ an area of land that is higher than the land surrounding it but that is smaller and lower than a mountain: *They climbed slowly to the top of the hill.*

hit /hɪt/ verb [I/T] ★★★ **1** to move quickly against something, or to move an object quickly against something, touching it with force: *The glass smashed as it hit the ground.* **2** to move your hand or an object hard against someone's body, so that you hurt them: *Stop hitting your brother!*

hold /həʊld/ verb [T] ★★★ **1** to carry something or someone using your hands or arms: *Can you hold my bag for a moment?* **2** to organise something such as a meeting or event: *The government agreed to hold a referendum.*

home time /'həʊm ˌtaɪm/ noun [U] the end of the school day when the students go home

homely /'həʊmli/ adj simple and pleasant in a way that makes you feel comfortable and at home

honest /'ɒnɪst/ adj ★ **1** a person who is honest does not tell lies or cheat people, and obeys the law: *an honest man* **2** telling the truth, or not cheating people: *I want you to give me an honest answer.*

honeymoon /ˈhʌnɪˌmuːn/ noun [C] a holiday that two people take after they get married

hood /hʊd/ noun [C] the part of a coat or jacket that covers your head

hoodie /ˈhʊdi/ noun [C] a piece of clothing with a hood that you wear on the top part of your body, usually made of thick cotton. Some people think that young men wear hoodies because they are trying to hide their face when they carry out criminal activities.

hopeless /ˈhəʊpləs/ adj **1** if a situation is hopeless, it seems very unlikely to succeed or improve **2** not skilful at all: *I am hopeless at tennis.*

horrible /ˈhɒrəb(ə)l/ adj ★ very unpleasant or unkind: *I've had a horrible day at work.*

horror /ˈhɒrə/ noun [C/U] a strong feeling of shock or fear, or the thing that makes you feel shocked or afraid: *Millions watched in horror as the disaster unfolded on TV.* noun [U] a type of book or film that is intended to frighten people: *a horror story/film*

human /ˈhjuːmən/ noun [C] ★★ a person: *The disease can be fatal in humans.*

humid /ˈhjuːmɪd/ adj hot and wet in a way that makes you feel uncomfortable: *a humid climate*

hunger /ˈhʌŋgə/ noun [U] **1** the feeling that you have when you need to eat: *a nutritious snack that will satisfy your hunger* **2** a lack of food that can cause illness or death: *a new chance to fight world hunger and poverty*

hurt /hɜːt/ verb [I] ★★★ to feel pain somewhere in your body: *Fred's knees hurt after skiing all day.* verb [I/T] ★★★ to cause someone physical pain or injury: *You're hurting my arm!*

husband /ˈhʌzbənd/ noun [C] ★★★ the man that a woman is married to

hygiene /ˈhaɪdʒiːn/ noun [U] the practice of keeping yourself and the things around you clean in order to prevent illness and disease

I i

ice /aɪs/ noun [U] ★★ water that has frozen and become solid: *a block/lump of ice*

ice cap /ˈaɪs ˌkæp/ noun [C] a large area of ice that covers the land and sea around the North or South Pole

ideal /aɪˈdɪəl/ adj ★ of the best or most suitable type: *Upgrading your computer seems the ideal solution.*

identification /aɪˌdentɪfɪˈkeɪʃ(ə)n/ noun [U] something that proves who you are, especially a document with your name and a photograph: *Can you show me some identification?*

identify /aɪˈdentɪˌfaɪ/ verb [T] ★★★ to recognise someone and be able to say who they are: *One of the thieves has been identified by witnesses.* verb [T] ★★★ to recognise something and to understand exactly what it is: *Several key problems have already been identified.*

identity /aɪˈdentɪti/ noun [C/U] ★★ the fact of who you are or what your name is: *Do you have any proof of identity?*

igloo /ˈɪgluː/ noun [C] a building made from snow or ice

illegal /ɪˈliːg(ə)l/ adj ★★ not allowed by the law: *illegal drugs*

illness /ˈɪlnəs/ noun [C] ★★★ a particular disease, or a period of being ill: *a serious illness*

image /ˈɪmɪdʒ/ noun [C] ★★★ a picture, especially one in a mirror or on a computer, television or cinema screen: *the flickering black-and-white images on the first cinema screens*

immediately /ɪˈmiːdiətli/ adv, conj ★★★ very quickly and without delay: *She decided to leave immediately.*

impact /ˈɪmpækt/ noun [C] ★★★ an effect or influence *Her paper discusses the likely impact of global warming.* noun [C/U] ★★★ the force or act of one object hitting another: *the point of impact*

import /ɪmˈpɔːt/ verb [T] ★ to buy a product from another country and bring it to your country: *We import most of our coal from other countries.*

impossible /ɪmˈpɒsəb(ə)l/ adj ★★★ if something is impossible, no one can do it or it cannot happen: *We were faced with an impossible task.*

improve /ɪmˈpruːv/ verb [I/T] ★★★ to become better, or to make something better: *Your English will improve with practice.*

improvement /ɪmˈpruːvmənt/ noun [C] ★★★ a change that you make to something in order to make it better: *home improvements*

incident /ˈɪnsɪd(ə)nt/ noun [C] ★★ something that happens that is unusual, violent or dangerous: *an embarrassing incident*

include /ɪnˈkluːd/ verb [T] ★★★ **1** to contain, or to have someone or something as a part: *The book includes activities, stories and practical advice.* **2** to make someone or something be part of a group, set, or collection of things: *Please include a photograph of yourself with your application.*

income /ˈɪnkʌm/ noun [C/U] ★★★ money that someone gets from working or from investing money: *What is your approximate annual income?*

incorrect /ˌɪnkəˈrekt/ adj wrong, or not accurate or true

increase /ɪnˈkriːs/ verb [I/T] ★★★ to become larger in number or amount, or to make something do this: *We have managed to increase the number of patients treated.*

indecisive /ˌɪndɪˈsaɪsɪv/ adj unable to make decisions

independence /ˌɪndɪˈpendəns/ noun [U] ★★ **1** freedom from control by another country or organisation: *Lithuania was the first of the Soviet republics to declare its independence.* **2** the ability to make decisions and live your life free from the control or influence of other people: *Employment gave young women a measure of independence.*

independent /ˌɪndɪˈpendənt/ adj ★★★ not depending on other people: *Michelle is young, independent and confident.*

indigenous /ɪnˈdɪdʒənəs/ adj **1** indigenous people lived in a place for a very long time before other people came to live there **2** indigenous plants and animals belong to a region because they developed there

influence /ˈɪnfluəns/ noun [C/U] ★★★ the effect that a person or thing has on someone or something: *He couldn't hope to exert any real influence in the new department.* noun [C] ★★★ a person or thing that has an effect on someone or something verb [T] ★★★ to affect someone or something: *What factors influenced your decision to take the job?*

inform /ɪnˈfɔːm/ verb [T] ★★★ to officially tell someone about something: *The President has been fully informed of developments.*

informal /ɪnˈfɔːm(ə)l/ adj ★ relaxed, friendly and not official: *The hotel has an informal atmosphere.*

information /ˌɪnfəˈmeɪʃ(ə)n/ noun [U] ★★★ knowledge or facts about someone or something: *We're not allowed to give you any information about our clients' medical records.*

informative /ɪnˈfɔːmətɪv/ adj giving a lot of useful information

ingot /ˈɪŋgət/ noun [C] a block of gold, silver or other metal

ingredient /ɪnˈgriːdiənt/ noun [C] one of the foods or liquids that you use in making a particular meal: *Mix all the ingredients together carefully.*

injection /ɪnˈdʒekʃ(ə)n/ noun [C/U] ★ a drug that is injected into your body, or the process of injecting it into your body: *vaccines that are given by injection*

injury /ˈɪndʒəri/ noun [C/U] ★★★ physical harm: *an eye/leg injury*

in-law noun [C] someone who you are related to by marriage, especially the father or mother of your husband or wife: *We're going to stay with the in-laws this weekend.*

innocence /ˈɪnəs(ə)ns/ noun [U] the state of not being guilty of a crime or anything bad: *This new evidence would hopefully prove his innocence.*

innovation /ˌɪnəʊˈveɪʃ(ə)n/ noun [C/U] a new idea or piece of equipment, or the use of new ideas or equipment

I

inquiry /ɪn'kwaɪri/ noun [C] ★★ a question that is intended to get information about someone or something: *There have already been over 300 inquiries from people interested.* noun [C/U] ★★ a process of trying to find out more information about something: *The public is demanding an official inquiry into the incident.*

insert /ɪn'sɜːt/ verb [T] to put something into something else: *Insert the plug into the earphone socket.*

inspiration /ˌɪnspə'reɪʃ(ə)n/ noun [C/U] someone or something that gives you the enthusiasm and new ideas to create something, or a feeling of enthusiasm like this: *Her short story was the original inspiration for the film.*

instead /ɪn'sted/ adv ★★★ used for saying that one person, thing, or action replaces another: *If you don't have olive oil, you can use sunflower oil instead.*

instrument /'ɪnstrʊmənt/ noun [C] ★★★ **1** a tool that is used in science, medicine or technology: *scientific instruments such as microscopes* **2** a musical instrument, for example a piano or a guitar: *Do you play an instrument?*

interaction /ˌɪntər'ækʃ(ə)n/ noun [C/U] ★★ the activity of being with and talking to other people, and the way that people react to each other: *I enjoy the constant interaction with people from other departments.*

interested /'ɪntrəstɪd/ adj ★★★ **1** wanting to know about or take part in something: *Joe's always been interested in politics.* **2** willing or keen to do something: *We're going to the cinema. Are you interested? Would you like to come too?*

J

K

interesting /'ɪntrəstɪŋ/ adj ★★★ making you want to pay attention or know more: *an interesting topic*

interpretation /ɪnˌtɜːprɪ'teɪʃ(ə)n/ noun [C/U] ★★ **1** an explanation of the meaning or importance of something: *The Catholic interpretation of the Bible is slightly different.* **2** a way of performing a piece of music, a part in a play etc that shows how you understand it and feel about it: *He was best known for his interpretation of English folk music.*

interpreter /ɪn'tɜːprɪtə/ noun [C] someone whose job is to translate what someone is saying into another language

intrigue /ɪn'triːg/ verb [T] to make someone very interested in knowing more about something: *That old house has always intrigued me.*

Inuit /'ɪnuɪt, 'ɪnjuɪt/ noun [C/U] a member of a group of people who live in northern Siberia, Canada, Alaska, and Greenland, or the language that they speak

invent /ɪn'vent/ verb [T] ★★ to design or create something that did not exist before: *Alfred Nobel invented dynamite.*

invention /ɪn'venʃ(ə)n/ noun [C/U] ★ something that someone has made, designed or thought of for the first time, or the act of inventing something: *Inventions like the electric light bulb changed the way people lived.*

inventor /ɪn'ventə/ noun [C] someone who has invented something, or whose job is to invent things

invest /ɪn'vest/ verb [I/T] ★ to use your money with the aim of making a profit from it, for example by buying shares in a company: *Banks invested £20 million in the scheme.*

invisible /ɪn'vɪzəb(ə)l/ adj something that is invisible cannot be seen

involve /ɪn'vɒlv/ verb [T] ★★★ to include something as a necessary part of an activity, event or situation: *The course involves a lot of hard work.*

iron /'aɪən/ noun [U] ★★ a hard heavy metal that is used for making steel

irregular /ɪ'regjʊlə/ adj **1** not happening regularly: *His breathing had become irregular.* **2** not following the usual rules of grammar. For example, 'eat' is an irregular verb because its past tense is 'ate' and its past participle is 'eaten'.

island /'aɪlənd/ noun [C] ★★★ a piece of land that is completely surrounded by water: *the best hotel on the island*

issue /'ɪʃuː, 'ɪsjuː/ noun [C] ★★★ **1** a subject or problem that people discuss or argue about: *environmental issues* **2** a magazine that is published at a particular time: *The article appeared in the November issue.*

Jj

jacket /'dʒækɪt/ noun [C] ★★ a short coat: *a linen/denim/leather jacket*

jam /dʒæm/ noun [C/U] a sweet sticky food made from boiled fruit and sugar, that is usually spread onto bread: *strawberry jam*

jar /dʒɑː/ noun [C] a glass container for food, with a lid and a wide opening: *a jar of marmalade*

jaywalking /'dʒeɪˌwɔːkɪŋ/ noun [U] a dangerous or illegal way of crossing a street at a place where cars do not usually stop. Someone who does this is called a jaywalker.

journalist /'dʒɜːnəlɪst/ noun [C] ★★ someone whose job is to report the news for a newspaper, magazine, radio programme or television programme

journey /'dʒɜːni/ noun [C] ★★★ an occasion when you travel from one place to another, especially over a long distance: *a train journey*

judge /dʒʌdʒ/ noun [C] ★★ **1** someone whose job is to make decisions in a court of law: *The judge sentenced her to ninety days in prison.* **2** someone who decides who the winner of a competition will be: *All entries will be examined by a panel of judges.* verb [I/T] ★★ to form an opinion about something after considering all the details or facts: *He left the room when he judged that she was asleep.* verb [T] ★★ to decide in a court of law whether or not someone is guilty

jump in /ˌdʒʌmp 'ɪn/ hr vb [I] to become involved in something without thinking carefully about it

jungle /'dʒʌŋg(ə)l/ noun [C/U] a thick tropical forest

Kk

keep up /ˌkiːp 'ʌp/ phr vb **1** to move or develop at the same speed as someone or something: *By studying hard, she managed to keep up.* **2** to continue to do something: *Keep up the good work.*

ketchup /'ketʃəp/ noun [U] a thick red sauce made from tomatoes

keyboard /'kiːˌbɔːd/ noun [C] **1** a piece of computer equipment with keys on it, used for putting information into a computer **2** a musical instrument that has a keyboard, especially an electric piano

kidnap /'kɪdnæp/ verb [T] to illegally take someone away and make them a prisoner, especially in order to make their family or a government give you money

kill /kɪl/ verb [I/T] ★★★ to make a person or other living thing die: *Each year thousands of people are killed and injured on the roads.*

kindergarten /'kɪndəˌgɑːt(ə)n/ noun [C/U] **1** a nursery school **2** the first year of formal education in the US, for children aged 5 or 6

king /kɪŋ/ noun [C] ★★★ a man who rules a country and is the senior male member of the royal family: *King George VI*

kingdom /'kɪŋdəm/ noun [C] a country or area that is ruled by a king or queen

kiwi /'kiːwiː/ noun [C] **1** the bird that is the symbol of New Zealand. It has a long thin beak and cannot fly. **2** someone from New Zealand

knee /niː/ noun [C] ★★★ the part in the middle of your leg, where it bends: *a serious knee injury*

knife /naɪf/ noun [C] ★★★ an object with a blade, used for cutting food or as a weapon: *knives and forks*

knowledge /'nɒlɪdʒ/ noun [U] ★★★ what you know, or what is known about a particular subject: *She had a lot of knowledge and experience.*

L l

laboratory /lə'bɒrət(ə)ri, 'læbrə,tɔːri/ noun [C] ★ a building or large room where people do scientific research: *our new research laboratory*

landscape /'læn(d),skeɪp/ noun [C] **1** an area of land that has particular features: *a green, rural landscape* **2** a painting of an area of land

laptop /'læp,tɒp/ noun [C] a small computer that you can carry with you

last /lɑːst/ verb [I] ★★★ to continue happening for a particular period, or until a particular time: *The game lasts 80 minutes.* verb [I/T] ★★★ to continue to be available, or to be enough for what people need: *The water won't last long.*

late /leɪt/ adj ★★★ **1** if you are late, you arrive somewhere after the correct or usual time: *She phoned to say she'd be late.* **2** near the end of a period of time such as a day, month or season: *the late 18th century* **3** near the end of an evening or night: *If it weren't so late I would give Donna a call.*

later /'leɪtə/ adv ★★★ at some time in the future, or after the time that you have been talking about: *She'll be home later.*

laugh /lɑːf/ verb [I] ★★★ to make the noise with your voice that shows that you think that something is funny: *We talked and laughed late into the night.*

law /lɔː/ noun [singular] ★★★ the law: the system of rules that must be obeyed in society: *Failing to declare any extra income is against the law.*

lawyer /'lɔːjə/ noun [C] ★★ someone whose profession is to provide people with legal advice and services: *Mayer's lawyer spoke to the press today.*

lazy /'leɪzi/ adj ★ not willing to work or do anything that involves effort: *Get out of bed, you lazy slob!*

leader /'liːdə/ noun [C] ★★★ **1** someone who is in charge of a group, organisation or country: *a political/military/religious leader* **2** someone or something that is the most successful, most popular, most advanced etc: *He is a world leader in his field.*

leadership /'liːdəʃɪp/ noun [U] ★★ the position of being a leader: *The war was fought under the emperor's leadership.*

leave /liːv/ verb [I/T] ★★★ **1** to go away from a place: *We left London at three in the afternoon.* **2** to end a relationship with someone and stop living with them: *His wife has threatened to leave him.* verb [T] ★★★ **1** to put something somewhere and forget to take it away with you: *I left my homework on the bus.* **2** to put something somewhere, especially in a place where it will stay: *Leave your things by the door.*

left-handed /,left 'hændɪd/ adj born with a natural tendency to use the left hand to do things

leg /leg/ noun [C] ★★★ **1** one of the parts of a person's or animal's body to which the feet are attached: *an exercise to strengthen the leg muscles* **2** the part of a piece of furniture that supports it and raises it off the floor: *a stool with three legs* **3** a part of a journey, race or competition

let /let/ verb [T] ★★★ to allow something to happen, or to allow someone to do something: *Alice's mum won't let her come with us.*

level /'lev(ə)l/ noun [C] ★★★ the amount of something that exists at a particular time: *Unemployment is now at its lowest level for 15 years.* noun [C/U] ★★★ **1** a standard of academic ability: *This is an excellent book for advanced level students.* **2** a part or stage in a system that has several parts or stages: *Decisions should be taken at local, not national, level.* **3** one of the floors in a building: *a garage at basement level*

library /'laɪbrəri/ noun [C] ★★★ **1** a place where books, documents, CDs etc are available for you to look at or borrow: *the university/school library* **2** a private collection of books, or the room that it is kept in

lie /laɪ/ verb [I] ★★★ **1** to be or put yourself in a position in which your body is flat on a surface such as the floor or a bed: *She was lying on the beach reading a book.* **2** to be on a particular surface: *The gun was lying on the ground next to him.* **3** to deliberately say something that is not true: *It was obvious that she was lying.*

lifestyle /'laɪf,staɪl/ noun [C/U] the type of life that someone has, for example the type of things that they own and the type of activities that they do: *a healthy, outdoor lifestyle*

lift /lɪft/ noun [C] ★ **1** an occasion when someone takes you somewhere in their car: *I can give you a lift into town.* **2** a machine that carries people up or down between different levels of a tall building

light /laɪt/ adj ★★★ **1** very bright because of light from the sun *The room is light and airy.* **2** if it is light, you can see because it is day and not night: *It gets light around 5 am.* **3** not weighing much, or weighing less than you expect: *The table is a lot lighter than it looks.*

light bulb /'laɪt ,bʌlb/ noun [C] a glass object that you put in an electric light to produce light

lightning /'laɪtnɪŋ/ noun [U] the bright flashes of light that you see in the sky during a storm: *The ship was struck by lightning soon after it left the port.*

lime /laɪm/ noun [C/U] a fruit with a hard green skin and sour juice

limit /'lɪmɪt/ noun [C] ★★★ **1** the greatest amount or level of something that is possible or allowed: *The speed limit here is 40 miles an hour.* **2** the outer edge of an area: *No bombs landed within the city limits.*

linguist /'lɪŋgwɪst/ noun [C] **1** someone who studies and speaks a lot of languages **2** someone who teaches or studies linguistics

link /lɪŋk/ verb [T] ★★★ to connect two or more places or things: *Several new roads will link the southern and northern regions of the country.*

litter /'lɪtə/ noun [U] things that people have dropped on the ground in a public place, making it untidy

live happily ever after /lɪv 'hæpɪli: evə(r) ,ɑːftə/ phrase to be happy for the rest of your life

lock /lɒk/ noun [C] ★ the thing that is used for fastening a door, drawer etc so that no one can open it: *All the windows were fitted with locks.* verb [I/T] ★★ to fasten something such as a door with a key, or to be fastened with a key: *Have you locked the car?*

logic /'lɒdʒɪk/ noun [U] **1** the way that someone connects ideas when they are explaining something or giving a reason **2** the study of the way that ideas can be connected and used to explain things

lonely /'ləʊnli/ adj ★ unhappy because you are alone or have no friends: *a lonely childhood*

look after /,lʊk 'ɑːftə/ phr vb to take care of someone or something: *It's hard work looking after three children all day.*

look ahead /,lʊk ə'hed/ phr vb to think about what is likely to happen, or to plan what you are going to do in the future: *Looking ahead, I think the company needs to develop some new services.*

look back /,lʊk 'bæk/ phr vb to think about a time or event in the past: *Most people look back on their schooldays with fondness.*

look for /'lʊk ,fɔː/ phr vb to search for someone or something: *I'm looking for Jim. Have you seen him?*

look forward to /,lʊk 'fɔːwəd tuː/ phr vb to feel happy and excited about something that is going to happen

look into /,lʊk 'ɪntuː/ phr vb to try to discover the facts about something such as a problem or crime: *The airline have promised to look into the matter.*

look out for /,lʊk 'aʊt fɔː/ phr vb to look carefully at people or things around you in order to try to find a particular person or thing: *We were told to look out for a blue van.*

look round /,lʊk 'raʊnd/ phr vb [I/T] to walk around a room, building or place and see what is there

look up /,lʊk 'ʌp/ phr vb to try to find a piece of information by looking in a book or on a list, or by using a computer: *I had to look the word up in a dictionary.*

lose /luːz/ verb [T] ★★★ **1** to no longer have something: *Mike lost his job last year.* **2** to be unable to find someone or something: *I've lost my bag. Have you seen it?* verb [I/T] ★★★ to not win a race or competition: *England lost 2–1 to Germany.*

lottery /ˈlɒtəri/ noun [C] a game in which people win money if they guess the correct numbers

loud /laʊd/ adj ★★ a loud sound is strong and very easy to hear: *There was a loud knocking on the door.*

lower /ˈləʊə/ verb [T] ★ **1** to move something or someone slowly down from a higher position: *He lowered himself into the chair.* **2** to reduce something in number, amount, value, or strength: *The voting age was lowered from 21 to 18 years.*

lucky /ˈlʌki/ adj ★★ if you are lucky, something good happens to you as a result of luck: *Five lucky winners will each receive £1,000.*

lyric /ˈlɪrɪk/ noun [C] the words of a song

Mm

mad /mæd/ adj ★ **1** very silly or stupid: *You'll think I'm mad – I've just left my job.* **2** an offensive way of describing someone who is mentally ill

madness /ˈmædnəs/ noun [U] ideas and actions that show a lack of good judgment and careful thought: *It would be madness to give up your job just now.*

magazine /ˌmægəˈziːn/ noun [C] ★★ a large thin book with a paper cover that is usually published once a month or once a week: *a fashion/gardening/motoring magazine*

magician /məˈdʒɪʃ(ə)n/ noun [C] someone whose job is to entertain people by performing magic tricks

main /meɪn/ adj ★★★ most important or largest: *We eat our main meal in the evening.*

M

mainly /ˈmeɪnli/ adv ★★★ **1** used for talking about the largest or most important part of something: *This sauce is made mainly of milk and flour.* **2** in most cases: *Our customers are mainly young mothers.*

make up /ˌmeɪk ˈʌp/ phr vb **1** to become friendly with someone again after an argument: *Why don't you two forget your differences and make up?* **2** to invent something such as a story or an explanation: *He made up some excuse about the dog eating his homework.*

make-up /ˈmeɪkʌp/ noun [U] substances that people put on their faces to make them look attractive: *Gina wears no make-up at all.*

manual /ˈmænjuəl/ noun [C] a book that contains instructions for doing something, especially for operating a machine

marriage /ˈmærɪdʒ/ noun [C/U] ★★★ the relationship between two people who are husband and wife: *a long and happy marriage*

marry /ˈmæri/ verb [T] ★★ to perform the ceremony in which two people become husband and wife

marvellous /ˈmɑːvələs/ adj extremely enjoyable, good or impressive: *a marvellous performance/trip/party*

master's degree /ˈmɑːstəz dɪˌgriː/ noun [C] a university degree that a student gets if they study for one or two years after their first degree

mate /meɪt/ noun [C] a friend

material /məˈtɪəriəl/ noun [C/U] ★★★ cloth: *What sort of material is your dress made from?*

matter /ˈmætə/ verb [I] ★★★ to be important: *Education matters.*

meal /miːl/ noun [C] ★★★ an occasion when you eat, such as breakfast or lunch, or the food that you eat at that time: *He cooked us a delicious meal.*

mean /miːn/ adj ★ **1** cruel or unkind: *Don't do that – it's mean.* **2** not willing to spend money: *She was too mean to put the heating on.* verb [T] ★★★ to have a particular meaning: *What does 'maudlin' mean?*

measles /ˈmiːz(ə)lz/ noun [U] an infectious disease in which you have red spots all over your body and a high temperature

mechanic /mɪˈkænɪk/ noun [C] someone whose job is to repair vehicles and machines

mechanical /mɪˈkænɪk(ə)l/ adj operated by a machine, or relating to machines: *a mechanical device*

meet /miːt/ verb [I/T] ★★★ **1** to come together in order to spend time with someone who you have arranged to see: *I'll meet you in the bar later.* **2** to be introduced to someone that you do not know: *Have you met my wife?*

melodramatic /ˌmelədrəˈmætɪk/ adj behaving in a way that is too emotional or too serious

melt /melt/ verb [I/T] ★ to change a solid substance into a liquid, or to be changed from a solid into a liquid: *Melt the butter in a small saucepan.*

member /ˈmembə/ noun [C] ★★★ someone who belongs to a group or an organisation: *a trade union member*

membership /ˈmembəʃɪp/ noun [U] ★ the fact of being a member of a club, organisation or group: *Several countries have applied for membership of the EU.*

memorise /ˈmeməˌraɪz/ verb [T] to learn something so that you can remember it perfectly: *The children had memorised a poem.*

memory /ˈmem(ə)ri/ noun [C] ★★★ **1** something that you remember: *What are your most vivid memories of that period?* **2** the part of a computer in which information is stored noun [singular] ★★★ the ability to remember things: *Your memory tends to get worse as you get older.*

mend /mend/ verb [T] to repair something that is broken or damaged: *Have you mended the gate?*

mention /ˈmenʃ(ə)n/ verb [T] ★★★ to refer to something, but not discuss it much: *He didn't mention her all evening.*

mess /mes/ noun [C/U] ★ a situation in which a place is dirty, untidy or in bad condition: *The garden was a real mess.* noun [singular] ★ a difficult situation with a lot of problems: *an economic mess*

message /ˈmesɪdʒ/ noun [C] ★★★ a piece of written or spoken information that you give or send to someone: *I got your email message, thank you.*

messy /ˈmesi/ adj dirty or very untidy

middle-aged /ˌmɪdlˈeɪdʒd/ adj no longer young but not yet old, usually between 40 and 60 years of age

military /ˈmɪlɪt(ə)ri/ adj ★★ relating to armed forces, or using armed forces: *military service*

mime /maɪm/ verb [I/T] to tell a story using only the movements of your body and face, not using words

mind /maɪnd/ noun [C/U] ★★★ your thoughts and attention, or the part of you that thinks, knows and remembers things: *You never know what's going on in her mind.* verb [I/T] ★★★ to feel annoyed, upset or unhappy about something: *We had to cancel, but Rosa didn't seem to mind.* verb [T] ★★★ to be careful about something: *Mind the step!*

miner /ˈmaɪnə/ noun [C] someone whose job is to dig coal from a mine

mirror /ˈmɪrə/ noun [C] ★★ a piece of special glass in which you can see yourself or what is behind you: *a bathroom mirror*

misbehave /ˌmɪsbɪˈheɪv/ verb [I] to behave badly

misery /ˈmɪzəri/ noun [U] the state of being extremely unhappy or uncomfortable

miss /mɪs/ verb [I/T] ★★★ to fail to catch, hit or reach something: *I tried to catch the ball but missed.* verb [T] **1** to fail to be present for someone or something: *I had to miss a week of school.* **2** to feel sad because someone is not with you any longer, or because you do not have or cannot do something any longer: *We miss him enormously.*

mission /ˈmɪʃ(ə)n/ noun [C] an important piece of work that a person or group of people has to do for a government or large organisation, especially one that involves travel: *a fact-finding/rescue mission* noun [singular] an aim that is very important to a person or organisation: *Helping homeless people was Gina's mission in life.*

mistake /mɪˈsteɪk/ noun [C] ★★ **1** something that you have not done correctly, or something you say or think that is not correct: *spelling/grammar mistakes* **2** something that you do that you later wish you had not done, because it causes a lot of problems: *You're making a big mistake.*

mix /mɪks/ verb [I/T] ★★ **1** to combine two or more substances so that they become a single substance: *Add the eggs and mix thoroughly.* **2** to combine things such as activities, ideas, or styles: *In this room, antique and modern furniture have been successfully mixed.*

mixture /'mɪkstʃə/ noun [singular] ★★ a combination of two or more different people or things: *Her face showed a mixture of fear and excitement.* noun [C/U] ★★ a substance such as food that is the result of mixing different things: *Spoon the mixture into the cake tins.*

modern /'mɒd(ə)n/ adj ★★★ **1** relating to or belonging to the present time: *the role of women in modern society* **2** using the most recent methods, ideas, designs or equipment: *We should replace the equipment with something more modern.*

month /mʌnθ/ noun [C] ★★★ **1** one of the 12 periods that a year is divided into, for example January or February: *Could we meet earlier in the month?* **2** a period of about four weeks: *They're getting married in a month's time.*

monument /'mɒnjʊmənt/ noun [C] **1** a structure that is built in a public place in order to celebrate an important person or event **2** a place of historical importance

mood /mu:d/ noun [C/U] ★★ the way that someone is feeling, or the way that a group of people is feeling at a particular time: *Politicians have to be in touch with the public mood.* noun [C] ★★ a group of verb forms that are used to show whether, for example, a sentence is a statement, question or order

moral /'mɒrəl/ adj ★ relating to right and wrong and the way that people should behave: *moral standards/principles/values*

mosque /mɒsk/ noun [C] a building in which Muslims worship

mother tongue /ˌmʌðə 'tʌŋ/ noun [C] the first language that you learn to speak

motherboard /'mʌðəˌbɔ:d/ noun [C] the main circuit board in a computer

mother-in-law /'mʌðə(r)ɪnˌlɔ:/ noun [C] the mother of your husband or wife

motorway /'məʊtəˌweɪ/ noun [C] a wide fast road with several lanes of traffic going in each direction

mountain /'maʊntɪn/ noun [C] ★★★ **1** a very high hill: *They went walking and climbing in the mountains.* **2** a large pile or amount of something: *a mountain of paperwork*

mountain range /'maʊntɪn ˌreɪndʒ/ noun [C] a long row of mountains

mouse /maʊs/ noun [C] ★★ **1** a small furry animal with a long tail **2** a small object connected to a computer that you move in order to do things on the computer screen: *Click on the left mouse button.*

mousepad /'maʊsˌpæd/ noun [C] the flat part on a laptop that you operate with your fingers to do things on a computer screen

moustache /mə'stɑ:ʃ/ noun [C] hair that grows above a man's mouth

movement /'mu:vmənt/ noun [C/U] ★★★ **1** a way of moving your body, or the ability to move your body: *rhythmic movements* **2** the process of moving something from one place to another: *The agreement governs the free movement of goods between countries.*

moving /'mu:vɪŋ/ adj **1** making you feel sad or sympathetic **2** a moving object is something that moves: *He was pushed from a moving train.*

mug /mʌg/ verb [T] to attack someone in a public place and steal their money or possessions

mugger /'mʌgə(r)/ noun [C] someone who attacks people in public places and steals their money, jewellery, or other possessions

mugging /'mʌgɪŋ/ noun [C/U] an attack on someone in a public place in order to steal their money, jewellery or other possessions

murder /'mɜ:də/ noun [C/U] ★★ the crime of deliberately killing someone: *The murder was committed over five years ago.*

murderer /'mɜ:dərə/ noun [C] someone who commits murder

muscle /'mʌs(ə)l/ noun [C/U] ★★ a piece of flesh that connects bones and moves a particular part of your body: *These exercises are good for your stomach muscles.*

mysterious /mɪ'stɪəriəs/ adj not explained, understood or known: *They are investigating the mysterious disappearance of a young man.*

mystery /'mɪst(ə)ri/ noun [C] ★ **1** something that you cannot understand, explain, or get information about: *The exact origin of the universe remains a mystery.* **2** a story, film or play in which events take place that are not explained until the end: *a murder mystery*

N n

native speaker /ˌneɪtɪv 'spi:kə/ noun [C] someone who speaks a particular language as their first language

navy /'neɪvi/ noun [C] the part of a country's armed forces that uses ships

necessary /'nesəs(ə)ri/ adj ★★★ if something is necessary, you must have it or must do it: *I don't want to be disturbed unless it's absolutely necessary.*

neck /nek/ noun [C] ★★★ **1** the part of your body that joins your head to the rest of your body **2** a long narrow part of something such as a bottle or a musical instrument

neighbour /'neɪbə/ noun [C] ★★ someone who lives near you: *friends and neighbours*

neighbourhood /'neɪbəˌhʊd/ noun [C] a particular area of a town

neither /'naɪðə(r), 'ni:ðə(r)/ conj, det, pron ★★★ used for showing that a negative statement also applies to someone or something else: *Adam was not invited, and neither were any of his friends.*

nephew /'nefju:, 'nevju:/ noun [C] a son of your brother or sister, or a son of your husband's or wife's brother or sister

net /net/ noun [C/U] ★★ a material made of string or rope that is woven into a loose pattern with spaces in it noun [C] ★★ **1** in some sports, an object made of net that you hit, kick or throw the ball over or into **2** the Net: the internet

news /nju:z/ noun [U] ★★★ **1** information about something that has happened recently: *I'm afraid I've got some bad news.* **2** information about recent events that is reported in newspapers or on television or radio: *foreign/sports/financial news*

newspaper /'nju:zˌpeɪpə/ noun [C] ★★★ a set of large printed sheets of folded paper containing news, articles and other information that is published every day or every week: *a local newspaper*

newsreader /'nju:zˌri:də/ noun [C] someone whose job is to read the news on television or radio

niece /ni:s/ noun [C] a daughter of your brother or sister, or a daughter of your husband's or wife's brother or sister

nightmare /'naɪtˌmeə/ noun [C] a very frightening and unpleasant dream: *I still have terrible nightmares about the crash.*

noisy /'nɔɪzi/ adj ★ making a lot of noise, or full of noise: *noisy neighbours*

non-alcoholic /ˌnɒnælkə'hɒlɪk/ adj non-alcoholic drink does not contain alcohol

non-resident /ˌnɒn'rezɪdənt/ adj **1** not based in a particular country: *The island does not tax non-resident companies.* **2** not living in a house that you own: *These houses all belong to non-resident owners.* **3** not living at the place where you work: *non-resident teaching staff*

non-smoking /ˌnɒn'sməʊkɪŋ/ adj a non-smoking area is one where you are not allowed to smoke

non-stop /ˌnɒn'stɒp/ adj continuing without stopping: *non-stop entertainment*

nose /nəʊz/ noun [C] ★★★ the part of your face that is above your mouth that you use for smelling and breathing: *I'd like to punch him on the nose.*

note /nəʊt/ noun [C] ★★★ **1** a short written message to someone: *I've written him a note asking him to meet me tonight.* **2** a piece of paper money: *a £5 note* noun [plural] ★★★ notes: details from something such as a lecture or a book that you write on a piece of paper so that you can remember them: *It'll help you later if you take notes.*

novel /'nɒv(ə)l/ noun [C] ★ a long written story about imaginary characters and events

novelist /'nɒvəlɪst/ noun [C] someone who writes novels

nowadays /'naʊəˌdeɪz/ adv ★★ at the present time: *Lots of people get divorced nowadays.*

nuclear /'nju:kliə/ adj ★★★ relating to energy that is produced by changing the structure of the central part of an atom: *nuclear power/energy*

N

O o

obey /ə'beɪ/ verb [I/T] ★ to do what a person, law or rule says that you must do: *Officers expect their troops to obey them without question.*

objective /əb'dʒektɪv/ noun [C] ★ something that you plan to achieve: *I'm not sure I understand the objective of this exercise.*

obvious /'ɒbviəs/ adj ★★★ clear to almost anyone: *an obvious mistake*

obviously /'ɒbviəsli/ adv ★★★ in a way that is clear for almost anyone to see or understand: *Richards was obviously disappointed at being left out of the team.*

occasionally /ə'keɪʒ(ə)nəli/ adv ★★ sometimes, but not frequently or regularly: *Simmer the sauce for ten minutes, stirring occasionally.*

offer /'ɒfə/ verb [T] ★★★ to let someone know that you will give them something or do something for them if they want it: *They haven't offered me the job yet.*

office /'ɒfɪs/ noun [C] ★★★ a room or building where the people in an organisation or department work, or the people who work there: *the company's Los Angeles office*

one-parent family /ˌwʌn peərənt 'fæməliː/ noun [C] a family in which only one parent lives in the home and looks after the children

online /'ɒnlaɪn/ adj ★★ connected to or available through a computer or a computer network , especially the Internet: *an online bookshop*

open-minded /ˌəʊpən'maɪndɪd/ adj willing to consider new ideas

operator /'ɒpəˌreɪtə/ noun [C] **1** someone who works for a telephone company and helps people with calls **2** someone whose job is to operate a machine or piece of equipment: *a crane operator*

opponent /ə'pəʊnənt/ noun [C] ★★ **1** someone who is competing against you: *His opponent received only 36 per cent of the vote.* **2** someone who disagrees with something and tries to change or stop it: *opponents of the legislation*

opportunity /ˌɒpə'tjuːnəti/ noun [C/U] ★★★ a chance to do something, or a situation in which it is easy for you to do something: *The trip sounds like a wonderful opportunity.*

opposite /'ɒpəzɪt/ adj ★★ **1** across from, or on the other side of, someone or something: *They sat at opposite ends of the room.* **2** completely different: *The car smashed into a lorry coming in the opposite direction.*

option /'ɒpʃ(ə)n/ noun [C] ★★★ something that you can choose to do: *We discussed all the marketing options and chose television advertising.*

order /'ɔːdə/ verb [T] ★★★ **1** to tell someone to do something, in a way that shows that you have authority: *The government has ordered an investigation into the cause of the accident.* **2** to put things in a particular order: *The list of books is ordered alphabetically.* verb [I/T] ★★★ to ask for something to be brought to you or be made for you: *Are you ready to order?*

ordinary /'ɔːd(ə)n(ə)ri/ adj ★★★ normal or average, and not unusual or special: *It was just an ordinary Saturday morning.*

organised /'ɔːgəˌnaɪzd/ adj **1** planned carefully and effectively **2** an organised person arranges and plans activities carefully and effectively

organiser /'ɔːgəˌnaɪzə/ noun [C] someone who makes all the arrangements for an event or activity

original /ə'rɪdʒ(ə)nəl/ adj ★★★ **1** existing at the beginning of a period or process, before any changes have been made: *Do you know who the car's original owner was?* **2** new, interesting, and different from anything else: *a highly original design* **3** not copied from something else: *The original painting is in a museum in Vienna.*

outdoors /ˌaʊt'dɔːz/ adv not in a building

outfit /'aʊtfɪt/ noun [C] a set of clothes that are worn together

outlaw /'aʊtˌlɔː/ noun [C] a criminal

outside /ˌaʊt'saɪd/ adj, adv, noun, prep ★★★ **1** not inside a building: *Outside the sun was shining.* **2** away from a particular country, area or town: *The postal service is better outside London.* **3** not within the limits of a particular time, range or situation: *classes held outside normal school hours*

over /'əʊvə(r)/ adv, prep ★★★ **1** moving across the space above someone or something: *Government troops fired a few shots over their heads.* **2** on someone or something and covering them: *She put her hands over her ears.* **3** on the opposite side of an area, line, road, river etc: *Sandra's brother lives just over the road from our house.* **4** falling, hanging or looking down from the edge of something: *Lava flowed over the rim of the volcano.* **5** more than a particular amount, number or age: *Yeltsin was elected by a large majority with over 45 million votes.*

overtime /'əʊvəˌtaɪm/ noun [U] extra hours that someone works at their job, or money that is paid for working extra hours

overweight /ˌəʊvə'weɪt/ adj heavier than you should be

owner /'əʊnə/ noun [C] ★★★ someone who owns something: *a restaurant/supermarket/hotel owner*

ozone layer /'əʊzəʊn ˌleɪə/ noun [singular] a layer of ozone in the Earth's atmosphere that protects the Earth from the harmful effects of the Sun

P p

pacifist /'pæsɪfɪst/ noun [C] someone who believes that violence is wrong and refuses to fight in wars

packaging /'pækɪdʒɪŋ/ noun [U] the boxes, plastic etc that are used for wrapping products

packet /'pækɪt/ noun [C] ★ **1** a box, bag or piece of plastic wrapping, containing food that is ready to be sold: *The ingredients should be listed on the packet.* **2** a small parcel or envelope containing a set of similar things: *A packet of brochures arrived in the post.*

pain /peɪn/ noun [C/U] ★★★ a bad feeling in part of your body when you are hurt or become ill: *An old injury was causing him intense pain.*

painful /'peɪnf(ə)l/ adj ★ causing physical pain: *The sting can be excruciatingly painful.*

painkiller /'peɪnˌkɪlə/ noun [C] a medicine that reduces pain

pair /peə/ noun [C] ★★★ **1** a set of two things of the same type: *The vases were sold as a pair.* **2** a single unit made up of two similar parts joined together: *My glasses are getting old and I probably need a new pair.*

pal /pæl/ noun [C] a friend

pale /peɪl/ adj ★★ **1** light and not bright in colour: *pale blue/yellow/green* **2** a pale person has skin that is lighter than usual because they are ill, shocked or worried: *He looked pale and weary.*

palm tree /'pɑːm ˌtriː/ noun [C] a tropical tree without branches that has large wide leaves growing from the top of its trunk

paperwork /'peɪpəˌwɜːk/ noun [U] the documents that you need for a particular activity or occasion

paracetamol /ˌpærə'siːtəmɒl, ˌpærə'setəmɒl/ noun [C/U] a common type of painkiller

parachuting /'pærəʃuːtɪŋ/ noun [U] the activity of jumping out of a plane wearing a parachute

parcel /'pɑːs(ə)l/ noun [C] something wrapped in paper or in a large envelope so that it can be sent by post

parrot /'pærət/ noun [C] a brightly coloured tropical bird that is often kept as a pet and can be taught to copy what people say

particle /'pɑːtɪk(ə)l/ noun [C] **1** an extremely small piece or amount of something **2** an adverb or preposition used with a verb to form a phrasal verb. For example in the sentence 'He quickly put on his clothes', 'on' is a particle.

particular /pə'tɪkjʊlə/ adj ★★★ used for emphasising that you are talking about one specific person or thing and not anyone or anything else: *Are there any particular topics that you would like me to explain further?*

partner /'pɑːtnə/ noun [C] ★★★ **1** someone who you live with and have a sexual relationship with: *Are partners invited to the office party?* **2** someone who you do a particular activity with: *John is my tennis partner.* **3** one of two or more people who own a company and share its profits and losses: *He became a partner in his father's law firm.*

part-time /ˌpɑːt'taɪm/ adj done for only part of the time that an activity is usually performed: *a part-time job*

party /'pɑːti/ noun [C] ★★★ **1** a social event at which people meet in order to celebrate something or have fun: *Did you invite her to your birthday party?* **2** an organised group of people who share the same ideas about how a country should be governed, and who try to get elected: *the two main political parties*

passion /'pæʃ(ə)n/ noun [C/U] ★ a powerful emotion such as love or anger: *She spoke with great passion about the plight of the refugees.* noun [C] ★ a strong enthusiasm or interest: *a passion for classical music*

password /'pɑːsˌwɜːd/ noun [C] a secret word or phrase that you need in order to get into a room, building or area

path /pɑːθ/ noun [C] ★★★ a way from one place to another that people can walk along: *Amy walked up the path to the house.*

patient /'peɪʃ(ə)nt/ adj ★★ someone who is patient is able to wait for a long time or deal with a difficult situation without becoming angry or upset: *Susan's very patient with the children.*

pattern /'pæt(ə)n/ noun [C] ★★★ **1** a series of actions or events that together show how things normally happen or are done: *The study examined patterns of behaviour in young children.* **2** a set of lines, shapes or colours that are repeated regularly: *a carpet with a pretty pattern* **3** a drawing or shape that you use when you are making something, so that you get the shape and size correct

PC /ˌpiː 'siː/ noun [C] **1** personal computer: a computer that is designed to be used by one person at home or in an office **2** police constable: a police officer of the lowest rank

peace /piːs/ noun [U] ★★★ **1** a situation in which there is no war between countries or groups: *For many years the agreement maintained peace in Europe.* **2** a calm quiet situation in which you are not annoyed by noise or other people: *He just wanted to read his newspaper in peace.*

peaceful /'piːsf(ə)l/ adj ★ **1** not involving war or violence: *talks aimed at finding a peaceful solution to the crisis* **2** calm and quiet: *The hotel is set in peaceful surroundings.*

per /pə, pɜː/ prep ★ used for stating the rate or cost for each unit of time, quantity, distance etc: *He is paid £10 per hour for the job.*

perfectionist /pə'fekʃ(ə)nɪst/ noun [C] someone who always wants things to be done in a perfect way

performance /pə'fɔːməns/ noun [C] ★★★ the act of performing a play, dance or other form of entertainment: *The first performance of the opera was in 1936.* noun [C/U] ★★★ the standard of success that someone or something achieves: *A healthy diet can improve a child's performance in school.*

perhaps /pə'hæps/ adv ★★★ **1** used for saying that you are not certain whether something is true: *I haven't seen them for months – perhaps they've moved away.* **2** used when you are making a suggestion, giving advice or making a polite request: *You don't look well – perhaps you should go to the doctor.*

permanent /'pɜːmənənt/ adj ★★ happening or existing for a long time, or for all time in the future: *The illness can cause permanent blindness.*

permission /pə'mɪʃ(ə)n/ noun [U] ★★ the right to do something that is given to you by someone in authority: *You are not allowed to camp here without permission.*

persuade /pə'sweɪd/ verb [T] ★★ **1** to make someone agree to do something by giving them reasons why they should: *He did finally come with us, although it took a long time to persuade him.* **2** to make someone believe that something is true: *I managed to persuade him that it was not his fault.*

petrol /'petrəl/ noun [U] ★ a liquid that is used as a fuel for cars and other vehicles:

petrol station /'petrəl ˌsteɪʃən/ noun [C] a garage that sells petrol for your car

pharmacy /'fɑːməsi/ noun [C] a place where medicines are prepared and sold

photographer /fə'tɒgrəfə/ noun [C] someone who takes photographs, especially as their job

physics /'fɪzɪks/ noun [U] ★ the science that deals with heat, light and other forms of energy and how they affect objects

picnic /'pɪknɪk/ noun [C] a meal that you eat outside

picturesque /ˌpɪktʃə'resk/ adj a picturesque place or scene is attractive

pill /pɪl/ noun [C] ★ a small piece of solid medicine that you swallow with water: *vitamin pills*

pin /pɪn/ noun [C] ★ a small thin piece of metal with a sharp point, used for holding cloth in place while you are sewing

PIN /pɪn/ noun [C] personal identification number: a set of four numbers that you put into a cash machine in order to take money out of your bank account

piracy /'paɪrəsi/ noun [U] **1** the crime of making and selling illegal copies of computer programs, books, videos or CDs **2** the crime of stealing things from ships while they are sailing

pirate /'paɪrət/ noun [C] someone who steals things from ships while they are sailing

pitch /pɪtʃ/ noun [C] ★ a flat area of ground that is used for playing sports on: *a football/cricket/rugby pitch*

place /pleɪs/ verb [T] ★★★ to put something somewhere, usually in a careful way: *Ella placed the dish on the table.*

plant /plɑːnt/ noun [C] ★★★ a living thing that grows in soil and has leaves and roots: *a strawberry plant*

platform /'plætˌfɔːm/ noun [C] ★ **1** a raised structure for people to stand on so that they can be seen by an audience: *The two candidates shared the platform for the question and answer session.* **2** an area next to a railway track where passengers get onto and off trains: *The train to Brussels will depart from platform 3.*

play /pleɪ/ noun [C] ★★★ a piece of writing that is intended to be performed by actors in a theatre or on television or the radio: *a Shakespeare/West End play*

player /'pleɪə/ noun [C] ★★★ **1** someone who plays a particular game or sport: *a tennis/cricket player* **2** someone who plays a musical instrument: *a piano player*

playground /'pleɪˌgraʊnd/ noun [C] an area of land where children can play, especially at a school

plot /plɒt/ noun [C/U] ★ a series of related events that make up the main story in a book, film etc noun [C] ★ a secret plan to do something bad, made by two or more people: *a kidnap plot*

plumber /'plʌmə/ noun [C] someone whose job is to fit and repair the pipes and equipment that are used for supplying and storing water

pocket /'pɒkɪt/ noun [C] ★★ a small bag that forms part of a piece of clothing and is used for holding small objects: *She searched her pockets for the car keys.*

poison /'pɔɪz(ə)n/ noun [C/U] a substance that can kill you or make you ill if you eat, drink or breathe it verb [T] **1** to kill someone, or make them very ill, by giving them poison: *He was suspected of poisoning his wife.* **2** to put poison in something: *Waste from the factories is poisoning the water supply.*

police force /'p(ə)liːs ˌfɔːs/ noun [C] an organised group of police officers in charge of a country or a particular area

police officer /'p(ə)liːs ˌɒfɪsə/ noun [C] a member of the police

politely /pə'laɪtli/ adv ★ in a polite way: *'Did you sleep well?' she asked politely.*

politician /ˌpɒlə'tɪʃ(ə)n/ noun [C] ★★ someone who has a job in politics

pollution /pə'luːʃ(ə)n/ noun [U] ★★ chemicals and other substances that have a harmful effect on air, water or land: *new measures to prevent pollution levels from rising*

poor /pɔː/ adj ★★★ **1** having little money and few possessions: *a poor family/area/country* **2** not as good as expected or needed: *poor health/eyesight/hearing* **3** used for showing that you feel sorry for someone: *The poor child had lost both his parents.*

popular /'pɒpjʊlə/ adj ★★★ liked by many people: *Jenny is one of the most popular girls in the school.*

population /ˌpɒpjʊ'leɪʃ(ə)n/ noun [singular] ★★★ **1** the number of people who live in a particular area: *Los Angeles has a population of over 3 million.* **2** all the people who live in a particular area: *Less than 40% of the population voted in the last election.*

positive /'pɒzətɪv/ adj ★★★ **1** completely certain: *We'd met before – I was positive about that.* **2** believing that good things will happen, or that a situation will get better: *a positive attitude* **3** a positive experience, situation, result etc is a good one: *School was a totally positive experience for me.*

P

possession /pəˈzeʃ(ə)n/ noun [C] ★★ something that you own: *Their family home and possessions were destroyed in the fire.*

post /pəʊst/ noun [U] ★★★ the letters and parcels that are delivered to someone, or the system used for collecting, carrying and delivering them: *There was no post for you today.* verb [T] **1** to send a letter or parcel to someone in the post **2** to put information or a message where the public can see it, for example on a wall: *The menu and prices are posted outside the door.* **3** to put information on the Internet: *New job openings are posted every day on their website.*

potion /ˈpəʊʃ(ə)n/ noun [C] a drink that is believed to be magic, poisonous or useful as a medicine

power /ˈpaʊə/ noun [U] ★★★ **1** the ability to influence or control people: *a power struggle within the party* **2** energy that is used for operating equipment and machines: *solar power* **3** physical force or strength: *The boy was thrown backwards by the power of the blast.*

practical /ˈpræktɪk(ə)l/ adj ★★★ **1** involving, or relating to, real situations rather than theories or ideas alone: *Unfortunately this research has no practical use.* **2** making sensible decisions and choices based on what can be successfully achieved: *Despite their wealth, they were always practical about money.* **3** intended to be useful or suitable, not just fashionable or attractive: *a practical car for the family* **4** able to make repairs or do things with your hands in a skilful way

practice /ˈpræktɪs/ noun [C/U] ★★★ occasions when you do something in order to become better at it, or the time that you spend doing this: *piano/basketball practice*

practise /ˈpræktɪs/ verb [I/T] ★★ to repeat an activity regularly so that you become better at it: *How many hours a day do you practise?*

pray /preɪ/ verb [I/T] ★ to speak to God or a saint, for example to give thanks or to ask for help: *They prayed for peace.*

predator /ˈpredətə/ noun [C] an animal that kills and eats other animals

predict /prɪˈdɪkt/ verb [T] ★ to say what you think will happen in the future: *They're predicting heavy rain for tomorrow.*

prescription /prɪˈskrɪpʃən/ noun [C] a piece of paper that a doctor gives you that says what type of medicine you need: *The drug is only available on prescription.*

press /pres/ noun ★★★ the press: newspapers and news magazines, or the journalists who work on them: *the national/local/American press*

pressure /ˈpreʃə/ noun [C/U] ★★★ **1** attempts to persuade or force someone to do something: *Pressure for political change increased in the 1990s.* **2** a worried feeling that you get when you have to deal with a difficult or complicated situation: *With greatly increased workloads, everyone is under pressure now.* noun [U] a physical force that is pressing on someone or something: *She became aware of the pressure of his hand on her shoulder.*

Q

previous /ˈpriːviəs/ adj ★★★ a previous event, period or thing happened or existed before the one that you are talking about: *Mark has two children from a previous marriage.*

priest /priːst/ noun [C] ★ **1** someone whose job is to perform religious duties and ceremonies in some Christian churches: *a Roman Catholic priest* **2** a man who performs religious duties in some religions that are not Christian

prime minister /ˌpraɪm ˈmɪnɪstə/ noun [C] ★★ the political leader in countries such as the UK that are governed by a parliament

print /prɪnt/ verb [I/T] ★★ to produce words, numbers, pictures etc on paper, using a printer or printing press: *The book is beautifully printed on quality paper.* verb [T] **1** to publish something in a newspaper or magazine: *They refused to print my letter.* **2** to produce a photograph on paper

printer /ˈprɪntə/ noun [C] ★ **1** a piece of equipment that you use for printing documents that you have created on a computer **2** a person or business that prints books, newspapers etc

prison /ˈprɪz(ə)n/ noun [C/U] ★★★ an institution where people are kept as a punishment for committing a crime: *He's currently in prison for tax fraud.*

prize /praɪz/ noun [C] ★★ a reward that you get for being successful in a competition, or for being good at something: *the Nobel Prize for chemistry*

product /ˈprɒdʌkt/ noun [C/U] ★★★ something that is made, grown or obtained in large quantities so that it can be sold: *dairy/pharmaceutical/software products*

professional /prəˈfeʃ(ə)nəl/ adj ★★★ **1** relating to work that needs special skills and qualifications: *Teachers must be free to exercise their professional judgment.* **2** playing a sport or taking part in an activity as a job rather than for enjoyment: *a professional actor/photographer*

professor /prəˈfesə/ noun [C] ★ a senior teacher in a college or university: *a professor of English*

programme /ˈprəʊgræm/ noun [C] ★★★ **1** a series of planned events: *a festival with an exciting musical programme* **2** a television or radio broadcast: *More people watch the news than any other programme.* **3** a document that tells you what will happen in a performance or event

programmer /ˈprəʊˌgræmə/ noun [C] someone whose job is to create computer programs

project /ˈprɒdʒekt, ˈprəʊdʒekt/ noun [C] ★★★ a piece of work that involves collecting information: *The university has set up a new research project to study language development in babies.*

promise /ˈprɒmɪs/ verb [I/T] ★★★ **1** to tell someone that you will definitely do something: *The police chief promised tougher action against young criminals.* **2** to make something seem likely: *This evening promises to be a lot of fun.*

property /ˈprɒpəti/ noun [U] ★★★ the things that you own: *The books are my personal property.* noun [C/U] ★★★ land and the buildings on it: *He owns several properties in London.*

protect /prəˈtekt/ verb [T] ★★★ to keep someone or something safe: *Are you prepared to protect yourself in case of attack?*

protection /prəˈtekʃ(ə)n/ noun [U] ★★★ the process of keeping someone or something safe: *the protection of the countryside*

protein /ˈprəʊtiːn/ noun [U] a substance in foods such as meat, eggs and milk that keeps you healthy

protest /ˈprəʊtest/ noun [C/U] ★★ a strong complaint or disagreement: *a formal protest against the nuclear testing* noun [C] ★★ an occasion when people show strong public opposition to something: *a protest march*

protest /prəˈtest/ verb [I] ★ to show publicly that you oppose something: *Workers are protesting against high unemployment.*

proud /praʊd/ adj ★ **1** feeling happy about your achievements, your possessions, or people who you are connected with: *We're so proud of her for telling the truth.* **2** a proud person does not like other people to help them or to think that they are weak: *a proud and independent nation*

publication /ˌpʌblɪˈkeɪʃ(ə)n/ noun [U] ★ the process of producing a book for people to buy: *She became famous after the publication of her first novel.* noun [C] ★ a magazine, newspaper or book: *a weekly financial publication*

publisher /ˈpʌblɪʃə/ noun [C] a person or company that produces and sells books

punish /ˈpʌnɪʃ/ verb [T] ★ to do something unpleasant to someone because they have done something bad or illegal: *He was punished for stealing.*

purse /pɜːs/ noun [C] ★ a small bag for carrying money

Qq

questionnaire /ˌkwestʃəˈneə/ noun [C] a set of questions that a lot of people are asked as a way of getting information about what people generally think or do

queue /kjuː/ noun [C] ★ a line of people that are waiting for something: *There was a long queue for tickets.*

quickly /ˈkwɪkli/ adv ★★★ at a fast speed: *We have to work quickly.*

R r

race /reɪs/ noun [C] ★★★ a competition that decides who is the fastest at doing something: *He is training for a big race.* noun [C/U] ★★★ a group of people who are similar because they have the same skin colour or other physical features, or because they speak the same language or have the same history or customs: *We do not discriminate on the basis of race or gender.*

rainforest /ˈreɪnˌfɒrɪst/ noun [C/U] a forest in a tropical region of the world where it rains a lot

raise your voice /ˌreɪz jə ˈvɔɪs/ phrase to speak in a loud angry way: *We told him not to raise his voice to our children.*

rash /ræʃ/ noun [C] an area of small red spots on your skin that is caused by an illness or a reaction to something

reach /riːtʃ/ verb [T] ★★★to arrive somewhere: *We hoped to reach the camp before dark.* verb [I] ★★★ to move your hand towards something you are trying to touch or pick up: *He turned round and reached for the phone.* verb [I/T] ★★★ to manage to touch something or pick it up by stretching out your arm: *We keep the bottles up here so the children can't reach them.*

read out /ˌriːd ˈaʊt/ phr vb to say the words that you are reading so that people can hear them: *He read the list of names out.*

read up on /ˌriːd ˈʌp ɒn/ phr vb to get information on a particular subject by reading a lot about it: *I need to read up on my British history.*

rebellious /rɪˈbeljəs/ adj opposing authority or the accepted rules of society

reboot /ˌriːˈbuːt/ verb [I/T] if a computer or system reboots, or if someone reboots it, it starts again after it has been turned off

receipt /rɪˈsiːt/ noun [C] ★ a document that you get from someone showing that you have given them money or goods: *Keep all your credit card receipts.*

recent /ˈriːs(ə)nt/ adj ★★★ happening or starting a short time ago: *a recent discovery*

receptionist /rɪˈsepʃ(ə)nɪst/ noun [C] someone who works in reception at a hotel or office and whose job is to welcome visitors, deal with questions etc

recipe /ˈresəpi/ noun [C] ★ a set of instructions for cooking or preparing a particular food: *a recipe for apple pie*

recommend /ˌrekəˈmend/ verb [T] ★★ to say that someone or something is good and worth using, having or experiencing: *Can you recommend a good restaurant?*

record /ˈrekɔːd/ noun [C] ★★★ **1** information that is kept about something that has happened or that someone has done: *medical/historical records* **2** the best achievement so far in a particular activity, especially a sport: *She holds the world record in the 800 metres.* **3** a large circular black piece of plastic containing music or other sounds: *an original Beatles' record*

record /rɪˈkɔːd/ verb [T] ★★★ to make a record of something that has happened, usually by writing it down: *They were asked to record the time at which the attack happened.* verb [I/T] ★★★ to put sounds or images onto a DVD, CD or video: *Can you record the football for me at 10 o'clock?*

recover /rɪˈkʌvə/ verb [I] ★★ to become fit and healthy again after an illness or injury: *I haven't fully recovered from the flu.* verb [T] ★★ to get back something that has been lost or stolen or is owed: *The thieves were caught, but many of the items were never recovered.*

recycle /riːˈsaɪk(ə)l/ verb [T] to treat waste materials so that they can be used again

reduce /rɪˈdjuːs/ verb [T] ★★★ to make something smaller or less in size, amount, importance, price etc: *Try to reduce the amount of fat in your diet.*

reef /riːf/ noun [C] a long line of rock or coral in the sea, with its top just below or just above the surface

referee /ˌrefəˈriː/ noun [C] someone whose job is to make sure that players in a game obey the rules

reference /ˈref(ə)rəns/ noun [C/U] ★★ a comment that mentions someone or something: *He made no reference to my untidy appearance.* noun [C] ★★ a statement giving information about you that you ask someone who knows you or has worked with you to provide when you apply for a new job: *Her former employer provided a reference for her.*

refine /rɪˈfaɪn/ verb [T] to remove things from a natural substance in order to make it pure

regular /ˈregjʊlə/ adj ★★★ **1** arranged so that there is the same amount of time or space between things: *regular monthly meetings* **2** doing something or done frequently: *a regular customer* **3** following the normal patterns of grammar: *regular verbs*

regularly /ˈregjʊləli/ adv ★★ **1** after equal amounts of time have passed: *The committee meets regularly.* **2** frequently: *The equipment needs to be checked regularly.*

related /rɪˈleɪtɪd/ adj ★ **1** connected: *We think the two crimes are related in some way.* **2** belonging to the same family: *Annie's related to the director.*

relationship /rɪˈleɪʃ(ə)nʃɪp/ noun [C] ★★★ **1** the way in which two or more people or things are connected: *There is a close relationship between poverty and crime.* **2** a situation in which two people are sexual or romantic partners: *I was already in a relationship when I met Ben.*

relatively /ˈrelətɪvli/ adv ★★★ in comparison with someone or something similar: *a relatively small flat*

relaxed /rɪˈlækst/ adj ★ calm and not worried: *Bill came back from his holiday looking relaxed and tanned.*

relaxing /rɪˈlæksɪŋ/ adj pleasant and making you feel relaxed

release /rɪˈliːs/ verb [T] ★★★ **1** to let someone leave a place where they have been kept: *The authorities had recently released two suspects.* **2** to stop holding someone or something: *She slowly released her grip on Louisa's hand.*

reliable /rɪˈlaɪəb(ə)l/ adj ★ able to be trusted: *a reliable workman/car*

rely on /rɪˈlaɪ ˌɒn/ phr vb **1** to need something in order to continue living, existing, or operating: *The museum relies on voluntary donations to keep open.* **2** to trust someone or something to do something for you: *Sometimes you just have to rely on your own judgment.*

remedy /ˈremədi/ noun [C] ★ **1** a solution to a particular problem: *There are no easy remedies for learning difficulties.* **2** a cure for pain or for a minor illness: *homeopathic/herbal remedies*

remote control /rɪˌməʊt kənˈtrəʊl/ noun [U] a system of controlling a machine or a vehicle from a distance

renewable /rɪˈnjuːəb(ə)l/ adj **1** a renewable contract or arrangement can be continued for a longer period of time **2** renewable energy and natural materials replace themselves by natural processes, so that they are never completely used up

reply /rɪˈplaɪ/ verb [I/T] ★★★ to say, write or do something as an answer: *'I know,' Corbett replied quietly.*

report /rɪˈpɔːt/ noun [C] ★★★ **1** a spoken or written description of a particular subject, situation or event: *A new report shows violent crime is on the increase.* **2** an article or broadcast that gives information about something in the news: *Did you see that report about house prices in London?* **3** a document that is written by a teacher, giving details of a student's school work verb [I/T] ★★★ to give information about something in a news article or broadcast: *Three journalists were sent to report on the conflict.* verb [T] ★★★ to produce an official statement or a written document about a particular subject: *The committee will report the results of its investigation tomorrow.*

reputation /ˌrepjʊˈteɪʃ(ə)n/ noun [C/U] ★★ the opinion people have about how good or bad someone or something is: *The town has a bad reputation.*

research /rɪˈsɜːtʃ, ˈriːsɜːtʃ/ noun [U] ★★ the detailed study of something in order to discover new facts: *medical/historical/linguistic research*

resident /ˈrezɪd(ə)nt/ noun [C] ★★ someone who lives in a particular place: *Many local residents have objected to the new road.*

respect /rɪˈspekt/ noun [U] ★★★ **1** the attitude that someone is important and should be admired, and that you should treat them politely: *She has worked hard to gain the respect of her colleagues.* **2** a feeling that something is important and deserves serious attention: *a healthy respect for the law* verb [T] ★★ to treat someone in a way that shows that you think they are important and should be admired: *He is highly respected in his profession.*

R

responsibility /rɪˌspɒnsəˈbɪləti/ noun [U] ★★★ something that you have to do as a duty or a job: *She has a lot of responsibility as a nurse.*

responsible /rɪˈspɒnsəb(ə)l/ adj ★★★ **1** if you are responsible for something that has happened, you caused it, or you deserve to be blamed for it: *Parents feel responsible when things go wrong.* **2** in charge of someone or something: *The manager is responsible for the running of the theatre.*

rest /rest/ noun [singular] ★★★ the part of something that remains, or the people or things that remain: *I'm not really hungry – do you want the rest?* noun [C/U] ★★★ a period of time that you spend relaxing or sleeping: *Can we stop for a minute? I need a rest.* verb [I] ★★★ **1** to spend a period of time relaxing or sleeping: *It would be nice to sit down and rest for a while.* **2** to not use a part of your body that is tired or injured, so that it can get better: *You'll need to rest your foot for at least two days.*

restriction /rɪˈstrɪkʃ(ə)n/ noun [C] something, for example a law, that limits what you can do

result /rɪˈzʌlt/ noun [C/U] ★★★ something that is caused directly by something else: *He said the argument was the result of a misunderstanding.* noun [C] ★★★ **1** the final score in a sports game, the number of votes that someone gets in an election or the number of points that someone gets in a competition: *The election result was a disaster for the party.* **2** a piece of information that you get by examining, studying or calculating something: *The results of the survey will be published shortly.* noun [plural] ★★★ results: success that you achieve: *He breaks rules, but he gets results.*

retire /rɪˈtaɪə/ verb [I] ★★ to stop working permanently, especially when you are old: *He retired from the army last month.*

retired /rɪˈtaɪəd/ adj no longer working at a job, especially when you are old: *a retired teacher/police officer*

reunion /riːˈjuːniən/ noun [C] a social event for people who have not seen each other for a long time: *a family reunion*

revise /rɪˈvaɪz/ verb [T] to change, improve or make additions to something: *a revised draft of the treaty* verb [I/T] to study your notes and information again in order to prepare for an examination

revision /rɪˈvɪʒ(ə)n/ noun [C/U] the process of changing, improving or making additions to something: *He intends to undertake a major revision of the constitution.* noun [U] the work of studying for an examination: *I can't go out – I've got to do some revision for my exams.*

rich /rɪtʃ/ adj ★★★ **1** having a lot of money, property or valuable possessions: *a rich man* **2** containing a lot of things such as butter, eggs or cream that make your stomach feel full very quickly: *a rich chocolate dessert*

ride /raɪd/ verb [I/T] ★★ to sit on a bicycle, motorcycle or an animal such as a horse and control it as it moves: *I learned to ride a bike when I was five.*

right-handed /ˌraɪt ˈhændɪd/ adj naturally tending to use your right hand rather than your left to do things such as writing

ring /rɪŋ/ noun [C] ★★★ **1** a piece of jewellery in the form of a circle that you wear on a finger: *She had a ring on every finger.* **2** something that is in the shape of a circle: *onion rings*

S

risk /rɪsk/ noun [C/U] ★★★ the possibility that something unpleasant or dangerous might happen: *The risks to consumers are being analysed.* verb [T] ★★ to do something although you know that something that is bad could happen as a result: *He risked a lot of money on the company.*

river bank /ˈrɪvə ˌbæŋk/ noun [C] the land at the side of a river

rob /rɒb/ verb [T] to take money or property from someone illegally: *They were planning to rob the museum.*

robber /ˈrɒbə/ noun [C] someone who steals money or property

robbery /ˈrɒbəri/ noun [C/U] the crime of stealing money or property

romance /rəʊˈmæns/ noun [U] the behaviour that is typical of two people who love each other: *She wasn't in a mood for romance.* noun [C] a book or film about a romantic relationship

roommate /ˈruːmˌmeɪt/ noun [C] someone who you share a room with

rope /rəʊp/ noun [C/U] ★★ a type of very thick string that can be used for tying or pulling things

route /ruːt/ noun [C] ★★ the roads or paths that you use when you go from one place to another: *The tunnel is the route taken by most drivers.*

rubbish /ˈrʌbɪʃ/ noun [U] ★ **1** things that you throw away because they are no longer useful: *The streets were littered with rubbish.* **2** things that someone says or writes that are not reasonable or sensible: *As usual, he was talking complete rubbish.* **3** something that is of very low quality: *Critics have described the paintings as worthless rubbish.*

rucksack /ˈrʌkˌsæk/ noun [C] a bag that you carry on your back

rude /ruːd/ adj ★ not polite: *I don't want to seem rude, but I'd rather be alone.*

ruin /ˈruːɪn/ verb [T] to spoil or destroy something: *She had ruined her mother's chances of getting a job.*

rule /ruːl/ noun [C] ★★★ a statement that explains what you can or cannot do in a particular situation: *grammatical rules* noun [U] ★★★ the person, group, or country that officially controls a place: *British rule over Hong Kong ended in 1997.*

runner /ˈrʌnə/ noun [C] a person or animal that runs in a race, or someone who runs for pleasure

Ss

sack /sæk/ verb [T] ★ to force someone to leave their job: *Hundreds of workers are to be sacked at the factory.*

sad /sæd/ adj ★★ feeling unhappy, making you feel unhappy or showing that you feel unhappy: *It was a sad day when we sold our home.*

sadness /ˈsædnəs/ noun [U] the feeling of being unhappy: *Joan's childhood was filled with pain and sadness.*

sailing /ˈseɪlɪŋ/ noun [U] the sport or activity of travelling across water in a sailing boat

salary /ˈsæləri/ noun [C] ★ a fixed amount of money that you earn each month or year from your job: *an annual salary of £25,000*

sand /sænd/ noun [U] ★★ a pale brown substance that you find at a beach or in the desert, formed from very small pieces of rock: *The children were playing in the sand.*

sauce /sɔːs/ noun [C/U] ★ a liquid food that you put on other foods to give them a particular flavour: *tomato sauce*

save /seɪv/ verb [T] ★★★ **1** to make it possible for someone or something to avoid danger, harm, injury etc: *campaigns to save the planet* **2** to avoid using something such as money, time or energy, or to use less of it: *You can save £25 if you buy your tickets before Saturday.* **3** to keep or store something so that you can use it in the future: *Save some energy for the end of the race.* verb [I/T] ★★★ if a goalkeeper saves a ball in a sport such as football, they prevent the ball from going into the net

scandal /ˈskænd(ə)l/ noun [C/U] a situation in which people behave in a dishonest or immoral way that shocks people: *a sex scandal*

scanner /ˈskænə/ noun [C] **1** a piece of equipment that you use for copying a picture or document into a computer **2** a piece of equipment that is used for producing a picture of the inside of an object or a part of your body

scar /skɑː/ noun [C] a permanent mark on your skin where you have been injured: *He has a scar under his left eye.*

scared /skeəd/ adj ★ frightened or worried: *I'm scared stiff of having the operation.*

scary /ˈskeəri/ adj frightening: *a scary story*

scholarship /ˈskɒləʃɪp/ noun [C] an amount of money that an organisation gives to someone so that they can study at a particular school or university: *Sophie was awarded a scholarship to attend Boston University.*

science /ˈsaɪəns/ noun [U] ★★★ the study and knowledge of the physical world and its behaviour, that is based on experiments and facts and is organised into a system: *recent advances in science*

science fiction /ˌsaɪəns ˈfɪkʃən/ noun [U] books and films about imaginary future events that often include space travel and creatures from other planets

scientist /'saɪəntɪst/ noun [C] ★★ someone who is trained in science, especially someone whose job is to do scientific research

score /skɔː/ noun [C] ★★ the number of points that someone gains in a game or test: *The average score for the test was 75.* verb [I/T] ★★ to get a point in a game or sport: *No one scored in the first half.*

screen /skriːn/ noun [C] ★★ the flat surface on a computer, television or piece of electronic equipment where words and pictures are shown: *Suddenly the screen went blank.*

scuba diving /'skuːbə ˌdaɪvɪŋ/ noun [U] the activity of swimming under water with a container of air on your back and a tube for breathing through

sea level /'siː ˌlevəl/ noun [U] the average level of the sea. It is used for measuring the height of parts of the land.

search engine /'sɜːtʃ ˌendʒɪn/ noun [C] a computer program that is used for searching for information on the Internet

seasick /'siːˌsɪk/ adj feeling ill from the movement of the boat that you are travelling on

seasickness /'siː sɪknɪs/ noun [U]

seaside /'siːˌsaɪd/ noun [singular] an area that is near the sea, especially one where people go for a holiday: *This was their first family holiday together at the seaside.*

seat /siːt/ noun [C] ★★★ something that you can sit on: *Some of the vans have leather seats.*

section /'sekʃ(ə)n/ noun [C] ★★★ **1** a person, group, part, or area that forms part of something larger: *The frozen-foods section is in the rear of the shop.* **2** a part of a newspaper, book, or other piece of writing that may be considered separately: *The story was reported on the front page of the business section.*

security /sɪ'kjʊərəti/ noun [U] ★★★ **1** safety from attack, harm, or damage: *The information received is highly confidential and relates to national security.* **2** the department within an organisation that protects buildings and workers: *If you won't leave, I'll have to call security.*

seed /siːd/ noun [C/U] ★★★ a small hard part produced by a plant that can grow into a new plant of the same type: *a packet of seeds*

seem /siːm/ verb [I] ★★★ to appear to be something, or to appear to have a particular quality: *John seems nice.*

selective /sɪ'lektɪv/ adj careful about what you choose or accept: *He is very selective in his reading.*

self-centred /ˌself'sentəd/ dj too interested in yourself, so that you do not think about what other people feel or need

self-confidence /ˌself'kɒnfɪdəns/ noun [U] the feeling that you can do things well and that people respect you

self-employed /ˌself ɪm'plɔɪd/ adj working for yourself rather than being employed directly by a company or organisation

selfish /'selfɪʃ/ adj thinking only about yourself and not caring about other people: *a greedy selfish man*

self-reliant /ˌselfrɪ'laɪənt/ adj able to do things for yourself without depending on other people

sell /sel/ verb [T] ★★★ to let someone have something in exchange for money: *We've decided to sell our house and move to Spain.*

senior citizen /ˌsiːniə 'sɪtɪzən/ noun [C] someone who is at or past the age when most people stop working

sensation /sen'seɪʃ(ə)n/ noun [C/U] the ability to feel something, or something that you feel: *When she awoke she had lost all sensation in her legs.*

sensationalism /sen'seɪʃ(ə)nəˌlɪz(ə)m/ noun [U] a way of reporting events, especially in a newspaper, that makes them seem as exciting or shocking as possible

sentence /'sentəns/ noun [C] ★★★ **1** a group of words, usually including a subject and a verb, that expresses a statement, question or instruction **2** a punishment that is officially given by a judge: *She received the maximum sentence of ten years.*

separate /'sep(ə)rət/ adj ★★★ **1** not together: *My brother and I always had separate rooms.* **2** not connected with something that is similar: *Police have arrested seven drug smugglers in three separate incidents this week.*

series /'sɪəriːz/ noun [C] ★★★ **1** a set of television or radio programmes that are all about a particular subject, person or group of people: *Tonight's programme is the second in a three-part series.* **2** a set of things that are made with the same design, or made in the same way: *a popular new series of children's books*

serious /'sɪəriəs/ adj ★★★ **1** bad or dangerous enough to make you worried: *It's not a serious problem.* **2** meaning what you say or do, and not making a joke: *I'm sorry, I didn't realise you were being serious.*

service /'sɜːvɪs/ noun [C] ★★★ **1** a system that provides things that the public needs: *transport/education services* **2** a religious ceremony: *a church service*

set up /ˌset 'ʌp/ phr vb [I/T] to start something such as a business, organisation or institution: *The group plans to set up an import business.*

ship /ʃɪp/ noun [C] ★★★ a very large boat that is used for carrying people or goods long distances: *His ship sailed from Pearl Harbor on Monday.*

shock /ʃɒk/ noun [singular/U] ★★ the feeling of being very surprised by something bad that happens unexpectedly: *Jessica's face was blank with shock.* noun [C] ★★ something that happens unexpectedly and makes you feel very surprised and upset: *The price of housing was quite a shock for us.*

shocked /ʃɒkt/ adj ★ **1** very surprised and upset by something bad that happens unexpectedly: *We were deeply shocked to hear of his sudden death.* **2** very offended or embarrassed by something that you consider immoral: *People were shocked by the sex scenes in the film.*

shoot /ʃuːt/ verb [I/T] ★★★ **1** to fire a gun: *We were ordered not to shoot until he gave the signal.* **2** in sport, to throw or kick a ball in an attempt to score points: *He shot the ball straight at the goalkeeper.* verb [T] ★★★ to hit someone or something with a bullet from a gun: *The man was shot in the head as he left the bar.*

shop assistant /'ʃɒp əˌsɪstənt/ noun [C] someone whose job is to serve people in a shop

shoplifting /'ʃɒpˌlɪftɪŋ/ noun [U] the crime of stealing things from a shop

short story /ˌʃɔːt 'stɔːri/ noun [C] a short piece of writing about an imaginary situation

shout /ʃaʊt/ verb [I/T] ★★★ **1** to say something in a loud voice: *He was one of those speakers who shout into the microphone.* **2** to make a sudden loud noise because you are afraid or you feel pain: *A man in the next bed was shouting wildly in pain.*

show /ʃəʊ/ noun [C] ★★★ **1** a performance in a theatre: *the new show at the Aldwych Theatre* **2** a television or radio programme: *It's the funniest comedy show on television.* **3** an exhibition: *a fashion/flower show*

shower /'ʃaʊə/ noun [C] ★ **1** a piece of equipment that forces small drops of water into the air and is used for washing your body, or a small area with a shower in it: *The shower isn't working.* **2** the activity of washing yourself by standing under a shower: *I'm going to have a shower.*

shy /ʃaɪ/ adj ★ nervous and embarrassed in the company of other people, especially people who you do not know: *I'd love to meet her but I'm too shy to introduce myself.*

sibling /'sɪblɪŋ/ noun [C] your siblings are your brothers and sisters

sick /sɪk/ adj ★★ if you are sick, food that you have eaten suddenly comes out of your stomach through your mouth: *I'm going to be sick!*

side road /'saɪd ˌrəʊd/ noun [C] a small road that is connected to a major road

sign /saɪn/ noun [C] ★★★ a flat object with words or pictures on it, put in a public place in order to provide information or to advertise something: *a flashing neon sign*

silent /'saɪlənt/ adj ★★ **1** not talking or making any noise: *a crowd of silent onlookers* **2** not pronounced: *The 'b' in 'thumb' is silent.*

silly /'sɪli/ adj ★ **1** not intelligent or sensible: *a silly mistake* **2** not important: *Don't get upset over silly things that people say.*

simple /'sɪmp(ə)l/ adj ★★★ **1** easy to understand or do: *Students were given a simple skills test.* **2** plain, without any complicated features or decoration: *a simple meal*

simplify /'sɪmplɪˌfaɪ/ verb [T] to make something less complicated or difficult

S

singer /'sɪŋə/ noun [C] someone who sings, especially someone who sings well or as their job

single /'sɪŋg(ə)l/ adj ★★★ **1** only one: *a single sheet of paper* **2** not married, or not in a romantic relationship: *Please state whether you are single, married or divorced.*

sinister /'sɪnɪstə/ adj threatening to do something harmful or evil: *a sinister remark*

sister /'sɪstə/ noun [C] ★★★ a girl or woman who has the same parents as you: *He has two brothers and two sisters.*

sister-in-law /'sɪstə(r)ɪn,lɔː/ noun [C] **1** the sister of your husband or wife **2** the wife of your brother

sitcom /'sɪt,kɒm/ noun [C] a humorous television or radio series about a group of characters

situation /,sɪtʃu'eɪʃ(ə)n/ noun [C] ★★★ the set of conditions that exist at a particular time in a particular place: *The country is facing a very difficult economic situation.*

size /saɪz/ noun [C/U] ★★★ a measurement of how large or small something is: *balloons of all shapes and sizes*

skate /skeɪt/ noun [C] **1** a type of shoe with a thin metal blade on the bottom, used for moving quickly on ice **2** a type of shoe with four thick wheels on the bottom, used for moving quickly on a smooth surface verb [I] to move over a surface using skates

ski /skiː/ verb [I] to slide over snow on skis

skill /skɪl/ noun [C/U] ★★★ the ability to do something well, usually as a result of experience and training: *I admired the skill and dedication of the nursing staff.*

skilled /skɪld/ adj skilful: *a skilled craftsman*

skinny /'skɪni/ adj very thin

slightly /'slaɪtli/ adv ★★★ a little: *I feel slightly better today.*

slip /slɪp/ verb [I] ★★ **1** if you slip, your feet slide accidentally and you fall or lose your balance: *Margaret slipped and broke her arm.* **2** if something slips, it slides out of the position it should be in: *The knife slipped and cut my finger.*

slow down /,sləʊ 'daʊn/ phr vb to move at a slower speed, or to make someone or something move at a slower speed: *Slow down! You're driving too fast.*

smart /smɑːt/ adj ★ **1** intelligent: *Sophie is a smart hard-working student.* **2** clean and tidy in appearance and dressed in nice clothes: *smart new clothes*

smoke /sməʊk/ verb [I/T] ★★ to suck smoke from a cigarette, pipe etc into your mouth and lungs: *Phil was reading the paper and smoking a cigarette.*

SMS /,es em 'es/ noun [U] short message service: a method of sending a written message using a mobile phone

snow /snəʊ/ noun [U] ★★ small soft white pieces of ice that fall from the sky and cover the ground: *The path was hidden under a blanket of snow.*

S

soap /səʊp/ noun [C/U] ★★ a substance that you use with water in order to wash your body or an object: *a bar of soap* noun [C] ★★ a soap opera

sociable /'səʊʃəb(ə)l/ adj a sociable person is friendly and enjoys being with other people

social /'səʊʃ(ə)l/ adj ★★★ **1** relating to society and to people's lives in general: *a period of enormous political and social change* **2** relating to activities that involve being with other people, especially activities that you do for pleasure: *a social activity/engagement*

software /'sɒf(t),weə/ noun [U] ★★★ the programs used by computers for doing particular jobs: *word-processing software*

soldier /'səʊldʒə/ noun [C] ★★ someone who is a member of an army

solid /'sɒlɪd/ adj ★★ a solid substance is firm and hard and is not a liquid or a gas: *The lake was frozen solid.*

solution /sə'luːʃ(ə)n/ noun [C] ★★ **1** a way to solve a problem or deal with a bad situation: *Putting children in prison is not the solution.* **2** the answer to a question in a game or a problem in mathematics

solve /sɒlv/ verb [T] ★★ **1** to find a solution to something that is causing difficulties: *solve a crisis/dispute/conflict* **2** to find the reason or explanation for something: *solve a mystery/puzzle/riddle*

son /sʌn/ noun [C] ★★★ your male child: *My younger son is a doctor.*

soon /suːn/ adv ★★★ within a short time: *If we don't leave soon, we're going to miss our bus.* **2** quickly: *How soon can this package be delivered to Brussels?*

sore /sɔː/ adj painful and uncomfortable, usually as a result of an injury, infection or too much exercise: *I always feel stiff and sore after gardening.*

sound /saʊnd/ noun [C] ★★★ something that you can hear: *Laura didn't make a sound as she left the room.* noun [U] ★★★ the loudness of a radio, television etc: *Turn the sound up a bit – I can't hear.*

soundtrack /'saʊn(d),træk/ noun [C] the music that is played during a film or television programme, or a CD of this music

space /speɪs/ noun [C/U] ★★★ an empty or available area: *We replaced the bath with a shower to create more space.* noun [U] ★★★ **1** the whole of the universe outside the Earth's atmosphere: *a space mission* **2** the area in which everything exists: *different points in space and time*

spare /speə/ adj ★ **1** kept in addition to other similar things, so that you can use it if you need it: *a spare key/battery* **2** available: *Have you got any spare room in your car?*

speaker /'spiːkə/ noun [C] ★★ **1** someone who talks about a subject to a group: *She's a very interesting speaker.* **2** someone who is able to speak a particular language: *an English speaker* **3** a piece of electrical equipment that sends out sound

specialist /'speʃəlɪst/ noun [C] ★ someone whose training, education, or experience makes them an expert in a particular subject: *a web design specialist*

species /'spiːʃiːz/ noun [C] ★★ a plant or animal group whose members all have similar general features and are able to produce young plants or animals together: *the human species*

spectacular /spek'tækjʊlə/ adj extremely impressive

speed /spiːd/ noun [C/U] ★★★ the rate at which something or someone moves or works: *They were working with incredible speed.*

spend /spend/ verb [I/T] ★★★ to use money to pay for things: *How much money did you spend?* verb [T] ★★★ to stay somewhere, or to do something, for a period of time: *We spent the day at the beach.*

spill /spɪl/ noun [C/U] an amount of liquid that has accidentally flowed out of its container: *an oil spill*

split up /,splɪt 'ʌp/ phr vb to end a sexual or romantic relationship

spread /spred/ verb [I/T] ★★ **1** to gradually affect a larger area or a large number of people or things, or to make something do this: *Rain will spread from the west this evening.* **2** to put things in many parts of an area, or to be present in many parts of a large area: *There are 54 community colleges spread across California.* **3** if information spreads, or if you spread it, it becomes known by more people than before: *Someone has been spreading nasty rumours about Stella's private life.*

spy /spaɪ/ verb [I] to work as a spy

stage /steɪdʒ/ noun [C] ★★★ **1** a particular point in time during a process or series of events: *We were now on the last stage of our journey.* **2** the part of a theatre where the actors or musicians perform: *They had now been on stage for over four hours.*

stare /steə/ verb [I] ★★ to look at someone or something very directly for a long time: *It's rude to stare.*

state school /'steɪt ,skuːl/ noun [C] in the UK, a school that is paid for by the government and that provides free education

station /'steɪʃ(ə)n/ noun [C] ★★★ **1** a building or place where trains or buses stop so that passengers can get on or off: *It was dark when we arrived at the station.* **2** a company that broadcasts television or radio programmes: *Listen to your local radio station for travel information.*

stay in /,steɪ 'ɪn/ phr vb to remain in your home and not go out: *I think I'd rather stay in tonight.*

steal /stiːl/ verb [I/T] ★★ to take something that belongs to someone else without permission: *She was caught stealing food from the supermarket.*

stepfather /'step,fɑːðə/ noun [C] the man who is married to your mother, but who is not your father

stepmother /ˈstepˌmʌðə/ noun [C] the woman who is married to your father, but who is not your mother

still /stɪl/ adv ★★★ used for saying that a situation continues to exist up to and including a particular time: *Her hair was still damp from her walk in the rain.*

stir /stɜː/ verb [I/T] ★ to move food or a liquid around using a spoon or other object: *Stir the sauce gently over a low heat.*

stomach /ˈstʌmək/ noun [C] ★★ **1** the soft part at the front of your body that is between your chest and your legs: *A horse had kicked her in the stomach.* **2** the organ inside your body where food goes when you have eaten it: *She'll feel better when she has some food in her stomach.*

stomach ache noun [C/U] pain in your stomach

stone /stəʊn/ noun [U] ★★★ the hard substance that rocks are made of: *a cottage built of stone* noun [C] ★★★ **1** a small piece of rock: *Children threw stones at him.* **2** a large hard seed that is inside a piece of fruit: *a peach stone*

storm /stɔːm/ noun [C] ★★ an occasion when a lot of rain or snow falls very quickly, often with very strong winds or thunder and lightning: *A fierce storm hit the west coast of Florida early this morning.*

strange /streɪndʒ/ adj ★★★ **1** unusual or unexpected in a way that surprises, worries or frightens you: *Ian is a very strange person.* **2** not familiar or known to you: *When you arrive in a new country, everything seems strange.*

stress /stres/ noun [C/U] ★ **1** a worried or nervous feeling that makes you unable to relax, or a situation that makes you feel like this: *the stresses and strains of everyday living* **2** the emphasis that you put on a particular word or part of a word by saying it more loudly

strict /strɪkt/ adj ★ **1** someone who is strict expects people to obey rules completely, or obeys rules completely themselves: *The coach is very strict about our diet.* **2** strict rules or conditions must be obeyed completely: *They operate within strict time limits.*

strong /strɒŋ/ adj ★★★ **1** physically powerful and healthy: *Are you strong enough to carry that?* **2** not easily broken, damaged or destroyed: *a strong fabric/glue/rope* **3** someone who is strong has confidence, determination and emotional strength: *You've got to be strong and not let their jokes bother you.* **4** very noticeable: *a strong light/colour*

stubborn /ˈstʌbən/ adj **1** not willing to change your ideas or decisions: *Stop being so stubborn!* **2** very difficult to change, defeat or remove: *stubborn opposition*

stuck /stʌk/ adj caught or held in a position so that you cannot move: *Carl's car got stuck in the mud.*

student /ˈstjuːd(ə)nt/ noun [C] ★★★ someone who goes to a university, college or school: *Jennifer is one of my best students.*

study /ˈstʌdi/ verb [I/T] ★★★ to learn about a subject by going to school, university etc: *She's studying history at university.* verb [I] ★★★ to do work such as reading and homework: *You need to study hard if you want to pass.*

stuff /stʌf/ noun [U] ★★★ **1** objects or things: *What's all this stuff on my desk?* **2** a material, or a substance: *The costumes were made of thin, gauzy stuff.* **3** general information: *I already know all that stuff.*

stylish /ˈstaɪlɪʃ/ adj attractive and fashionable: *stylish clothes*

subtitle /ˈsʌbˌtaɪt(ə)l/ noun [plural] subtitles: a translation of what people are saying in a foreign language film or television programme which appears at the bottom of the screen noun [C] an additional title that appears after the main title of a piece of writing

succeed /səkˈsiːd/ verb [I] ★★★ to achieve something that you planned to do or attempted to do: *Everyone wants the peace process to succeed.*

successful /səkˈsesf(ə)l/ adj ★★★ **1** achieving the result that you want: *The team has had a highly successful season.* **2** a successful person does well in their career: *a successful businesswoman* **3** a successful business makes a lot of money: *It was another very successful year for the bank.*

suddenly /ˈsʌd(ə)nli/ adv ★★★ quickly and without any warning: *A strange feeling suddenly came over him.*

suffer /ˈsʌfə/ verb [I/T] ★★★ to experience something very unpleasant or painful: *In wars, it's usually innocent civilians that suffer.*

sufficient /səˈfɪʃ(ə)nt/ adj ★★ as much as is needed: *The wages were not sufficient for people to live on.*

suggest /səˈdʒest/ verb [T] ★★★ **1** to offer an idea or a plan for someone to consider: *He suggested that we have dinner first, and then watch the film.* **2** to make people think that something exists or is true: *Evidence suggests a link between asthma and pollution.*

suggestion /səˈdʒestʃ(ə)n/ noun [C] ★★★ an idea or plan that you offer for someone to consider: *Could I make a suggestion?* noun [U] ★★★ the act of suggesting something: *It was at Larry's suggestion that I attended the meeting.*

suit /suːt/ noun [C] ★★ **1** a set of clothes made from the same cloth, usually a jacket with trousers or a skirt: *He was wearing a dark suit and a tie.* **2** a type of clothing that you wear for a particular activity: *a diving/jogging suit*

sum up /ˌsʌm ˈʌp/ phr vb to give a summary of something

summary /ˈsʌməri/ noun [C] ★★ a short account of something that gives only the most important information: *The text provides summaries of the plots of Shakespeare's plays.*

summer /ˈsʌmə/ noun [C/U] ★★★ the season between spring and autumn, when the weather is hottest: *the summer of 1973*

sunglasses /ˈsʌnˌglɑːsɪz/ noun [plural] dark glasses that you wear to protect your eyes when the sun is bright

support /səˈpɔːt/ noun [U] ★★★ **1** help and approval that you give to a particular idea, politician, organisation etc: *I urge my colleagues to join me in support of this plan.* **2** help and kindness that you give to someone who is having a difficult time: *I am grateful to my family for their love and support.* noun [C/U] ★★★ something that holds the weight of an object, building or structure so that it does not move or fall verb [T] ★★★ **1** to help someone and be kind to them when they are in a difficult situation: *My friends have supported me through the entire trial.* **2** to hold the weight of someone or something so that they do not move or fall: *The plants were supported with wire.* **3** to like a particular sports team and always want them to win: *I support West Ham – who do you support?*

suppose /səˈpəʊz/ verb [T] ★★★ to think that something is probably true, right or possible: *I suppose she must be delighted about getting the job.*

sure /ʃɔː, ʃʊə/ adj ★★★ **1** certain that something is real, true or correct: *I think she's called Monica, but I'm not sure.* **2** certain to happen or succeed: *Everyone thought that the deal was a sure thing.*

surf /sɜːf/ verb [I] to ride on waves in the sea on a surfboard verb [I/T] to look at various places one after another on the Internet or on television: *She spends hours every day just surfing the Net.*

surfing /ˈsɜːfɪŋ/ noun [U] **1** a sport in which people ride on waves using surfboards **2** the activity of looking at different places on the Internet or on television in order to find something interesting

surgeon /ˈsɜːdʒ(ə)n/ noun [C] a doctor who does operations

surgery /ˈsɜːdʒəri/ noun [U] ★ medical treatment in which a doctor cuts open someone's body noun [C] ★ a place where people can visit a doctor or a dentist

surprise /səˈpraɪz/ noun [C] ★★★ an unusual event, or an unexpected piece of news: *The news came as a big surprise to everyone.* noun [U] ★★★ the feeling that you have when something unusual or unexpected happens: *Many students expressed surprise at the news.*

surprised /səˈpraɪzd/ adj ★★ feeling surprise because something unexpected has happened: *We were surprised by Ben's reaction to the news.*

surprising /səˈpraɪzɪŋ/ adj ★★ unusual or unexpected: *It's not at all surprising that she's angry, considering what you said.*

surroundings /səˈraʊndɪŋz/ noun [plural] a place and all the things in it: *She soon became accustomed to her new surroundings.*

survive /səˈvaɪv/ verb [I/T] ★★★ **1** to continue to exist or live in a difficult situation: *Only one of the museum's paintings survived the fire.* **2** to stay alive after an injury, illness or attack: *Doctors don't think the victims will survive.*

S

survivor /sə'vaɪvə/ noun [C] someone who is still alive after an accident, illness or attack

suspect /'sʌspekt/ noun [C] someone who might have committed a crime: *a murder suspect*

suspect /sə'spekt/ verb [T] ★★ to believe that something is true: *Police suspected that she had some connection with the robbery.*

suspicious /sə'spɪʃəs/ adj **1** if you are suspicious, you do not trust someone or you think that something bad might have happened: *Colleagues became suspicious when he started acting strangely.* **2** if something is suspicious, you think that it might be bad or dangerous: *Customers noticed a suspicious package by the door.*

sweet /swiːt/ adj ★★ **1** foods and drinks that are sweet taste like sugar: *I'd like something sweet, like a piece of cake.* **2** something that is sweet has a nice smell, sound or appearance: *The room is filled with the sweet fragrance of flowers.* **3** kind and gentle: *He's such a sweet man.*

switch off /ˌswɪtʃ 'ɒf/ phr vb **1** to stop listening to someone, or to stop thinking about something: *He just switches off and ignores me.* **2** if you switch off something such as a light or a machine, or if it switches off, it stops working: *The heating has switched off.*

switch on /ˌswɪtʃ 'ɒn/ phr vb if you switch on something such as a light or a machine, or if it switches on, it starts working: *Don't switch on the light.*

Tt

tabloid /'tæblɔɪd/ noun [C] a newspaper that has small pages and not much serious news

take over /ˌteɪk 'əʊvə/ phr vb **1** to begin to do something that someone else was doing: *Jane took over as director after Richard retired.* **2** to take control of something, especially another company

talkative /'tɔːkətɪv/ adj someone who is talkative talks a lot

taste /teɪst/ verb [linking verb] ★★ to have a particular flavour: *Although the meal was cold, it tasted delicious.* verb [T] ★★ to eat or drink something and experience its flavour: *The dinner was one of the best meals I have ever tasted.* noun [C/U] ★★★ **1** the flavour that something creates in your mouth when you eat or drink it: *I love the taste of chocolate.* **2** the types of thing that you like: *The meals are designed to suit all tastes.*

teacher /'tiːtʃə/ noun [C] ★★★ someone whose job is to teach: *a French/maths/piano teacher*

team /tiːm/ noun [C] ★★★ **1** a group of people who play a sport or game against another group: *a football/basketball team* **2** a group of people who work together: *a negotiating team*

technician /tek'nɪʃ(ə)n/ noun [C] someone with technical training whose job involves working with and taking care of special equipment

technology /tek'nɒlədʒi/ noun [C/U] ★★★ advanced scientific knowledge that is used for practical purposes, especially in industry: *computer/military technology*

teenager /'tiːnˌeɪdʒə/ noun [C] ★ a young person between the ages of 13 and 19

temperature /'temprɪˌtʃə/ noun [C/U] ★★★ a measurement of how hot or cold a place or object is: *The plants need a temperature of at least 15°C to grow well.*

temporary /'temp(ə)rəri/ adj ★★★ **1** existing, done or used for only a limited period of time: *These measures are only temporary.* **2** temporary workers do a job for a limited period of time: *a temporary lecturer*

term /tɜːm/ noun [C] ★★★ **1** a word or phrase that is used for referring to or describing someone or something: *a technical/medical term* **2** one of the periods of time that the year is divided into for students: *What classes are you taking this term?*

terrified /'terəfaɪd/ adj extremely frightened

terrifying /'terəˌfaɪɪŋ/ adj extremely frightening: *a terrifying experience*

textbook /'teks(t)ˌbʊk/ noun [C] a book that contains information about a particular subject

theft /θeft/ noun [C/U] the crime of stealing something

theme park /'θiːm ˌpɑːk/ noun [C] a large park where people pay to play games and have fun and where all the entertainment is designed according to one theme

thick /θɪk/ adj ★★★ **1** a thick object or material has a long distance between two opposite sides, edges or surfaces: *a thick woollen sweater* **2** used for stating the distance between the opposite surfaces or edges of a solid object: *The walls are only a few inches thick.* **3** a thick liquid is more stiff or solid than normal and does not flow easily: *a thick cream sauce* **4** stupid

thief /θiːf/ noun [C] someone who steals something

thin /θɪn/ adj ★★★ **1** a thin object or material has only a short distance between two opposite sides, edges or surfaces: *a thin layer of dust* **2** someone who is thin has very little fat on their body: *Charles was thin and very tall.* **3** a thin liquid contains mostly water, so that it flows easily: *a plate of meat covered with thin gravy*

thirsty /'θɜːsti/ adj ★ feeling that you want or need to drink something: *I'm really thirsty – could I have a glass of water?*

though /ðəʊ/ adv, conj ★★★ **1** but: *I really enjoyed your lecture, though there were some parts I didn't quite understand.* **2** used when adding a statement or question that seems surprising after the previous statement: *'The Savoy's a very nice hotel.' 'Isn't it rather expensive, though?'*

thriller /'θrɪlə/ noun [C] a book, play or film that tells an exciting story

throat /θrəʊt/ noun [C] ★★ **1** the area at the back of your mouth and inside your neck: *She's in bed with a throat infection.* **2** the front part of your neck: *The bigger man grabbed him by the throat.*

thunder /'θʌndə/ noun [U] the loud noise that you sometimes hear in the sky during a storm

on time /ˌɒn 'taɪm/ phrase arriving at the correct time and not late: *The train was on time.*

tiny /'taɪni/ adj ★★ extremely small: *She is one of a tiny minority of female motoring journalists.*

tip /tɪp/ noun [C] ★ **1** a narrow or pointed end, especially of something long or thin: *the tip of your nose/finger* **2** an amount of money that you give to someone in addition to the price of a service: *Shall we leave a tip for the waiter?* **3** a useful suggestion or piece of information that someone gives you: *The booklet gives some good tips on getting the most out of your software.*

tired /'taɪəd/ adj ★★★ needing to rest or sleep: *Your mother looked tired.*

tiring /'taɪərɪŋ/ adj making you feel tired

toe /təʊ/ noun [C] ★ one of the five individual parts at the end of your foot: *Vera slipped off her shoes and wriggled her toes.*

together /tə'geðə/ adv ★★★ **1** if you put or join two or more things together, you combine or connect them: *Mix together the flour, eggs, and water.* **2** with each other: *Kevin, Jack and Dave share a house together.*

tolerant /'tɒlərənt/ adj willing to accept other people's beliefs, way of life etc without criticising them, even if you disagree with them

tonne /tʌn/ noun [C] a unit for measuring weight, equal to 1,000 kilograms

tool /tuːl/ noun [C] ★★ **1** a piece of equipment that you hold to do a particular type of work: *kitchen/gardening tools* **2** something that you use in order to perform a job or achieve an aim: *The Internet has become an important research tool for students.*

tooth /tuːθ/ noun [C] ★★★ any of the hard white objects inside your mouth that you use for biting: *a loose/missing/broken tooth*

toothache /'tuːθeɪk/ noun [singular/U] a pain in one or more of your teeth

toothbrush /'tuːθˌbrʌʃ/ noun [C] a small brush that you use for cleaning your teeth

toothpaste /ˈtuːθ,peɪst/ noun [C/U] a soft thick substance that you put on a toothbrush to clean your teeth

top /tɒp/ noun [C] ★★★ **1** the highest place, point, part or surface of something: *We could see mountain tops in the distance.* **2** a lid or cover for a container or pen: *the top of the shampoo bottle* **3** a piece of clothing that covers the upper part of your body: *She was wearing a red skirt and a black top.*

tower /ˈtaʊə/ noun [C] ★★ a tall narrow structure, building or part of a building: *a water tower*

tradition /trəˈdɪʃ(ə)n/ noun [C/U] ★★★ a very old custom, belief or story: *Native American culture and traditions*

traditional /trəˈdɪʃ(ə)nəl/ adj ★★★ **1** relating to very old customs, beliefs or stories: *traditional Mediterranean cooking* **2** typical of the things people have usually done: *Our house was built in a traditional style.*

traffic jam /ˈtræfɪk ˌdʒæm/ noun [C] a line of vehicles waiting behind something that is blocking the road

trainers /ˈtreɪnəz/ noun [plural] a type of comfortable shoe that you wear in informal situations or for doing sport

transistor /trænˈzɪstə/ noun [C] an object that controls the flow of electricity inside electronic equipment

translate /trænsˈleɪt/ verb [I/T] ★ to change spoken or written words into a different language: *I don't speak Russian, so someone will have to translate.* verb [I] ★ to cause a particular situation or result: *Will the sales increase translate into more jobs?*

translation /trænsˈleɪʃ(ə)n/ noun [C] ★ a piece of work in which spoken or written words have been changed into a different language: *Some people like to make lists of words with translations in their own language.* noun [U] ★ the activity of changing spoken or written words into a different language: *Most legal translation is done by lawyers with foreign language training.*

translator /trænsˈleɪtə/ noun [C] someone whose job is to translate spoken or written words into a different language

transmission /trænzˈmɪʃ(ə)n/ noun [C/U] the process of sending electronic signals such as radio or television signals, or a signal that is sent in this way: *New telephone lines allow faster data transmission by fax or modem.* noun [U] the process by which something spreads from one person to another: *the transmission of disease*

transmit /trænzˈmɪt/ verb [T] **1** to send an electronic signal such as a radio or television signal: *The Cup Final was transmitted via satellite to over 20 countries.* **2** to pass information, beliefs or attitudes to other people: *We transmit our values to our children.* **3** to spread a disease from one person to another: *HIV can be transmitted by sexual contact.*

tribe /traɪb/ noun [C] a large group of related families who live in the same area and share a common language, religion and customs: *Native American tribes*

trip /trɪp/ noun [C] ★★ an occasion when you go somewhere and come back again: *a fishing/camping/sightseeing trip*

troll /trɒl, trəʊl/ noun [C] **1** an imaginary, very ugly, creature in old Scandinavian stories that lives in a cave and is either very small or very tall **2** an ugly or unpleasant person

trolley /ˈtrɒli/ noun [C] a large container with wheels that you push and use for carrying things in a supermarket or at an airport

trust /trʌst/ noun [U] ★★ a feeling that you trust someone or something: *The doctor-patient relationship has to be based on trust.* verb [T] ★★ to believe that someone or something is good, honest or reliable: *Both communities have to trust each other.*

trustworthy /ˈtrʌs(t),wɜːðɪ/ adj someone who is trustworthy can be trusted

try /traɪ/ verb [I/T] ★★★ to attempt to do something: *Owen tried a shot at goal, but the ball went wide.* verb [T] ★★★ to do something in order to find out whether it is enjoyable, suitable or effective: *Have you tried these biscuits? They're great!*

tube /tjuːb/ noun [C] ★ **1** a long narrow object similar to a pipe that liquid or gas can move through: *Nurses had to feed Dan through a tube.* **2** a long narrow plastic or metal container that you squeeze in order to push out the soft substance inside: *a tube of toothpaste* noun [singular] ★ the tube: the system of underground trains in London: *a tube station/train*

turn into /ˌtɜːn ˈɪntuː/ phr vb to change or develop into something different, or to make something change or develop into something different: *Our holiday turned into a nightmare.*

turn on /ˌtɜːn ˈɒn/ phr vb to start using a piece of equipment or a supply of gas, electricity or water by pressing, turning, or moving something: *Is your computer turned on?*

turn off /ˌtɜːn ˈɒf/ phr vb **1** to leave the road that you are travelling along in order to go along another one: *If you're coming on the M4, turn off at junction 26.* **2** to stop using a piece of equipment or a supply of gas, electricity or water by pressing, turning or moving something: *Will you turn the television off, please?*

turn over /ˌtɜːn ˈəʊvə/ phr vb **1** to stop watching one television station and start watching another: *Let's turn over – this is really boring.* **2** to turn a page in a book or a sheet of paper so that the other side is towards you: *You may turn over your exam papers now.*

turn round /ˌtɜːn ˈraʊnd/ phr vb to change the position of your body or head so that you are facing in a different direction: *The girls in front turned round and grinned.*

turn up /ˌtɜːn ˈʌp/ phr vb **1** to arrive somewhere: *She failed to turn up for work on Monday.* **2** to increase the amount of sound, heat or light that is produced by a piece of equipment, by pressing a button or by moving a switch: *Can you turn the volume up a bit?*

twice /twaɪs/ adv ★★★ two times: *He's phoned twice already this morning.*

twin /twɪn/ noun [C] ★ one of two children who were born at the same time to the same mother: *my twin brother/sister*

twist /twɪst/ verb [I/T] ★ to bend or turn into a different shape, or to force something out of its original shape by bending it or turning it: *The force of the explosion had twisted the metal.* verb [T] ★ **1** to injure a part of your body by suddenly bending it too much: *I've twisted my ankle so I won't be able to play.* **2** to change the intended meaning of something slightly, so that it means what you want it to mean: *You're twisting my words.*

U u

ugly /ˈʌgli/ adj ★ **1** unpleasant to look at **2** an ugly situation involves violent or angry behaviour: *an ugly confrontation*

umpire /ˈʌmpaɪə/ noun [C] someone whose job is to make sure that players obey the rules in some sports, for example tennis, baseball and cricket

uncle /ˈʌŋk(ə)l/ noun [C] ★ the brother of one of your parents, or the husband of your aunt: *The business was owned by my uncle.*

undergraduate /ˌʌndəˈgrædʒʊət/ noun [C] a student who is studying for a first degree at a college or university

unemployed /ˌʌnɪmˈplɔɪd/ adj ★ without a job: *Have you been unemployed for a year or more?*

unexpectedly /ˌʌnɪkˈspektɪdli/ adv something that is surprising because you did not expect it at all, or you expected it to happen in a different way: *His response was unexpectedly positive.*

unhappy /ʌnˈhæpi/ adj ★★ **1** feeling sad or upset: *Why are you so unhappy?* **2** not satisfied: *People are very unhappy about the high ticket prices.*

unhealthy /ʌnˈhelθi/ adj **1** ill, or not physically fit **2** not good for you

uniform /ˈjuːnɪˌfɔːm/ noun [C] ★★ a set of clothes that you wear to show that you are part of a particular organisation or school: *He was still wearing his school uniform.*

unkind /ʌnˈkaɪnd/ adj ★ unfriendly, insulting or cruel: *an unkind remark*

unleaded /ʌnˈledɪd/ adj unleaded petrol does not contain lead

unnecessary /ʌnˈnesəs(ə)ri/ adj ★ not needed: *Remove all unnecessary files from your computer.*

unofficial /ˌʌnəˈfɪʃ(ə)l/ adj **1** not organised or formally approved by anyone in authority **2** not having an official position or status

U

untidy /ʌn'taɪdi/ adj **1** not arranged in a way that is tidy: *an untidy desk* **2** not keeping things tidy: *He's always criticising me for being untidy.*

unusual /ʌn'ju:ʒʊəl/ adj ★★ **1** not normal, common or ordinary: *You're in a very unusual situation.* **2** different from other people or things in a way that is interesting, attractive or impressive: *The designers have chosen unusual colour combinations.*

upset /ʌp'set/ adj ★ **1** sad, worried or angry about something: *Why are you so upset?* **2** if your stomach is upset, you have an illness affecting your stomach, usually caused by something that you have eaten or drunk: *Phone and tell them you've got an upset stomach.* verb [T] ★ to make someone feel sad, worried or angry: *I'm sorry, I didn't mean to upset you.*

urban /'ɜ:bən/ adj ★ relating to towns and cities: *People moved to the urban areas for jobs.*

urgent /'ɜ:dʒ(ə)nt/ adj ★ urgent things are things that you need to deal with immediately: *He had some urgent business to attend to.*

USB port /ju: es 'bi: pɔ:t/ noun [C] a place on a computer where you can attach a cable for connecting a printer, keyboard, modem etc

useful /'ju:sf(ə)l/ adj ★★★ helpful for doing or achieving something: *a useful tool/technique/gadget*

V v

vacancy /'veɪkənsi/ noun [C] **1** a job that is available: *We have several vacancies to fill in the Sales Department.* **2** a room in a hotel that is available: *We have no vacancies at all during July.*

valley /'væli/ noun [C] ★ a low area of land between two mountains or hills, often with a river flowing through it: *Their house has wonderful views across the valley.*

vandal /'vænd(ə)l/ noun [C] someone who deliberately damages or destroys things, especially public property

vandalise /'vændəˌlaɪz/ verb [T] to deliberately damage or destroy things, especially public property

variety /və'raɪəti/ noun [singular] ★★★ a number of different people or things: *Adults study for a variety of reasons.* noun [C] ★★★ a particular type of thing: *a new variety of tomato*

various /'veəriəs/ adj ★★★ several different: *There are various ways of solving the problem.*

vegetarian /ˌvedʒə'teəriən/ adj relating to or intended for vegetarians: *a vegetarian diet/cookbook/restaurant*

version /'vɜ:ʃ(ə)n/ noun [C] ★ a form of something that is different from other forms or from the original: *The software comes in several different versions.*

victim /'vɪktɪm/ noun [C] ★★★ **1** someone who has been harmed or killed as the result of a crime: *a murder victim* **2** someone who has been affected by something such as an accident or illness: *flood/earthquake victims*

violence /'vaɪələns/ noun [U] ★★ **1** violent behaviour: *acts of violence* **2** a strong force that something has, often one that causes a lot of damage: *the violence of the storm*

violent /'vaɪələnt/ adj ★★★ **1** using physical force to hurt people or damage property: *There were several violent incidents on the streets.* **2** a violent wind, storm or explosion happens with a lot of force and causes serious damage

virus /'vaɪrəs/ noun [C] ★ **1** a very small living thing that can enter your body and make you ill, or a disease or illness caused by this: *Malaria is caused by a virus.* **2** a program that enters your computer and damages or destroys information that you have stored: *Most viruses are spread over the Internet.*

vocational /vəʊ'keɪʃ(ə)nəl/ adj relating to the skills that you need for a particular job: *a vocational course/qualification*

volleyball /'vɒliˌbɔ:l/ noun [U] a sport in which two teams use their hands and arms to hit a ball to each other over a high net

vowel /'vaʊəl/ noun [C] one of the letters a, e, i, o or u, or the sounds that they represent

W w

wage /weɪdʒ/ noun [C] ★★★ a regular amount of money that you earn for working: *a daily/hourly/weekly wage*

waiting room /'weɪtɪŋ ˌru:m/ noun [C] a room where you wait for something such as a train, or for someone such as a doctor to be ready to see you

walking stick /'wɔ:kɪŋ ˌstɪk/ noun [C] a stick that some people use to help them to walk

waste /weɪst/ verb [T] ★★ to use more of something than is necessary, or to use it in a way that does not produce the best results: *There were accusations that the government was wasting public money.*

water /'wɔ:tə/ verb [T] to pour water on plants in order to keep them healthy verb [I] **1** if your eyes water, tears form in them because something is hurting them **2** if your mouth waters when you see or smell nice food, saliva begins to form in your mouth

wave /weɪv/ noun [C] ★★ **1** a line of water that rises up on the surface of a sea, lake or river: *The boat was smashed by a huge wave.* **2** a movement that you make with your hand or with an object as a way of saying hello or goodbye to someone or as a signal to them verb [I/T] ★★ to move your hand in order to say hello or goodbye: *He smiled and waved when he saw me.* verb [T] ★★ to move something around in the air: *People clapped and cheered and children waved flags.*

weak /wi:k/ adj ★★ **1** lacking physical strength or good health: *The illness had left him too weak to speak.* **2** lacking determination and easily persuaded to do something that you should not do: *weak, indecisive leadership* **3** bad in quality or ability: *Her written work is good, but her oral skills are rather weak.*

weakness /'wi:knəs/ noun [U] ★ the state or condition of being weak: *the increasing weakness of the government* noun [C] ★ a fault or problem that makes someone or something less effective or attractive: *They listed the strengths and weaknesses of their product.*

wealthy /'welθi/ adj rich: *a wealthy businessman*

webcam /'webˌkæm/ noun [C] a camera that is connected to a computer and produces images on a website

website /'webˌsaɪt/ noun [C] a place on the Internet where information is available about a particular subject, company, university etc

wedding anniversary /'wedɪŋ ænɪ'vɜ:səri/ noun [C] a celebration of the number of years that two people have been married

weight /weɪt/ noun [U] ★★★ a measurement of how heavy a person or thing is: *It was about 12 pounds in weight.* noun [C] ★★★ a piece of heavy metal that is designed for lifting for exercise or as a sport

well-behaved /ˌwel bɪ'heɪvd/ adj behaving in a way that is polite and quiet and does not upset people

well-built /ˌwel 'bɪlt/ adj a well-built person has an attractive, strong body

well-known /'welˌnəʊn/ adj known by many people, or by the people involved in a particular situation

well-off /'welˌɒf/ dj rich

well-paid /'welˌpeɪd/ adj receiving a satisfactory amount of money for the work that you do

whisper /'wɪspə/ verb [I/T] ★ to speak very quietly to someone, so that other people cannot hear you: *Stop whispering, you two!*

whole /həʊl/ adj ★★★ **1** all of something: *My whole family came to watch me playing in the concert.* **2** not divided or broken: *Add three whole eggs plus two additional yolks.*

wicked /'wɪkɪd/ adj morally wrong and deliberately intending to hurt people

wife /waɪf/ noun [C] ★★★ the woman that a man is married to: *I'd better phone my wife and tell her I'll be late.*

wild /waɪld/ adj ★★ **1** a wild animal or plant lives or grows on its own in natural conditions and is not raised by humans: *The wild rose is a familiar sight in woods and hedges.* **2** a wild area is one where people do not live or cannot live: *wild, mountainous regions* **3** exciting and enjoyable: *They have some pretty wild parties.*

V W

wing /wɪŋ/ noun [C] ★★ **1** one of the parts on a bird or insect that move up and down and allow it to fly: *a moth's delicate wings* **2** one of the long flat parts on both sides of a plane that allow it to fly

winter /ˈwɪntə/ noun [C/U] ★★★ the season after autumn and before spring, when it is usually cold: *a cold/severe/hard winter*

wireless /ˈwaɪələs/ adj not using wires: *wireless phones*

wisdom /ˈwɪzdəm/ noun [U] the ability to make good decisions based on knowledge and experience: *The Egyptian leader was praised for his courage and wisdom.*

wise /waɪz/ adj ★ **1** a wise action or decision is sensible and shows that you have good judgment: *You made a wise decision when you chose to study Spanish.* **2** a wise person is able to make good choices and decisions because they have a lot of experience

witch /wɪtʃ/ noun [C] a woman with magic powers

without /wɪðˈaʊt/ adv, prep ★★★ used for saying what someone or something does not have: *I can't find the answer without a calculator.*

wolf /wʊlf/ noun [C] a wild animal that looks like a large dog

wonder /ˈwʌndə/ verb [I/T] ★★★ to think about something because you want to know more facts, or because you are worried: *'How did they find out?' she wondered.* verb [I] ★★★ to be very impressed or surprised by something: *It's hard not to wonder at the miracle of a newborn baby.*

wooden /ˈwʊd(ə)n/ adj ★★ made of wood: *a wooden box*

work out /ˌwɜːk ˈaʊt/ phr vb **1** to do physical exercise as a way of keeping fit **2** to find an answer to something by calculating it: *Use the chart to work out how much tax you have to pay.*

the World Wide Web /ðə ˌwɜːld waɪd ˈweb/ noun [singular] a very large collection of documents, pictures, sounds etc stored on computers in many different places and connected through the Internet

worried /ˈwʌrid/ adj ★ nervous and upset because you are thinking about your problems or about bad things that could happen: *Everyone was very worried when John didn't show up.*

worrying /ˈwʌriɪŋ/ adj making you feel worried

wrap /ræp/ verb [T] ★ to cover someone or something by putting paper, cloth etc round them: *Keep the cheeses fresh by wrapping each one individually.*

wreck /rek/ noun [C] **1** something that has been badly damaged or is in very bad condition **2** someone who looks or feels very ill or tired

wrinkle /ˈrɪŋk(ə)l/ noun [C] a line that appears on your skin when you get older, or when your skin has been damaged by the sun

write down /ˌraɪt ˈdaʊn/ phr vb to write something on a piece of paper

writer /ˈraɪtə/ noun [C] ★★★ someone who writes books, stories or articles as their job

Xx

X-ray /ˈeks ˌreɪ/ noun [C] **1** a type of radiation that is used for looking inside things such as your body **2** a picture of the inside of someone's body that is taken using X-rays

Yy

yell /jel/ verb [I/T] to shout loudly

yoghurt /ˈjɒɡə(r)t/ noun [C/U] a food made from milk that has become thick and slightly sour

Zz

zone /zəʊn/ noun [C] ★ an area where a particular thing happens: *an earthquake zone*

Macmillan Education
4 Crinan Street
London N1 9XW
A division of Macmillan Publishers Limited
Companies and representatives throughout the world

ISBN 978-0-230-72345-0

Page make-up by Carolyn Gibson
Illustrated by Vlademir Aleksic (p42); Fred Blunt (pp41, 64); Paul Daviz (pp38, 74); Jim Hansen (pp16, 40, 66); Peter Harper (pp36, 47); Joanna Kerr (pp22, 94); Peter Lubach (pp28, 48); Ed McClachlan (pp7, 10, 13, 15, 39, 79); Julian Mosedale (pp23, 49, 51, 58, 77, 87); Oxford Designers and Illustrators (pp46); Gary Wing (p31).
Cover design by Andrew Oliver

Author's acknowledgements
I would like to thank the whole Macmillan team in Oxford for their dedication and hard work during the creation of this book. A big thanks also to all the students that I have had the pleasure of teaching at Colegio Europeo Aristos, Getafe and to my colleagues there. Finally, writing this book would not have been possible without the support of my wonderful family. All my love and thanks to Gemma, Jamie and Becky.

The publishers would like to thank all of those who reviewed or piloted Gateway: Agnieska Orlińska, Barbara Ścibor, Katarzyna Sochacka, Katarzyna Zaremba-Jaworska and Katarzyna Zadrożna-Attia, Anna Ciereszynska, Barbara Nowak, Marta Piotrowska, Joanna Spoz, Luiza Gervescu, Stela Halmageanu, Eva Ellederovan, Prilipko, Vladyko, H Fouad, N Reda, Mag. Annemarie Kammerhofer, Katharina Schatz, Jutta Habringer, Regina Culver, Stephanie Sutter, Nicole Ioakimidis, Lisa Durham, Benjamin Affolter, Gabriela Liptakova, Ondrej Dosedel, Evelyn Andorfer, Pia Wimmer, Andrea Hutterer, Dagmar Eder, Roswitha Schwarz, Sonja Lengauer, Isabel González Bueno, María Cristina Maggi, Marisol Suppan, Sabrina Funes, Silvia Miranda and María Paula Palou.

The author and publishers would like to thank the following for permission to reproduce their photographs:
Alamy/ Blend Images p8(t), Alamy/ David Gee 5 p53, Alamy/ Glowimages RM p56(5), Alamy/ Ken Weingart p56(6), Alamy/ paul prescot p56(8), Alamy/ david pearson p60(t), Alamy/ Photofusion Picture Library p60(b), Alamy/ van Hilversum p62(t), Alamy/ Dennis Chang - CZ Prague p67(2), Alamy/ Picture Partners p78, Alamy/ Indigo Photo Agency p82(2 and 5), Alamy/ imagebroker p82(6), Alamy/ Georgios Alexandris p82(7), Alamy/ Darren Matthews p82(8); **Jane Barlow** p57(b); **Bridgeman Art Library**/ Private Collection / Peter Newark American Pictures / Bridgeman Giraudon p14(t), Bridgeman Art Library/ Private Collection / Peter Newark American Pictures / Bridgeman Giraudon p14(b), Bridgeman Art Library/ Private Collection p76(3); **Corbis**/ moodboard p5(4), Corbis/ Bettmann p24(b), Corbis/ Don Hammond/Design Pics p26(b), Corbis/ Jose Luis Pelaez, Inc. p34(t), Corbis/ ERproductions Ltd/Blend Images p34(b), Corbis/ Heide Benser p44(t), Corbis/ Peter M. Fisher p52(t), Corbis/ Richard Morrell p56(4), Corbis/ Terry Vine/Blend Images p56(7), Corbis/ Mike Kowalski/ Illustration Works p67(1), Corbis/ Juice Images p71(l), Corbis/ Ulises Rodríguez/epa p73, Corbis/ MedioImages p82(3), Corbis/ James Hardy/ PhotoAlto p88(A), Corbis/ Richard Morrell p88(4); **FANCY** pp5(2), 65(b); **Getty Images**/ Jeffrey Braverman p3, Getty/ Annie Marie Musselman p5(1), Getty/ Matthew Brookes p5(3), Getty/ Christopher Leggett p5(5), Getty/ AFP p7, Getty/ Popperfoto p12, Getty/ Flying Colours Ltd p16(b), Getty/ YOSHIKAZU TSUNO p19, Getty/ Loren Santow p26(t), Getty/ Ron Levine p29, Getty/ Ebby May p44(b), Getty/ Oliver Rossi p52(b), Getty/ Paul Thomas p56(1), Getty/ Bob Barkany p56(2), Getty/ Jose Luis Pelaez p56(3), Getty/ Christopher Bissell p56(t)r, Getty/ Mike Clarke p57(t), Getty/ Image Source pp62(b) and 83, Getty/ Stockbyte p65(t), Getty/ Emmanuel Faure p67(4), Getty/ LatinContent p69, Getty/ AE Pictures Inc. p70(l), Getty/ Stockbyte p71(r), Getty/ Time & Life Pictures p76(1), Getty/ Dave Hogan p76(2), Getty/ Keren Su p80(t), Getty/ Yellow Dog Productions p80(b), Getty/ Thomas Northcut p82(1), Getty/ Photodisc p82(4), Getty/ Lester Lefkowitz p88(B), Getty/ Chev Wilkinson p88(5);**GOODSHOOT** pp27, 81(t); **Guardian News & Media Ltd 2008** p86; **Hippocrene Books** p88(2); **IMAGE SOURCE** pp8b, 24(tl), 88(3); **Macmillan**/ CORBIS p88(1); **Mary Evans Picture Library** p37; **Photolibrary**/ Bay Hippisley p16(t), Photolibrary/ Thierry Lauzun p24(tr), Photolibrary/ Jeremy Woodhouse p55, Photolibrary/ Kablonk! Kablonk! p70(r) **Reuters**/ China Daily China Daily Information Corp - CDIC p11, Reuters/ Felix Ordonez p75; **Rex**/ Isifa Image Service/Rex Features p42, Rex/ Michael Stroud p67(3), Rex/ KPA/Zuma p67(5); **The Picture Desk**/ Kobal Collection p32(t), The Picture Desk/ 20TH CENTURY FOX / THE KOBAL COLLECTION p68, The Picture Desk/ PARAMOUNT / THE KOBAL COLLECTION p88(6); SUPERSTOCK p81(b); **Wellcome Library**, London p32(m and b).

Commissioned photographs by Dean Ryan p91

The author(s) and publishers are grateful for permission to reprint the following copyright material:
Extract/Material from '50,000 pupils stay away from school every day in the UK' by Melanie Clarkson copyright © Telegraph Group Limited 2000, first published in The Daily Telegraph 28.10.00, reprinted by permission of the publisher; Adfero Ltd for extract adapted from 'Chief inspector calls for single-sex language classes' copyright © Adfero Ltd, 2005 www.teachers.org.uk/, granted with permission; The New York Times for an extract adapted from 'And the word of the airwaves is in Latin: The Finns have a word for it' by Barry James, IHT (One Shot) 15 April 1998 www.iht.com, copyright © The New York Times; ABC News for an extract adapted from'British woman awakes from coma with Jamaican accent' by Stephanie Kennedy, *The World Today*, 5 July 2006, www.abc.net.au/worldtoday/content/2006/s1679266.htm, copyright © ABC News; USA Today for an extract adapted from 'Ad glut turns off viewers' by Gary Levin, *USA Today* 11 October 2005. Reprinted with permission; Walker Books Ltd and Curtis Brown (Aust) Pty Ltd, Australia for an extract from *After Summer* by Nick Earls, text copyright © 2004 Nick Earls. Reproduced by permission of Walker Books Ltd, London SE11 5HJ, and Curtis Brown (Aust) Pty Ltd by arrangement with the Licensor, Nick Earls; Extract from 'Barry Cox: Shelf-stacker to Chinese crooner' copyright © Telegraph Group Limited 2007, first published in *The Daily Telegraph* 06.12.07, reprinted by permission of the publisher; Extract from 'From a cleaner to a concert pianist' by Andy McSmith copyright © The Independent 2007, first published in *The Independent* 07.12.07, reprinted by permission of the publisher; Hobby Farm News for an extract adapted from 'Hobby Farm News - Milk Carton helps Welsh farmer finds love' www.hobbyfarms.com/farm-industry-news/welsh-farmer-finds-love.aspx, granted with permission; Abner Stein for the speech "I want to tell you a story" by Paul Auster, upon acceptance of the Prince of Asturias Prize for Letters in Spain, 2006 granted with permission of Abner Stein; Central Library, Liverpool City Council for an extract adapted from 'Children's library Services' www.liverpool.gov.uk/Leisure_and_culture/Libraries/Childrens_library_service/index.asp, granted with permission; Extract from 'How one clumsy ship cut off the web for 75 million people' by Bobbie Johnson copyright © Bobbie Johnson 2008 first published in *The Guardian* 01.02.08, reprinted by permission of the publisher.

Every effort has been made to trace the copyright holders, but if any have been inadvertently overlooked the publishers will be pleased to make the necessary arrangements at the first opportunity.

Dictionary extracts taken from Macmillan Essential Dictionary copyright © Macmillan Publishers Limited 2003 and Macmillan English Dictionary 2nd Edition copyright © Macmillan Publishers Limited 2007

Printed and bound in Thailand

2019 2018 2017 2016
21 20 19 18 17 16 15 14